THE SIMPLE TRUTH

THE SIMPLE TRUTH
THE MONOCHROME IN MODERN ART

SIMON MORLEY

REAKTION BOOKS

Published by Reaktion Books Ltd
Unit 32, Waterside
44–48 Wharf Road
London N1 7UX, UK
www.reaktionbooks.co.uk

First published 2020

Printed and bound in Great Britain by TJ Books Ltd, Padstow, Cornwall

A catalogue record for this book is available from the British Library

ISBN 978 1 78914 231 0

CONTENTS

INTRODUCTIONS

'I see nobody on the road,' said Alice.
Lewis Carroll, *Through the Looking-glass* (1871)

Yasmina Reza's hit play *Art* (1994) casts a fictitious white monochrome painting as the emblem of all that is most baffling and infuriating about modern art. What, the two friends in the play ask with increasing consternation, are the grounds for their mutual friend's expensive purchase of a seemingly blank canvas, something that anyone could have made? Were his decisions based on obscure aesthetic taste or some equally obscure intellectual justification? Perhaps more mundane aspects of social life are involved, such as concern for status, the desire to be fashionable, or the making of a speculative economic investment? Or is their friend the victim of a hoax, the foolish dupe of a charlatan?

Reza chose a monochrome because this troubling artefact – the one-colour-all-over painting – stands at the centre of the heroic modernist project, representing its most uncompromising spirit.[1] The monochrome began life as the most minimal or extreme possibility, the beginning and the end, the point towards which to converge or from which to depart or fly free. It took what was considered merely arbitrary and visually meaningless and elevated it to the status of 'art worthy of the name'. A monochrome could be the outcome of exploring the spiritual and contemplative mind, but also equally of a mind dedicated to the empirical and literal. It was made in pursuit of both the most ethereal and extra-sensory experiences, and the most concrete and sensory. In the monochrome's heyday, between 1915 and the mid-1960s, artists who made them could claim to be concerned with the seemingly vastly different but in fact closely linked experiences of emptiness, nothingness, absence, silence, spiritual or intellectual transcendence, immateriality, infinity, purity, origins, essence, autonomy, absoluteness, specificity, materiality, repetition, seriality, rigour, recklessness and boredom. Monochrome artists explored the dialectics of the limit and the limitless, the bounded and boundless, form and formlessness, being and nothingness.

In *The Century* (2005) the philosopher Alain Badiou, like Reza, also elects a monochrome – Kazimir Malevich's *White on White* (1918) – as the emblematic image of what he calls the twentieth century's 'passion for the real'.[2] This was a passion stoked by an overwhelming sense of crisis, but also by an acute awareness of the new intellectual and practical possibilities which the heady experience of modernity offered. Artists felt it was both necessary and possible to start over, to rid themselves of all the barnacle-like accretions of the past. As a poster and leaflet printed by a group of German artists who called themselves Zero, and who made their fair share of monochromes, declared in 1963:

> Zero is silence. Zero is the beginning. Zero is round. Zero spins. Zero is the moon. The sun is Zero. Zero is white. The desert zero. The sky Zero. The night – . Zero flows. The eye Zero.

> Navel. Mouth. Kiss. The milk is round. The flower Zero the bird. Silently. Floating. I eat Zero, I drink Zero, I sleep Zero, I am awake Zero, I love zero. Zero is beautiful . . .[3]

The struggle to be 'zero' was necessarily directed both externally and internally. It required a purge of the social world and the resources of art itself. The repudiation of familiar subject-matter, the desire to free art of all its familiar apparatus and the rejection of the conventional skills taught in schools and academies were part and parcel of the larger desire to make a fresh start – to begin with a *tabula rasa* through returning to the 'real', to the point of origin. Under the extraordinary conditions created by the forces of modernity, it seemed self-evident to many artists that to produce art as such – rather than simply design, decoration, fashion, a commodity or a reflection of the ideology of the ruling class – it was necessary constantly to negate both art's place in the world and its own traditions. To this end, an act of negation was understood to be a cleansing palliative.

Strictly speaking, all works in black and white (drawings, ink paintings, prints, photographs and grisailles – paintings executed in grey or near-grey tones that were a commonplace from the Renaissance to the modern period) can be described as 'monochrome'.[4] In most discussions of modern art, however, the term, which unites the Greek words *mono*, meaning alone, single or one, and *chroma*, colour or hue, specifically defines a type of art in which a single colour becomes the sustained object of attention.

But what is discussed under the name 'monochrome' in what follows does not only include examples of the 'ideal' version, which is probably best epitomized by the work of Yves Klein – who, it should be noted, liked to call himself 'Yves le Monochrome'. His *Blue Monochrome* (1961) (illus. 1), for example, consists of an evenly coated and roughly textured layer of a single hue of ultramarine blue paint that has been applied using a house painter's roller to the front and narrow sides of a rectangular canvas with slightly rounded corners. Kazimir Malevich's *Black Square* of 1915 is often described as the very first monochrome, but it isn't as pure or essential as Klein's. Malevich's is a painted black square within a painted white square that is also the shape of the canvas itself. His *White on White* (1918) is closer to the 'ideal' as it features a greyish-white square within an only slightly differently hued white square canvas.[5] But by the standard of Klein's painting, *White on White* is also still quite a bit more complex.

Malevich's monochromes lie a short distance downstream from the essential and ideal state epitomized by Klein, Robert Rauschenberg and Ad Reinhardt, which brings us to the verge of the blank canvas, and instead tend in the direction of slightly greater visual activity or complexity. This kind of work is better described as monochromatic as opposed to monochrome, and belong in what the German artist and Zero member Heinz Mack, writing in 1958, called 'a continuum of deviations from an ideal monochrome'.[6] Examples of less essential monochromes also feature in this book, and some readers may be surprised to discover discussions of, for example, paintings by Mark Rothko, Barnett Newman, Agnes Martin and Lucio Fontana. But for the sake of style, I will henceforth refer simply to the 'monochrome', even when I sometimes, strictly speaking, mean 'monochromatic'. Readers may also be surprised that I include monochrome sculptures (Donald Judd, Hélio Oiticica, Anish Kapoor), monochrome installations (James Turrell, Olafur Eliasson), film (Derek Jarman), monochrome (not just black-and-white) photographs (Hiroshi Sugimoto) and photographs of readymade or 'found' monochromes (David Batchelor). Clearly, there is no well-defined borderline at which a monochromatic work of art ceases to be 'monochromatic' and becomes simply a minimally oriented painting, object or installation. Furthermore, readers may well find that artists they expected to be included are absent. But *The Simple Truth* does not aim to be a comprehensive survey.

In practice, even the 'ideal' monochrome painting can be made in numerous ways. It is the result of an additive process and of the act of erasure. As we saw with Malevich, it can be painted with a brush, in the traditional fashion, or like the paintings of Yves Klein, using a house painter's roller. At least one contemporary artist uses an inkjet printer (see Chapter Seventeen). The American artist Robert Rauschenberg described his *Erased de Kooning Drawing* (1953), for which he patiently rubbed out with an eraser a charcoal sketch by the Abstract Expressionist artist Willem de Kooning, as a 'monochrome no-image',[7] suggesting that a monochrome need not be painted, and that the subtractive process can be literal and a focus of sustained attention. The contemporary artists James Turrell and Olafur Eliasson make monochromes out of coloured electric light. In fact, a monochrome need not even be 'made' at all. It can be 'found', and thus related to the Duchampian readymade. At its most extreme, a monochrome is not even necessarily a spatially extended object; it can be an idea or concept, or an action. Already in 1958 Yves Klein had staged an exhibition entitled 'The Void', in which the gallery was completely empty of objects but was suffused, or so Klein insisted, with the 'pure pictorial sensibility' of his blue monochromes.[8]

My task is made more complicated by the fact that there have not been many full-time, full-blown monochrome artists – especially of the 'ideal' variety. None of the 'pioneers' went on to make monochromes as an exclusive enterprise. Focusing on something called 'the monochrome' as I do in this book might be seen as misleading to the extent that it implies we are dealing with a genre or a style.[9] In fact I think it is more useful to see the monochrome as a medium – not in the sense of a historically determined set of material practices, like painting, but rather as an agent or means of doing something. Like any agent, the monochrome possesses specific properties through which to achieve circumscribed goals, but these are not necessarily limited to a particular historical form, as is the case with 'painting' for example. (Although *The Simple Truth* is indeed mostly about painting.)

A monochrome seemingly tells us nothing, often not even the story of its own genesis. Compared to most paintings, monochromes are anonymous-seeming and as a result often have an air of cool detachment, one that can make them seem almost 'unmade' or uninteresting. Artists who make monochromes usually avoid the autographic or expressive mark, the 'indexical' gesture that brings to attention their own authorial presence. In other words, their methods often seem deliberately intended to conceal the manual or expressive processes that go into an artwork's making. A monochrome is usually the result of ritualized brain-to-hand action, and is a special kind of meeting of thought and gesture enacted according to a set of rules and using circumscribed procedures. It is therefore often cast as an ascetic medium, one that is characterized by a parsimonious attitude, by a restraining or constraining discipline. But in fact, as we will see, the monochrome may also be a medium through which the utmost passion is condensed and concentrated and the imagination given free rein.

The monochrome was born out of a powerful fantasy of purity and origins, and within a climate of dogmatism in which faith in an inviolable essence meant any deviation from what was deemed to be the path of truth was ruthlessly condemned.[10] Writing in the late 1940s, the American artist Barnett Newman argued that the process of cultural renewal is always inhibited by 'the nostalgic glasses of history', and in order to protect oneself from this contamination, it was necessary for an artist to remain as close as possible to the autonomous sanctuary of their work, which would then permit them and their audience to see with the 'glasses' of the now.[11]

Such hostility to the past, bolstered by the confident belief that it was possible to escape the limits of the European tradition, amounted for a while to a compelling possibility for the monochrome in the United States: it was a work of art without a past, one that functioned as a point of origin. Robert Rauschenberg noted that what he sought to avoid at all costs in his own monochromes were 'superficial subconscious relationships that I'm familiar with – clichés of association'.[12] In the course of defending his monochromes in an interview in the early 1960s, Frank Stella declared that for him the enemy of modern art was 'the old values in painting – the humanistic values'.[13] Donald Judd, when asked in the same interview why he found it necessary to avoid compositional effects involving variations in colour and form, replied: 'Well, those effects tend to carry with them all the structures, values, feelings of the whole European tradition. It suits me fine if that's all down the drain.'[14] Eventually, this animus against the past would motivate several artists to move beyond the rectangle of the canvas into three dimensions, and thereby into real space. 'That gets rid of the problem of illusionism and of literal space, space in and around marks and colours,' Judd declared. Only the minimally organized work in three dimensions could purge art of the totality of the tradition of a European art hopelessly wedded to illusionism – 'one of the salient and most objectionable relics of European art,' according to Judd.[15]

While much was made in its heyday of the monochrome's status as a *tabula rasa* or point of origin, in retrospect we can see that it has its roots firmly within the history of Western art since the Renaissance, and in particular within nineteenth-century developments in art. But the characteristic properties of a monochrome also place it within a much deeper context that links it with art forms and ideas from prior to the Renaissance, for example, with 'anonymous stone work, the object quality of the artefacts, the fact that the work was more important than the artist's personality', as the American artist Ellsworth Kelly noted while discussing his own one-colour paintings.[16]

We also need to take into account the converging and parallel existence of monochromes and monochromatic art outside Europe and North America – for example Brazilian Neoconcretismo (Neo-Concrete) of the 1950s and '60s, the work of the Japanese Gutai group of the 1950s, and Korean Dansaekhwa (literally one-colour painting') of the 1970s and '80s, and beyond into contemporary global practices. The works associated with these tendencies may at first seem typical of those produced by artists living at what have been called the 'margins' – as the products of artists struggling to assimilate the admired characteristics of the 'centre'. But while instances of modern non-Western monochromy did not develop in isolation from Western models, they must also be regarded as original extensions of the possibilities of the Western monochrome, or as further explorations of issues that in one way or another remained unresolved within the Western avant-garde, and which often draw on indigenous traditions that are distinct from those of the West, and that make the monochrome a compelling possibility.

IN ONE WAY or another, all the artists in this book are involved in what Yves Klein called the 'monochrome adventure'.[17] Within this narrative we will detect the presence of an unresolved tension between justifications and interpretations that seek to understand the monochrome in relation to discourse, code, text and meaning on the one hand, and those concerned with feeling, emotion, intuition and sensation on the other. There is also a tension that pits the declarative, which deals with explicit, consciously articulated acts, against the nondeclarative, which is implicit and doesn't require conscious thought. What is perhaps most interesting about the various iterations of the monochrome is that they in one way or another bring into manifest relationship what may at first seem to be mutually exclusive experiences. We encounter something abstract and intangible, but at the same time very real and up close. A monochrome can be considered by one viewer to be a flat two-dimensional object, but the same work may seem infinitely deep to someone else. It can be interpreted as empty of imagery but full of paint, or as a negation of reality and a new kind of realism. While a monochrome is composed of the most ubiquitous of elements – colour – it often addresses the most esoteric of meanings. It can be made by anyone, and yet is usually the province of the most intellectually questioning and challenging of artists.

The interpretative frameworks offered by these artists, which are consciously articulated in relation to what the artists do, are especially important resources when seeking to understand their work. As we will also see, artists who make monochromes are often highly articulate, and for good reason. It can sometimes seem as though the number of words they deploy in order to verbally communicate the meaning of their monochromes is in inverse proportion to the visual complexity they possess.

But such exegesis provided by the artist is only part of how to understand a monochrome. It does not serve their work well to assume that the meaning of what they have made is sufficiently exhausted by reference to what they say.

In fact, behind the fronts of confident rhetoric, the pioneers of the new art were often torn between extremes of fear and hope. 'What is to replace the missing object?' asked the first artist to push towards abstraction, Wassily Kandinsky, in 1913.[18] Despite relentless aesthetic and philosophical explorations, Kandinsky was painfully aware that the newly discovered abstract, objectless or non-objective pictorial space might simply be one of a 'dead semblance of stylized forms', and he confessed that 'a terrifying abyss of all kinds of questions, a wealth of responsibilities stretched before me.'[19] By stripping art of so much, the new art exposed the whole cultural edifice to potential destruction. As a result, wish-fulfilment plays an important part in the story of modern art, and especially the story of the monochrome. What, for example, are we to make of this declaration by Yves Klein: 'I can say at thirty years of age in 1958, that when Malevich burst into space like a tourist around 1915 or 1916, I welcomed him and he visited me because I was already, since always, owner, inhabitant.'[20] Considered from beyond the heady aura of significance that Klein managed to cast around his art, such a statement can seem little more than a product of magical thinking – what Sigmund Freud called the 'omnipotence of thought', which has its origins in the narcissism of childhood. In this light, an artist pursuing the 'monochrome adventure' evokes someone who believes that their imagination is capable of shaping and transforming reality at will, someone wholly untroubled by the 'reality principle'.

MONOCHROME PAINTINGS are still very much with us. As you read this book, a new one is probably being made or exhibited somewhere. They now coexist with monochrome sculptures, monochrome photographs, monochrome movies and monochrome installations. The medium of the monochrome won't go away just yet. But how are we to judge these new monochromes, and their relationship to their modernist predecessors?

There are continuities but also significant discontinuities. In fact, as we will see, already by the mid-1960s there was the sense among many art world 'insiders' that monochrome painting had exhausted its capacity to deliver any kind of shock or challenge. To the cognoscenti, it seemed to depend too much on novelty value, on its capacity to be temporarily 'incomprehensible'. Once the monochrome had been accommodated as a stylistic option, one that existed alongside all the other avant-garde gambits, it seemed fatally close to becoming a futile and redundant gesture.

So, while in 1994 Yasmina Reza presented a white monochrome as the apogee of artistic inscrutability, since the 1970s it has been increasingly perceived by younger artists and many in the art world as stranded a long way short of the cutting edge. It was even a retrogressive tendency. Worst of all, the monochrome painting was in danger of being banal. It used to be cast as the 'end of art', but now it often seemed to be art of the most accommodating kind – one suitable for museum exhibitions, corporate lobbies and boardrooms, and for placing above sofas. As with any discussion of the history of the monochrome, a new monochrome painting must also be seen in the light of the fading of the modernist dream, and the fall from grace of this, its greatest icon. Today, we begin with the recognition that a type of art that once claimed to be the 'end', the 'origin', 'zero', the 'last', the 'ground of being', the 'infinite', or the 'death' of art, now has a hundred-year-long history. Modern art, as the art historian and curator Kirk Varnedoe puts it, used to be envisaged as 'an inverted pyramidal progression pointing down toward the black square, the ultimate end, the effort to produce the last painting'.[21] But today we need another model. Varnedoe suggests it should be one that acknowledges that 'the line between A and B goes out in a million possible and ever more complex directions, where artists along the line from A and B find that A′ and A″ is a window opening onto an entire universe.'[22] This non-linear model, Varnedoe writes, can be compared with a digital hypertext. It could also be described using another metaphor, one derived from nature: the 'rhizomatic' structure theorized by Gilles Deleuze and Félix Guattari. The rhizome, as they write, 'is reducible neither to the One nor the multiple, it is comprised not of units but of dimensions, or rather directions in motion'.[23] An expansive field is explored in which a meshwork of interwoven lines of growthand movement replaces the once dominant idea of hierarchic organization based on connections and linear chronology, and on notions of purity and autonomy.

These analogies – the hypertext and the rhizome – foreground the importance of taking into account the network when studying cultural formations, and the discussion of the monochrome's role within modern art that is undertaken in *The Simple Truth* is especially aided by keeping in mind four kinds of such network: the experiential, the neural, the global and the digital.

Attending to the 'experiential' network means recognizing that, as the philosopher Alva Noë puts it, 'perception is [an] activity of doing and undergoing, a transaction with the world around us.'[24] To see the monochrome as an 'experience' means proceeding from the understanding that the mind is embodied, and continuously involved in organism–environmental interactions. All experience occurs within an embodied mind located within a social network involving others, who contribute to how meaning is propagated, and how we understand our experiences. But, as Noë emphasizes, this also means that often 'it is the existence of art objects themselves that gets in the way of understanding the nature of art. We look to the things themselves. But art is experience. It isn't the things that matter. It is the experience of those things.'[25]

Meaning arises from unconscious bodily perceptions and activities. As the philosopher Mark Johnson writes: 'Concepts that we think of as utterly divorced from physical things and sensorimotor experiences . . . are never really independent of our embodiment, because the semantic and inferential structure of these abstract concepts is drawn from our sensorimotor interactions.'[26] To acknowledge this is also to recognize that on important levels there are valuable meanings that can never be verbally articulated. Words fail us. This recognition will impose considerable limitations on what we consider to be the scope and manner of interpretation in relation to the monochrome or any work of art. After clearing the decks of explicit and declarative knowledge we are left having to account for properties that are fundamentally ungraspable or indeed ineffable. It remains unclear if it is valuable, or indeed possible or feasible, to attempt to provide a convincing verbal account of these properties and experiences within a secular framework that is dedicated to rational analysis.

Specifically, the monochrome encourages a range of experience triggered by a visually simple object. Within the human cultural narrative, which is characterized by incessant activity and ever-increasing levels of complexity, the simple has proven to be an especially compelling quality, and is so today more than ever. Etymologically, the English word 'simple' derives from the Latin *simplex*, from *semel*, meaning 'once', and *plecto* meaning 'pleat', 'fold' or 'weave'. These roots reminds us that the 'simple', which is only a small step away from the 'unfolded', is close to an unbroken totality. Engaging with the simple – examining the 'once pleated' – is an uncompromising way of becoming more conscious of the nature of one's experiences. But how the meaning of the 'simple' is interpreted has varied greatly. Often it is deemed unworthy of attention because it is equated with the naive, primitive, childlike or untutored. But other times, the 'simple' is cherished and cultivated for just such reasons, and because it provides a glimpse of the holistic unity before the divisive impact of human intervention. Trans-historically and trans-culturally, the idea of the 'simple' is closely associated with ideas pertaining to the untouched, unworked and unmade, and purity, essence and truth. When simplicity is valued it is because it is understood not as the elimination of complexity but rather as its incorporation. Thus simplicity is central to the search for spiritual enlightenment, scientific acuity and utility, and artistic originality. When a mystic, scientist or artist says they are interested in the 'simple' it is usually because in one way or another they are in search of some revitalizing or clarifying insight into the deeper meaning of life.

The second network is the 'neural'. Nowadays, we can use what the neurosciences have revealed about the relationship between basic biological resources and cognitive processes. How art activates and reveals, making us conscious of the interrelated processes of perception and cognition, has, for example, been greatly aided by discoveries concerning the brain's plasticity, which reveal that exposure to objects or events reinforces neural networks throughout life, not just in the early years.[27] This recognition has implications both for how we understand the processes involved in the creation of a work of art, and how a work is received by an audience. From the point of view of the artist, neuroplasticity means that any phenomenon looked at frequently and with focused attention will affect and consolidate neural formations, and thereby subconsciously guide choices. For the audience of art, the brain's plasticity explains how gaining increased familiarity with what is initially a new and alienating phenomenon – a monochrome, say – can eventually lead to its assimilation within a worldview; we arrive at a mental state in which our neural network has expanded to accommodate the new stimulus. The neurosciences have also shown the extent to which art functions on implicit and non-declarative levels that are preconscious and closely related to the movements of the body. Knowledge of the cortical correlates of movement in relation to perceiving a work of art, for example, means that any discussion of a monochrome's meaning must be supplemented by addressing the role played by forms of implicitly or unconsciously registered affective imitation.[28] The recognition of the neural basis for the interrelationship between vision, touch and movement suggests that preceding any *conscious* assessment of an image, complex, unconscious, embodied processes are at work and it may be these that ultimately constitute the indispensable core of art. This means that we should consider that when we look at a work of art, in a sense we are 'enacting' it as much as 'perceiving' it.[29] But another interesting insight from cognitive neuroscience takes us in the opposite direction. In addition to primary visual experience, verbal prompts and cues have been shown to play a major role in the experience of art, and they have direct biological correlates. This recognition is especially important in relation to the monochrome, which often depends much more heavily than other kinds of visual art on the information and cues provided by an artist, critic or art historian. The role of theory in relation to the monochrome has always been acknowledged, but it is now possible to see how it resonates not only on a cultural level but biologically through the supplying of a neurochemical reward.[30]

The third network is the global. The rethinking of the monochrome's status within the history of modern art, and the reassessment of its importance within the contemporary context, is bolstered by the expansion of the critical horizon beyond a narrowly Western paradigm. But while the exploration of the monochrome as a feature of the global network widens the geographical basis for its understanding, it also obliges us to reconsider what we think we already know. We recognize that non-Western monochromes both continue to develop already familiar themes and introduce new possibilities. In an interview in 2006 given by Park Seo-bo, a Korean artist who began making monochromes in the early 1970s, Park tried to clarify in broad terms how his approach differs from the Western monochromes with which he is often compared:

> People say my current work is similar to minimal art, but I don't agree. My work is more related to the oriental tradition and its

> spiritual concept of space. I am more interested in space from the point of view of nature. Even though my paintings may represent an idea about culture, the main focus is always based on nature. In other words, I want to reduce the idea and emotion in my work, to express my interest in space from the point of view of nature. Then I want to reduce that – to create pure emptiness. This has been an old value that still exists in oriental philosophy where nature and men are one. This tendency is evident in my work from the '70s and '80s – not just in recent years.[31]

Somehow, we need to try to assimilate into any global discussion of the monochrome the intentions and contents articulated by Park and other non-Western artists, which derive from specific cultural backgrounds, and may from a purely Western perspective be unfamiliar. Ultimately, taking a more transcultural approach means decentring modernism and postmodernism, thereby recognizing that, as the art historian and curator Ming Tiampo writes, 'the issue that needs to be addressed . . . is not a question of priority but rather a question of how historical value is ascribed. In other words, how does one add value to this [the art] system.'[32]

The fourth network is the digital. Courtesy of the Internet, without leaving home we can at the click of a mouse easily find out about the monochrome and its relationship to neuroscience or to global tendencies, or anything else that might spark our interest. If you do an image search for the name 'Yves Klein' you will be rewarded with a rich mosaic of imagery, interspersing black-and-white photos of the artist himself with his characteristic blue rectangles and other assorted examples of his oeuvre. Never before has so much information been at our fingertips, nor have we been so likely to be seduced away from actual, physical encounters with works of art in the here and now by the allure of the virtual. This dematerialization of art, which involves the transformation of artefacts from unique forms into universally on-demand availability, makes the Internet far more than simply a tool. It allows us to muster vast amounts of data, but it also transforms our relationship to the world. However, the shift to looking at visual images primarily on the Internet also involves a subtle but pervasive transformation in our status as agents. It physically isolates us, while simultaneously connecting us on the level of representations communicated via a technological apparatus. There is an instrumental dimension to the computer interface that is absent from books, and even more so when we look at art in person. We say a 'user' of a computer, not a 'reader' or 'viewer', but while we are working at the interface, we rarely bother to think about the complex technology that is hidden from view.[33] We have what seems to be a familiar kind of encounter between ourselves and the mediated information we access, but the new digital reality is a very different one from the analogue, and we are still uncertain of how it is transforming our consciousness, and what the consequences will be.[34] The massive disconnect between the relatively unproblematic and straightforward relationship we have with a digital interface – the computer or smartphone – and the exponentially complex nature of the technology that makes these devices work, is changing how we construe once relatively stable notions of such basic qualities as 'complexity' and 'simplicity'. Where before we interacted with discrete systems and structures of information, these are increasingly merging or being subsumed into a massively integrated totality.

THE STRUCTURE of *The Simple Truth* is essentially thematic, although it also follows a broadly chronological and narrative structure. It is not meant to be a comprehensive survey, but it does aim to offer a useful overview of the subject, one that considers the monochrome within a global context and with an eye on its continued relevance today. The first two chapters set the scene, defining terms and discussing the various contexts within which monochromes are viewed, and presenting a brief history of their critical reception. Chapters Three and Four look at their basic formal characteristics – colour and surface – putting them in wider cultural, neurological and psychological contexts. Chapters Five to Nine consider the possible meanings of the monochrome in relation to metaphysical, spiritual and experiential interpretations of emptiness and nothingness, including, in Chapter Nine, a discussion of the monochrome's relationship to the non-Western philosophy-religion of Zen Buddhism. In Chapters Ten and Eleven we shift focus to consider the monochrome as a new form of realism – that is, as an art form that rejects extra-visual associations and focuses on material properties. Chapter Twelve takes an opposing position, considering the monochrome as a sign, as an especially rarefied code-carrying surface, while in Chapter Thirteen the monochrome's transformation into a concept is discussed. This paves the way for a look at the postmodern 'allegorical' monochrome in Chapter Fourteen, a tendency subsequently countered in Chapter Fifteen, which discusses the development of the monochrome in other media since the 1980s. The next chapter heads east and focuses on an important instance of monochrome painting from beyond the Euro-American context called Dansaekhwa in South Korea during the 1970s and '80s. In Chapter Seventeen the status of the monochrome today is considered, and this is followed by a concluding section in which I speculate about potential roles for the contemporary monochrome.

I have tried to write a 'global' history of the monochrome. But inevitably there is a bias towards the West – the monochrome as we understand it today is, after all, a Western invention. Since I am British there is also a bias towards the Anglo-Saxon West, which is regrettable; but, as the monochrome found a particularly welcome home in the United States, not so unforgivable. This bias is at least in part countered, however, by discussions of South American monochrome art, and in particular, the East Asian monochrome. That there is a specific focus on Dansaekhwa painting is a reflection of the fact that I live in the Republic of Korea, and much of *The Simple Truth* was written there.

1

SETTING

The immaterialization of the invisible and intangible canvas.[1]
Yves Klein (1958)

What happens to a painting when it is illustrated in a book like this? Illus. 1 is a photograph of a characteristic work by Yves Klein, currently in the Museum of Modern Art, New York, and it might seem that almost everything that makes the actual painting significant as a visual experience is absent.

The colour, which, along with the rectangular format, is the only visual content, is actually *substance* – pigment suspended in a synthetic polymer medium – and it is therefore completely different from the colour you see in a reproduction. If you hold up a print or a screen image next to the real painting by Klein you will immediately notice that the blue is not the same. But you will also be aware that you cannot perceive the painting's real surface terrain, which is textured and powdery like a coated wall and catches the light, creating tiny shadows. If you're looking at a printed book right now, the reproduction's surface will be smooth, with the very slight texture of the paper; if you're in front of a computer screen, what you see is a completely glass-smooth, backlit surface. In either case, the painting's surface will seem more or less glossy and flat, while the original is rough and very matte.

If you are reading this book on a paper substrate, what you see is printing ink; if reading on-screen, you'll be seeing digitally generated colour. Book printing used to employ the four-colour, or CMYK, process, in which four inks – cyan, magenta, yellow and key (black) – are blended; more recently, however, six-colour printing has added orange and green to the palette. Where two inks overlap on the paper due to sequential printing impressions, a primary colour is perceived, in this case blue. A monitor or TV screen, on the other hand, generates red-, green- and blue-coloured light. Each pixel on your computer screen or smartphone contains three or four subpixels coated with phosphor, which is excited with UV light emitted by Xenon or Neon gas that turn to a plasma state once an electric current is passed through. Three separate phosphors produce red, green and blue light, which is emitted when struck by electron beams produced by the electron guns at the rear of the tube. The different colours we see on a screen arise from different combinations and intensities of the three primary colours.

Also, when we see Klein's painting on a screen rather than a book page, we are likely to experience a strong sense that inner light is being emitted from it, courtesy of the blue-light bias of the backlit liquid-crystal display (LCD). On a book page, the blue of Klein's painting seems darker and is obdurately inert, flat and concrete. But while the experience of the real blue surface of Klein's painting is not as substantial as it is on a paper page, neither is it quite so ethereal and luminous as the screen makes it seem. The real blue has both a curiously dense tangibility and an elusive intangibility, giving us a powerful sense that we are confronting a textured surface, combined, seemingly paradoxically, with the sensation of lightness and infinite depth.

From a photograph it is not possible to get a direct awareness of the actual size of Klein's painting, or indeed its scale (which, unlike 'size', is relative – to the human body for example). In fact, his painting is the size and shape of a largish window or a small doorway. You can only get information about these real dimensions through reading the caption, from which you can then infer what it might be like were you to be standing in front of it. As an object hanging on a wall, the real painting can be seen from oblique angles, up close or further away. You can experience it kinaesthetically – in relation to body movement and position – and tactilely, and examine how light is reflected and refracted from its surface. What would you see if you were close enough that the blue completely filled your field of vision? When you stand back, does the intensity of the painting's blue pigment suffuse the surrounding space, or generate a 'ghost' on the white wall of blue's complementary colour, orange?

In a photograph you see the painting from one fixed viewpoint and distance, that chosen by the photographer, which is recorded by his or her apparatus – directly in front of and perpendicular to the surface of the painting. You can't see the sides of the painting, which are at right angles to the wall. These, too, are painted blue. Nor can you fully appraise the effect of the curiously rounded corners, which are unlike the usual right angles of paintings. Nor can you tell how this shape is related to the wall that supports it – Klein hung his works away from the wall, not snug against it. In addition, it is very important to note that the white frame around this painting was added after the work was purchased, and that Klein himself deliberately did not frame his paintings. So as it is displayed today, the work looks very different from the way Klein intended. The fact that it is framed, and that this frame is included in the photograph, significantly shifts how it is perceived in relation not only to the wall but to the whole history of art.

According to the visual criteria given by the photograph/reproduction, you will probably agree that, on reflection, what you see is a nugatory approximation of the original. The result of recording Klein's painting using a stationary mechanical viewing device that employs a single lens to focus on a surface. This is a device that captures a cyclopean view of its subject, one that only such technology can construct, and is very different from how the human eye perceives.

Subsequently, this curious artefact has been edited, and through a process of cropping to delete extraneous information (but not the white frame), it has been excised from the wider context within which it was originally photographed, which was a gallery or an artist's studio, or the photography studio at MOMA, and relocated to a page or screen. The painting has begun its existence as an image that is located within the formal constraints and protocols laid down for a medium designed to convey information optimally through the horizontal organization of lines – writing – and within the parameters determined by an academic discipline: art history.

If you were looking at a photographic reproduction of a representational painting, or one with compositional content, you would at least receive relatively accurate information about the work. Its status as a re-presentation will mean you can refer to its function as a coded system in which you 'read' content on the surface of the work. If it is a figurative work, this content will have a correlation with not only the visible world around you but a long and familiar history of other figurative images. In the case of a more conventional kind of abstract painting – a Mondrian, say –

a photograph will supply an accurate copy of its compositional organization in terms of proportion and the position of shapes. In the case of a Mondrian, the nature of the work is certainly impaired by the translation in medium, but this is to a far lesser extent than is the case with Klein's painting, which seems to lack both narrative *and* formal content – unless, that is, we read it as a decidedly uncompromising picture of the sky or sea seen through a window (something the reproduction of the painting in a book format tends to encourage and which, as we will see, was in fact a reference Klein himself was not averse to endorsing).

THE DEVELOPMENT OF digital photography has made the status of the technologically reproduced image far more complicated than it ever was in the old analogue days. On the one hand, the quality of reproductions has vastly improved. Focus, light exposure, colour hue and tone can be controlled to a much greater extent than was possible with analogue photography. New printing technologies mean it is less expensive to produce photographs and to print or display them on a screen in colour, so that in a book like this one it is now normal to expect colour reproductions rather than black-and-white ones.

But a digital image is at a much greater remove than an analogue one from the source it re-presents. There is no longer necessarily any direct, imprinted relationship between the source and the representation. Using software like Photoshop, or nowadays simply the preset options that are available on any smartphone, a photographic image is infinitely malleable. In fact, in a certain sense, thanks to digitization, a photograph now has the same status as a handmade image, in that it can no longer claim to possess an indexical relationship to the real. Taking a photograph is no longer 'seizing the light' so much as manipulating pixels within a digital matrix.[2]

But at the risk of taking my point too far, it could be argued that any photographic reproduction of a work of art – analogue or digital – gratuitously perverts its meaning, making it vulnerable to a specific kind of intellectualized analysis, the kind at home within the pages of a book rather than in the more open and non-linear spaces of art. While an encounter with a real painting brings significant perceptual and multimodal stimulation – what psychologists call 'bottom-up' stimuli, coming from the body – an encounter with a photograph of a painting depends far more on 'top-down' information: data coming from our memory, prior knowledge, imagination, education and cultural worldview. Making sense of an encounter with a real work of art always includes input from 'top-down' information, but a photograph of an artwork depends far more substantially on this storehouse to give it substance and meaning.

For example, I can recall seeing for the first time in my teens the works of Mark Rothko in an art book and immediately dismissing them as some kind of con or joke. This was not only because I knew almost nothing about abstract art, but because I had never seen a *real* Rothko, nor hardly any examples of abstract art in general. As a result, I was unable to augment my experience of the tiny little photograph of coloured and black-and-white blurry shapes with useful memories of, and imaginative extrapolations from, the actual painting.

But we need to go back to the cave paintings of the Upper Palaeolithic, the earliest of which it is currently believed date to around 40,000 years ago, to find pictures that are perhaps unpolluted by verbal language.[3] In the Renaissance, the mutual dependency of word and image was freely acknowledged under the classical maxim *ut pictura poesis* (as is painting, so is poetry). In other words, painting is mute poetry, and poetry is spoken painting. But powerful arguments have been made to claim that modern art, and especially abstract art, resists language. In reality, however, the situation was much more confused, and will be especially so in relation to the monochrome. As W.J.T. Mitchell argues, paradoxically, the dependence on verbal discourse was especially heavy in relation to abstract art, and one could even assert that 'The entire antiverbal ideology of abstraction, its depiction as a rigorous "barrier" between vision and language, is a myth that needs to be understood and not just debunked.'[4]

But reading about and looking at art take place in very different locations, and involve very different customs and cognitive and social skills. The book you are reading (whether printed or digital) and the art it discusses exist in different, though linked, ontological, epistemological, semantic and social domains. In a book, you will be confronted with a flat blue rectangle inside a white frame, placed symmetrically upon a larger white rectangle (the page), which it will also probably share with small black shapes organized in neat clusters in horizontal rows (alphabetic letters). On a computer screen, unless you're seeing a traditional book format reproduced online, the same image will be obliged to share the visual field with advertisements or other only marginally relevant or completely unconnected fragments of data.

But this kind of division is also carried over into the three-dimensional world of social spaces. The gallery wall label strives to import into the art viewing space something of the reassuringly clear and distinct protocols of reading space, and in a certain sense a museum is like a three-dimensional projection of the book space –

with the entrance as the cover, and each numbered gallery functioning as a chapter. The wall labels and commentaries constantly call us back to the realm of the discursive. More recently, the guiding metaphor has shifted to that of cyberspace, but with uncertain interpretative benefits. In the typical viewing conditions imposed on the gallery- and museum-goer, the closest encounter with an artwork you are likely to have physically is when you read the wall label sited next to the work. In fact, people often spend more time reading these labels than they do looking at the actual art. Barriers (now often programmed to trigger an alarm) and nearby guards also effectively keep us at a distance.

Taking all these points into consideration, you may be tempted to conclude that there is very little purpose in looking at an illustration – especially a black-and-white one – of a monochrome. They cannot be duplicated mechanically in anything but the most notional way. The absence of compositional complexity, the reduction of the painted surface to one single colour, means that a monochrome is especially resistant to photographic reproduction. In short, much more than with other kinds of art – even abstract art – a photograph of a monochrome is more comparable to hearsay than to the experience of seeing one in person.

But the lack of a visible 'hook' might force us to consider that Klein's painting is not just something to apprehend in relation to the visual, but rather possesses something invisible, intangible and immaterial. An encounter with a real Yves Klein monochrome can force on us a much greater awareness of perceptual limits, of the invisible, or the unrepresentable – all that exceeds our capacities for control and organization. At the same time, and seemingly paradoxically, however, Klein's painting also has a powerful impact as a physically present object, and in this sense is very far from conveying the immaterial. This ambiguous awareness clearly cannot be accounted for on the level of signs – as a coded message, and therefore as something we can intellectually infer. It is communicated affectively and has a directly phenomenological dimension. In which case, we will certainly need to be in front of the real work in order to sense and experience it.

But perhaps Klein's painting's lack of visual complexity can also lead to another conclusion: a monochrome is not really about seeing at all. It is the idea that counts. After all, Klein's monochromes are more similar to each other than almost any other artist's paintings, even to the extent that they may seem to be identical: 'Once you've seen one, you've seen them all.' The content, which is supposed to be manifest through formal configuration rather than added on through a theoretical supplement, can be considered of such generality that it is exactly the same in every instance. A specific monochrome is in a sense a clone or repetition of a prototype. If this is true, then it would follow that it is not necessary to actually *see* a specific example. An image of a monochrome, albeit far removed from the actual thing, is sufficient to trigger the necessary intellectual work of viewing one. In fact, this being the case, working with reproductions may benefit this process by diminishing the distracting physical presence and aura of the real work, turning it into a much weaker visual cipher. Being aware of the possibility or the fact that a real object – a monochrome – has been made might on this reading be considered sufficient to make it a work of art.

If the monochrome ultimately brings to the fore the invisible and non-perceptual aspects of an encounter with art, then it is also closely involved with the cognitive dimension, which includes knowledge, imagination, beliefs, memories, fantasies and dreams.

In fact, for this reason one can argue that in a certain sense the meaning of any particular monochrome is *less* travestied by a photograph than any other kind of painting would be. Because they are so sensually under-stimulating, a real monochrome is a useful visual token for generating and attracting ideas and concepts. If a monochrome's meaning is not crucially dependent on a visual encounter, and emanates substantially from within the realm of abstract thought, then the less sensually imposing and potentially transformative the visual evidence, the more our mind is free to do its work. So, for those intent on intellectualizing art, it is perhaps better to deal with a photograph of a monochrome than a real one – preferably in black and white. Even a verbal description will do. As the critic Benjamin H. D. Buchloh argues in an essay discussing Klein, if we consider that the monochrome is 'a conceptual metalanguage', then one monochrome is more or less the same as any other.[5] In fact, the monochrome is ideally suited for such transformation into a 'conceptual' artefact, accompanied by copious exegesis; it is work destined from birth to hang on the wall of a museum and to have its meaning outlined in wall text, and discussed in great detail in books and on websites.[6]

But what if a monochrome isn't just about the absence of an image, or at least, what if the way in which the absence is communicated depends on the specific material reality of the work – on its real presence? What if, as I suggested above, an encounter with Klein's painting affects the kinds of thoughts and feelings we have when in front of it? What if it isn't just a passive trigger but an active agent? What if each monochrome invokes different associations and memories? Or, at least, what if the kind of conceptual space opened up by seeing Klein's painting is qualitatively different from the one opened by seeing it as a photograph? Then, it isn't even simply that we must recall in words what the real encounter was like, because such experiences refuse translation into words.

Does looking at the photograph of the Klein painting convey a powerful sense of primal, spiritually charged unity beyond all differences, as Klein intended, or is all we see a simple blue rectangle? Of course, looking at the real painting by Klein might also fail to deliver the kind of experience Klein hoped to invoke. After all, one would have to recognize that the 'unity' we see is much more than simply that of a well-painted wall, for example. We cannot, and surely would not want to, claim that the content of the Klein somehow imposes itself on all viewers, like a commandment from on high. Indeed, as we will see, it is precisely because the content of a monochrome is so underdetermined – that is, provides less evidence than the amount needed for proof or certainty – that it is so fascinating.

THERE IS VERY little chance that you will be able to verify in a directly experiential way the concrete nature of the Klein while reading *The Simple Truth*, or even soon afterwards or perhaps ever. It is certainly possible that you have already seen this particular painting in the flesh, and more likely that you have seen a similar one by Klein. As Klein's monochromes are so alike, we can assume they have a generic quality that makes seeing a specific example much less important than is usually the case. If you have seen a real Klein painting, you can use this reproduction as a memory aid to conjure up something of the absent original. The last time I saw this particular painting was several years ago, so I have been drawing on my memories, and relating it to another Klein seen much more recently at the Centre Pompidou in Paris (and unencumbered by a white frame).

For those readers who have never seen a real Klein painting, the situation is more complex. You only have this photograph to go on, bolstered by my description in words, plus your memory of seeing real works by other artists that seem to have similar stylistic characteristics, and also by your general background knowledge of this kind of thing. In such cases, it seems very likely that any content you draw from the Klein will be a supplement that has been provided through a verbal commentary.

There are practical, social, political and institutional dimensions to the issues discussed here, dimensions that are especially pressing if one considers that many people studying art nowadays live far from metropolitan centres supplied with well-stocked museums. One significant aspect of the globalization of culture is that this book may well be read by people in vastly different places, including ones that do not have museums with paintings by Yves Klein. People will have to make a journey to gain the acquaintance of a *real* Yves Klein, so they may not bother. This means that it is necessary to assimilate into any discussion of the monochrome (and art in general, of course) the fact that an encounter will often be indirect, highly mediated, and/or based on the kind of basic criteria that in many ways is typical of the first forms of art writing, which were discursive texts whose purpose was to call to mind and bring to life something the author had seen that lies far away. Before photography we only had words, and copies of originals handmade in print media such as etchings, to assist in this goal. With photography, things became easier – or they seemed to. However, any difficulty we may have in encountering a real Klein is more than compensated for by the dubious ease with which we can see one in reproduction on the Internet.

2

RECEPTION

> A non-entertainment, not for art commerce or mass-art publics, non-expressionist, not for oneself.[1]
>
> Ad Reinhardt (1955)

On 17 November 1977, the *New York Times* reported that 'a vandal or an angry art lover punched holes Tuesday in a "black" painting at Christie's by the late abstractionist painter Ad Reinhardt [(1913–1967)].' It continued:

> As a result, the painting was removed from those scheduled to be auctioned there tonight.
>
> The 5-square-foot painting appears to be nothing but a black canvas. Actually, there are subtle, close-valued tones that appear black to the naked eye.
>
> Mr Reinhardt's black paintings have been physically attacked in the past, and one at the Museum of Modern Art was roped off to keep it from harm. The one scheduled to have been auctioned tonight was estimated in the catalogue to be worth $35,000.[2]

Attacks like this on modern art, and on monochromes in particular, are fortunately not common, but the fact that they sometimes occur is evidence that works of art have the capacity to stir powerful negative emotions.[3] They even seem to function as surrogates for social relationships, and in this case, Reinhardt's painting was construed by the attacker as profoundly antisocial, and so he responded with an equally antisocial action.

It is fairly obvious what the 'vandal' or 'angry art lover' found so provocative. First of all, Reinhardt's monochrome appears to lack any recognizable content. This absence, which is made all the more blatant by the choice of black as the single colour, may have been especially unsettling if the man expected to find in an exhibition the traditional kind of representational content, and the lack may have been similarly felt even if he had been prepared to find evidence of the kind of expressionistic distortion typical of, say, Matisse or Picasso. But Reinhardt's painting also doesn't really seem to function as an *abstract* work of art. It doesn't contain shapes or colours arranged in an order that is likely to evoke an emotional or aesthetic response. A quick look at the painting will suggest that is it just a blank black square, while, as the *Times* article notes, on more sustained analysis what at first appears to be one solid square is actually nine closely valued black-hued squares arranged in a grid or cruciform structure. But recognizing this subtle level of compositional organization is unlikely to have made the painting any more appealing for the vandal. In other words, it seems to stand in obdurate opposition not only to the old idea of what makes a work of art interesting, but even to the newer ones proposed by the mid-twentieth-century avant-garde.

The apparent simplicity of Reinhardt's painting may also have communicated to the attacker an unsettling level of emptiness, even the possibility that Reinhardt had engaged in an act of deliberate and nihilistic voiding of everything that art is supposed to hold dear. Reinhardt himself did indeed make much of this process of negation in his statements. Here is one from 1955 in which he declares that he believed that an artwork should be

> A clearly defined object, independent and separate from all other objects and circumstances, in which we cannot see whatever we choose or make of it anything we want, whose meaning is not detachable or translatable. A free, unmanipulated and unmanipulable, useless, unmarketable, irreducible, unphotographable, unreproducible, inexplicable icon. A non-entertainment, not for art commerce or mass-art publics, non-expressionist, not for oneself.[4]

On the face of it, Reinhardt's work also looks as if it was produced with the minimum of technical skill. It may have suggested to the attacker the possibility that anyone could have made it, and so this invalidated it as 'art'. In fact, in 1951 another American artist, Robert Rauschenberg, wrote to his New York gallerist, Betty Parsons, concerning his own all-white monochrome paintings, declaring precisely this as being one of the important virtues of his new work. Since the pristine paint layer was applied with a roller, the activity of renewal could be done by anyone, declared Rauschenberg. 'It is completely irrelevant that I am making them. *Today* is their creator.'[5] But if this is indeed the case, then we (and the vandal) might be led to wonder how it is possible to tell the difference between a rectangular black or white surface hung on the wall, and a black or white 'monochrome painting' endowed with the status of 'art'. Under such circumstances, it is possible to imagine two works – one made by a renowned artist, the other by a complete unknown – that look identical but are accredited wholly different cultural (and economic) value.

Ultimately, Reinhardt's painting probably suggested to the attacker that it was the result of its maker's deliberate intention to shut people out, to generate an intimidating aura of elitist exclusivity. The painting precluded so much of what is normally expected from our relationships with art. For him, Reinhardt had evidently failed to keep his side of the bargain; he had failed to uphold the pact or contract that is supposed to govern our relationship with art.

In fact, by the time the attacker punched holes in the painting, the monochrome had already for over fifty years been playing a leading role in a drama that Susan Sontag described in 1969 as the systematic severance of the dialogue between art and its potential public. She wrote:

> Most valuable art in our time has been experienced by audiences as a move into silence (or unintelligibility or invisibility or inaudibility); a dismantling of the artist's competence, his responsible sense of vocation – and therefore as an aggression against them.[6]

One way of expressing this 'move into silence' is to see it as a basic assault on taste, on the very notion of 'beauty'. From the beginning of the twentieth century, avant-gardes set about destroying the terms by which the pacts traditionally binding the taste of an audience to its art had been written.[7] The most time-honoured kind of pact is that built on the will of a whole community. But this had already been shattered by the destabilizing rhythms of incessant change characteristic of modernity, and any hope of establishing such a consensus remained only the dream of the revolutionary and reactionary. But in pre-modern society the pact had also been based on an audience's recognition of a work of art's truthfulness in relation to prior experience, or its similarity to other admired representations. The avant-garde also deliberately jeopardized any possibility of this accord by using unfamiliar subject-matter, employing distorted representational styles, abstraction, collage, the readymade, and other unfamiliar and non-traditional styles and media. A third type of pact had been based on faith in a credible authority that gave validity to a work, but this, too, modern artists very consciously undermined through the radical embrace of the new and deliberate strategies of deconstruction and scandal-mongering, while at the same time setting themselves up as a new authority deliberately at odds with the old. A fourth kind of pact, grounded in the recognition that a work embodies values that are greatly hoped for or considered ideal, was also systematically challenged by deliberate acts of nihilistic destruction, or by the artists embracing political and spiritual goals that were inimical to large sections of the bourgeois art-going public. At the same time, the avant-garde also demanded that their audience adopt the new hopes and ideals in which they, the artists, believed.

As a result, modern art is intellectually demanding. This fact alone renders it marginal to most people's lives. This alienating potential is compounded by the fact that, unlike literature, there is a tacit assumption that because art typically uses the visual modality, it should be about representing the world we all see. What therefore makes the monochrome in particular one of the most demanding kinds of visual art is the fact that it so obviously refuses to function as a representation of any recognizable kind. It not only uncouples painting from the old syntax of representational art, in which figurative content is rendered through a composition comprising divisions that produce a hierarchy of signs, but it uncouples it from the much newer syntax of abstract art, in which traditional representational space is abandoned and emphasis shifts to a formal visual semantics determined by the organization of shape and colour on a two-dimensional surface. The monochrome therefore undermines the essential binary opposition that is necessary if art is to function as a stable and meaningful language – as a pictorial code. It takes the familiar resources of painting and forces them to elude both the old representational order and the new non-representational one. It pushes painting towards non-relational and anti-structural unity, or, more accurately, it negates the relation between parts from within the four edges or frame of a work, pushing them over its edges, and, potentially, beyond the object itself onto the wall, the exhibiting space, the culture in general – and yet further outwards from the initial encounter with the work.

Furthermore, because monochromes are composed of very few parts, the same small number of basic elements are shared by examples that have been made with very different agendas and that carry very different meanings. Imagine, for example, a hypothetical exhibition comprised solely of black monochromes. First, we encounter one that, so we learn from the exhibition guide, has been made to suggest that something has been left out, erased or concealed. But next to this there is another that we discover aims to evoke the existential void, the nothingness at the heart of being, or death. Nearby hangs another whose creator wants to suggest the mystical 'ground of being', the Absolute, the source of life itself. Next to it is another that is cast as a simple negation to be read in the light of what it is not, or what has deliberately been left out – lines, colour relations, imagery, symbolism, narrative. Next to this one is a monochrome that is supposed to embody pure potential, a suggestive vacancy signifying possibilities that are in direct proportion to the work's lack of easy readability. Yet another celebrates the 'impossible', the infinite, the transubstantiation of the art object into a refined and intangible feeling, and is neither a representation nor an abstraction but rather pure potential. Near this work hangs one that is simply announcing its obdurate materiality, the fact that it is black paint on a rectangular plane. Next to this is a black monochrome that aims to narrow or even erase the gap between art and life by being an object among other objects. Finally, in addition to all these is one that claims to be a 'meta-monochrome' – a black monochrome painting *about* all the possible meanings of black monochrome paintings, and about how black monochromes function in the elaborate institutional framework within which they all exist.

My hypothetical exhibition is only credible on paper, of course. A real one would oblige me to discuss in much more detail what kind of black each monochrome possesses. Is it entirely black or, like Ad Reinhardt's, subtly varied, or like Robert Rauschenberg's, painted on top of newspaper? Is the black glossy or matt, rough or smooth, opaque or transparent? What size is each work? But all the same, the conclusion is a reasonable one: monochromes seriously 'underdetermine their interpretations', as the philosopher and critic Arthur Danto put it.[8]

ANY WORK OF art will be perceived in a sociocultural context or setting, as part of a tradition, and therefore with the active involvement of memory. There is no real distinction between direct perception of an image and one consolidated by memory or even completely recalled or imagined. What psychologists call 'bottom-up' rules and 'top-down' processes – cognitive activity caused by stimuli coming from the body, on the one hand, and from information coming from memory (that is, encompassing history, knowledge and so on) on the other – produce the 'horizon' of meaning within which any work of art can be turned into a functioning code.[9] The eye 'is a product of history reproduced by education', as the sociologist Pierre Bourdieu puts it.[10]

As any novel phenomenon can only be understood by comparing it with something that is already known, a confrontation with something new and unfamiliar will always bring with it a sense of being at a disadvantage or a feeling of lack. Context determines the grounds for any comparison. We observe differences, seek similarities and try to draw conclusions. A work of art has meaning and interest for someone only if they are in possession of what Bourdieu calls 'cultural competence', that is, when they have know-how, and it is encoded. Without such a code, Bourdieu writes, someone will inevitably feel 'lost in a chaos of sounds and rhythms, colours and lines, without rhyme or reason'.[11] The cognitive model we use to understand a work will determine what we find, and with what we choose to compare this newly encountered work of art will determine which aspects stand forward and which recede in our conscious understanding.

Where an encounter with a monochrome is concerned, the importance of our mindset and the setting in which the encounter takes place are especially vital. To make a blank canvas seem meaningful, rather than just a dull object or the raw material needed to make art, it is necessary to be trained and acquainted with a specific history. A storehouse of 'top-down' information is called upon. Such resources are especially important in relation to the monochrome because, to a much greater extent than with other kinds of art, a monochrome's meaning is often related to a viewer's ability to make a convincing correlation between a minimal visual stimulus and a complex extra-sensory premise. In other words, in order to make sense of a monochrome, we must call on the inner space of thought rather than on our visual knowledge of the world.

For whatever reason, the man who attacked the Reinhardt clearly lacked the appropriately trained and acquainted eye needed to fully 'get' a Reinhardt. He was unable or unwilling to engage imaginatively or intellectually in ways that could make the painting acceptable to him as a work of art. He did not possess the specific mindset, but he also did not possess the specific 'setting' – the physical, mental, social and environmental context – that must be brought to the encounter with Reinhardt's art. He was not an 'insider' who could believe that Reinhardt had made something worthy of being called art, and that was therefore worth paying attention to, and a good deal of money for, at an art auction. Furthermore, the man clearly sensed this feeling of exclusion as a personal threat, and so responded with direct action. It is as if abstract art often seems to say: '"You, who are not qualified to speak about this art, keep your mouth shut."'[12] The attacker must have had a profound sense not only of incomprehension, but that he had not been invited into the 'magic circle' comprising those capable of understanding the value – aesthetic, and therefore financial – of such things. A sense of betrayal was felt on a personal and visceral level and led to violent, desperate action.

When the first monochromatic works, Malevich's *Black Square* (illus. 3) and *White on White*, made their appearance more than sixty years before Reinhardt's painting was assaulted, it was the absence of representational reference and compositional complexity that was so shocking. Malevich's intention inevitably cast the monochrome as a negation of what art is. His paintings were apprehended by everyone who saw them as unprecedented assaults on art, and they must have seemed akin to an act of blinding. 'The critics along with the public exclaimed, "everything we love has disappeared. Before us is a black square in a white frame",' wrote Malevich with evident satisfaction some years after he first exhibited *Black Square*.[13] He had deliberately made his paintings as devoid as possible of the familiar cues or prompts that aided a viewer of the period – progressive or reactionary – when looking at a painting. He used the monochrome to push art relentlessly towards a state that would be read as bordering on the meaningless, recognizing that the less familiar a work of art is – the further it strays from a context within which it can be compared with the already known and habitual – the more chance it will have of being directly perceived as an uncoded phenomenon, and therefore as a genuine *experience*.

Betty Parsons, Robert Rauschenberg's New York gallerist, mentioned earlier, was definitely an art 'insider' of the period, but she was nevertheless unconvinced by white monochromes that could be repainted by anyone, and so she declined to show them. But in 1953 Rauschenberg exhibited the works at the newly opened Stable Gallery in Manhattan, and among those who visited was the progressive art critic Hubert Crehan. He too was unconvinced. Rauschenberg's paintings, Crehan declared, were 'a *chef-d'oeuvre* of duck [meaning cotton duck, or canvas] pressed to the point of no return . . . White canvas . . . conceived as a work of art, is beyond the artistic pale.'[14]

Two years later, and across the Atlantic in Paris, Yves Klein submitted a large matt orange monochrome to the progressive Salon des Réalités Nouvelles, which was devoted to abstract art. It too was rejected. Once again, a monochrome was successfully deployed to test the institutions of art at their 'cutting edge'. As far as the committee of the salon was concerned, the 27-year-old Klein's submission crossed a boundary beyond which even their advanced aesthetics could not go. It eradicated all compositional divisions, all relations, by eliminating the fundamental prerequisite of the projection of an image onto a surface. In Klein's painting, the image or 'figure' had become coequal with the field or 'ground'. The painting's title did little to help convince the committee of the work's seriousness: it was called *Expression de l'univers de la couleur mine orange* (Expression of the Colour World of Lead-orange, or Expression of the World of the Colour Lead-orange). Klein had even failed to relate his minimal visual idiom to some kind of acceptable content via an appropriate label. 'Untitled' would have been less unacceptable.

As a result, the members of the committee could only announce to Klein's mother, the painter Marie Raymond – who, it is important to note, was herself a regular exhibitor at the Salon des Réalités Nouvelles – 'One single, uniform colour, no, no, truly that is not enough, that is impossible,' or so Klein later reported.[15] The painting was just too simple and too pure, and therefore, in the opinion of the committee, not art worthy of the name. The monochrome threw down a challenge that questioned the very basis of painting, even abstract painting. According to the dominant narrative of the time, the best in avant-garde art originated in the explorations begun in the mid-nineteenth century in the work of Édouard Manet and the Impressionists. Their art was important, it was argued, because it was involved in continuous reduction and purification, as painting searched for the essence of itself within its own formal resources. In the case of painting, as Clement Greenberg wrote in 'Modernist Painting' (1961), in what amounts to the most uncompromising version of this narrative, the quest for purity meant the concentration on the visual faculty detached from any other sense or mental activity, and the reduction of optical stimulation to the flatness of the surface, which, so Greenberg argued, was the most fundamental process within painting. For only flatness was the unique, indivisible concern of painting. He wrote, 'The enclosing shape of the picture was a limiting condition, or norm, that was shared with the art of the theater; color was a norm and a means shared not only with the theater, but also with sculpture.'[16]

Inevitably, applying such formalist procedures in practice meant an artist would potentially veer close to the singularity of a monochrome canvas. As Greenberg observed, 'a monochromatic flatness that could be seen as limited in extension and different from a wall henceforth automatically declared itself to be a picture, to be art.'[17] But Greenberg also noted that while colour was a primary vehicle for achieving planarity, it was also a characteristic that painting shared with theatre and sculpture. Only flatness was unique and indispensable to painting as a medium, and commitment to flatness did not preclude the display of 'heightened sensitivity to the picture plane', the continued play of the optical, as the work of the artists advocated by Greenberg demonstrated. Michael Fried, another important American formalist critic of the period, expressed this concern clearly:

> At the same time that the spectator may have gained the ability to see a length of fabric as a potential painting, he may also

> have acquired the tendency to regard a modernist painting of the highest quality as nothing more than a length of coloured fabric. Because all sorts of large and small items that used to belong entirely to the realm of the arbitrary and the visually meaningless may now be experienced pictorially or in a meaningful relationship to the pictorial, the risk is greatly increased that first-rate modernist painting will appear arbitrary and visually meaningless.[18]

Writing in 1967, Greenberg recalled his own first encounter with Rauschenberg's monochromes at the Stable Gallery and noted that the initial shock of seeing a seemingly empty painting had soon worn off. 'I was surprised by how easy they were to "get," how familiar-looking and even slick,' Greenberg wrote:

> It was no different afterwards when I first saw Reinhardt's, Sally Hazlett's, and Yves Klein's monochromatic or near-monochromatic pictures. These too, looked familiar and slick . . . The look of accident was not the only 'wild' thing that Abstract Expressionism first acclimatized and then domesticated in painting: it did the same to emptiness, to the look of the 'void.'[19]

For Greenberg, the problem wasn't that the monochrome was not art, it was that it wasn't good enough art. It just didn't have the capacity to push modern painting towards the kinds of refinements of taste that were central to his version of formalist theory.

But for formalists, the monochrome was also a potentially pernicious influence. It jeopardized the capacity of other kinds of purist abstract painting to address important aesthetic concerns successfully. When a painting is perceived to be no different from a blank canvas, for example, it has been reduced to the status of something that is already made prior to artistic interventions – it is a 'readymade'. In this sense, the destiny for the monochrome is to become another iteration of the subversive challenge thrown down by Marcel Duchamp around the same time as the birth of the monochrome when he began presenting found objects as works of art. But a monochrome becomes a readymade that relates to the properties of the genre of painting. As the art historian Thierry de Duve writes, 'unlike Duchamp's bottlerack or urinal, the blank canvas is a *specific* readymade.'[20] Thus a monochrome produces a relationship between painting and the criteria explored by Duchamp, that is, the manner in which an artist's election of an object as 'art' becomes sufficient grounds for it becoming 'art'.

What Greenberg saw was that through exploiting to an extreme the legitimately reductive practices of abstract art, the monochrome ends up presenting the quasi-blank canvas as a work of art, and thereby risks undermining the formalist project in general. The simple unity of the monochrome suggested the unsettling possibility that anything can be art. Greenberg and Fried, like the formalists on the committee of the Paris salon who rejected Klein's orange monochrome, were therefore right to be wary. The purity of the monochrome produced a paradox that ultimately undermined formalist principles. An artist pursuing modernist painting will often arrive at the literal flatness of a monochrome, but 'at that point they would cease to be painters and would merely be producing "arbitrary objects".'[21]

Eighty years after Malevich's *Black Square* presented viewers with a 'desert', 42 after Klein's orange monochrome was rejected by the

Salon des Réalités Nouvelles, 36 after Betty Parson refused to show Rauschenberg's white paintings and 17 after the 'vandal' or 'angry art lover' attacked Reinhardt's black painting, Yasmina Reza's hit play *Art* (1994), mentioned in the Introduction, appeared. Reza's choice of the monochrome as her play's focus seems broadly appropriate, given the history just sketched. Nevertheless, as already noted, by the time she wrote her play a proportion of the potential audience for the monochrome – and her play – had already become over-familiar with its artful blankness. When Malevich exhibited his monochromes, almost all viewers found what they saw so unexpected and improbable as to judge them meaningless and unacceptable as art. It also seems that when Klein entered his monochrome to the salon in 1955, substantial numbers even of progressives still found the one-colour painting beyond the pale. But by the time the man assaulted the Reinhardt, and even more so by the time Reza wrote her play, the monochrome's subversive, negating role had been greatly diminished. The capacity of the monochrome to communicate the 'spiritual' or an unsettling sense of nothingness – metaphysical, existential, formal – was evaporating through familiarity. The act of negation was in danger of becoming mere design.

By the late 1960s, avant-garde strategies had shifted away from the explorations of purity and formal autonomy towards the analysis of the conceptual dimension of art, and art's role within an institutional framework. In the 1970s and '80s, across the USA and Europe, artists increasingly dedicated themselves to the dethroning or reframing of the products of modernism through the application of linguistically based structuralist and semiotic models and procedures. The socially constructed nature of vision, the extent to which visual perception and visual meaning are fused, and how artworks are compromisingly implicated in an economic system that seems to reduce everything to exchange value, were now central to the critical analysis and practice of art. In this context, the modernist faith in the work of art's autonomy and in the purity of vision was simply no longer credible.

For Benjamin Buchloh, writing in 1998, for example, the monochrome had already been played out by the 1960s. He passed scornful judgement on Klein's paintings, writing that 'in Klein's hands the withdrawal of perceptual data – rather than wean his audience from the dependence upon an ontologically and phenomenologically grounded visuality – functioned as well calibrated *choc* for the already initiated.'[22] Many 'insiders' concluded that the monochrome was little more than a historical artefact. As the artist Jeff Wall wrote in 1993, a year before Reza's play premiered in Paris:

> For us, a new piece of canvas is already a monochrome; that is, it is already a certain kind of painting . . . It is the historical identity and character of what we call 'avant-gardism' that compels us to experience an empty canvas this way . . . The aesthetic categories created or revolutionized by the avant-garde have become objectivities for us, inescapable and necessary structures, transcendental conditions of the experience of works of art.[23]

From being a powerfully subversive medium, one through which to address the notion of the terminal point, the limit, the origin, boundaries, negation, emptiness or the transcendent, the monochrome had become just one stylistic option among many. At least for the 'us' evoked by Wall and Danto, the monochrome painting was thoroughly domesticated. Nevertheless, more than two decades since Reza wrote her play, Buchloh passed judgement and Wall and Danto concluded that the monochrome was an over-familiar piece of the furniture of the avant-garde, it still seems likely that, at least for 'outsiders' and the uninitiated intent on becoming an 'insider', there will still be a monochrome painting standing at the entrance to the mysterious world of modern art, barring the way.

BUT THE DESTRUCTION of the old pacts binding art and audience that was wrought by the avant-garde of the nineteenth and first half of the twentieth century was matched by the gradual creation of a new pact that is uniquely modern and now firmly in place – one that forged a more fluid relationship with the viewer, who is recast as a collaborator in the development of a kind of work-in-progress.

Even the arch-modernist Ad Reinhardt seems to have understood modern art in these terms, at least some of the time. Somewhat surprisingly, the austere painter of black monochromes also doubled as a cartoonist who commented on the vagaries of the art world.[24] In one cartoon from the 1950s, Reinhardt shows what is at stake within the new pact. He draws the same abstract painting twice. In the top drawing, a man in a trilby is mockingly smiling, pointing at the painting and saying, 'Ha, Ha, What does this represent?' In the bottom drawing, it is the painting's turn to respond. Some of the lines on its surface have turned into an accusatory face, and it has sprouted legs and an arm, which points accusingly at the now dumbfounded man as the painting says, 'What do *you* represent?'[25]

The style of the painting Reinhardt depicts is characteristically Abstract Expressionist and looks rather like something he himself might have painted at the time. But it is surely the monochromes that he went on to make that even better represent the status of the new art, which was to be encountered by a viewer who is now figured as an interlocutor in a process involving the critical analysis both of the work of art and of themselves. In this context, monochromes are the most explicit instances of a modern art that, while established by the artist, is dependent on the viewer for realization. They are not predetermined and are actualized during the act of contemplation.

Reinhardt attributes to his cartoon-painting the kind of agency normally reserved for living things, and dramatizes the encounter with art through suggesting that it emanates a force that directly impacts on the viewer, even against his or her will. In this sense, the artist is positioned as the author of a network or field of forces, with the viewer – the recipient or the one affected by the network – participating in an active way in how the work is experienced as well as in what it means. Reinhardt suggests, and Reza's play entertainingly demonstrates, that this dynamic encounter will be potentially confrontational, or at least discomforting, because it is inevitably characterized by distrust on both sides. But it is also one that turns the audience of art into an active participant in a potentially transformational experience.

3

COLOUR

Color . . . is the natural and human measure;
it bathes in a cosmic sensibility.[1]
Yves Klein (1958)

For the monochromist, colour is supposed to be painting's final usable property, and it is cast as the salvation of painting. For Yves Klein, the history of art was a perpetual struggle between line and colour. 'Ordinary painting, painting as it is commonly understood, is a prison window whose lines, contours, forms, and composition are all determined by bars,' Klein announced.[2] 'Line' represented the oppressive forces of reason and authority, while 'colour' embodied feeling and the freedom of the imagination:

> The line concretizes our mortality, our emotional life, our reason, and even our spirituality. They are psychological boundaries, our historical past, our skeletal framework; they are our weakness and our desires, our faculties, and our contrivances. Color, on the other hand, is the natural and human measure; it bathes in a cosmic sensibility.[3]

Perceptually speaking, colour permits differential spatial readings and as a result is inherently weak as a code-bearing entity. It brings to the fore awareness of the mobility of forms, the ambiguity of locations and the fluidity of contours, thereby directly manifesting the deeper and unstable nature of consciousness – but also undermining any ability to organize and establish firm cognitive boundaries.

Klein was also pitting himself against the idea that colour's ubiquity, its normative, everyday quality and its role as sensory stimulant made it an inferior property of art. He stood firm against a whole cultural predisposition – against 'chromophobia', as the contemporary artist and writer David Batchelor terms it.[4] For among those seeking to bind art closely to the life of the mind, the consensus has always been that colour is superficial and illusory, even deceitful, carnal and corrupting. Classical philosophers, Church Fathers and Renaissance humanists all concurred in the need to denigrate colour. The will of God or human knowledge was understood to be communicated through the clear and stable medium of the line, which imposes structure and order on the visual and is the means through which form appears from out of the chaotic flux of sensory stimulations.

Renaissance theoretical treatises on painting followed a deep-rooted convention in which 'line' was given much greater importance than 'colour' because their authors aimed to distance 'fine art' from craft and the artisanal trades, and to elevate it to the same level as the truly 'spiritual' or intellectual arts such as poetry. In Leon Battista Alberti's *On Painting* (1435), for example, the linear organization of composition is described as the most important skill for a painter, who 'must understand that he will become an excellent artist only if he knows well the borderlines of surfaces and their proportions'.[5]

In Giorgio Vasari's *Lives of the Artists* (1550), Florentine art is deemed superior to all others because Florentine artists had gained mastery of *disegno* – drawing. Venetian artists were well known by that time for their exploitation of transparent glazes and the rich chromatic properties of oil paint, and for producing paintings with intense colour saturation, soft contours and luminous tinted atmospheres that evoked the fluidity of a native environment characterized by the co-presence of architecture and water, but the art of Venice barely features in Vasari's *Lives*.[6] In the Renaissance, linear contour was understood to provide the conceptual and formal architecture that was necessary for the establishment of a stable and timeless order of learning. It facilitated the exercise of both the spiritual and the reasoning faculties, guaranteeing the intellectual powers necessary for invention and access to the inner world of absolute truth. Colour, on the other hand, was deemed to be inherently fickle from a rational point of view, and merely sensual and decorative.

The cultural animus against colour among the learned is especially striking because colour has always been so central to almost all artists' practices. Before the nineteenth century, the mortar and pestle needed for grinding pigment for paint were almost as important as the paintbrush and the wood panel or canvas. Artists often had to go to great lengths and expense to find and prepare colours, purchasing the pigments from apothecaries, and later in the shops of professional colourmen. A manual of reliable colour recipes was an important workshop tool. One from fifteenth-century Bologna lists a large number of bizarre-sounding recipes. Several are for producing 'azure', a blue hue, including this one:

> To make azure from the juice of herbs. – First collect in the beginning of the month of July those violet flowers which grow

> in the fields, and with the juice of them fill a glass flask, and pour strong vinegar or urine into it until it is full; let it be well covered over, and put it in dung or a heap of quicklime, or in the refuse of grapes for a fortnight, then take it out, and you will find your azure made.[7]

To apply coloured pigment to a surface it is necessary to mix it with a binder so that the powdered particles hold together and remain attached to the support after drying. Upper Palaeolithic humans living some 35,000 years ago used spit or animal fat. In the Middle Ages the most frequently used binder was the yolk of an egg, which produced a medium known as tempera. In the Renaissance, a new medium, oil paint, which usually mixed pigment with linseed oil, developed to supersede tempera. Since the 1950s, a plastic polymer emulsion binder has become popular and is known as acrylic paint. Each of these media has its own special properties. Tempera is fast-drying and opaque, while oil dries more slowly but can be used to produce semi-transparent layers, called glazes, and can be built up into terrains, a technique called impasto. Acrylic, which is essentially liquid plastic, is mixed with water; it is fast-drying and can be used like oil paint to build up variegated surfaces, or like tempera, to produce smooth, opaque grounds.

The paint medium can be applied in numerous ways and to numerous surfaces. Upper Palaeolithic painters brushed, smeared, dabbed and blew paint onto the uneven surfaces of dark caves. Since records began to be kept, the most frequently used tool for applying colour has been the hand-held brush. This was traditionally made using animal hair attached to a wooden shaft. More recently, paint has also been applied to surfaces using a roller, pressurized spraying devices, and with the assistance of computers. In the

Middle Ages, the surface onto which paint was applied was usually the flat panel of a rectangular piece of wood, although paint was also applied directly to the still wet plaster of a wall, a technique known as fresco. In the Renaissance, a new support – the woven canvas used for the sails of ships, stretched over a wooden frame – gradually superseded wood panels. This textile substrate in linen or cotton offered greater durability and flexibility, and the possibility of working on a large scale.

Today we are accustomed to chemically synthesized colours that come readymade in tubes or cans, so it is worth recalling that until the beginning of the nineteenth century all colours were derived from natural sources. The first known images in Europe, painted in the Chauvet Cave, southwest France, are in a restricted palette of reds and blacks, occasionally yellows, browns and whites, as the pigments derive from iron ore, manganese oxide, coal, charcoal, iron oxides, soil ochres and clays. Many thousands of years later, in the Renaissance, the same pigments were still in use but had been greatly augmented by other soil ochres – such as burnt sienna, which is derived from iron oxide, clay and quartz and takes its name from the Italian city where it was mined in large quantities –and by more expensive pigments ground from precious stones like gold, or semi-precious ones like lapis lazuli (the latter of which produces a brilliant blue pigment which in the Middle Ages was more expensive than gold because it was mined only in Afghanistan – hence the pigment's name, ultramarine, from the Latin *ultramarinus*, 'beyond the sea'). A cheaper blue in the Middle Ages and early Renaissance period was made from azurite, which was produced by the weathering of copper ore deposits. But this, unfortunately, has a tendency to turn green with age. Pigments were also derived from extremely unlikely and obscure sources, such as the bones of an Egyptian mummy. Called mummy brown, this pigment was originally made in the sixteenth century and was a favourite of the Pre-Raphaelites in the nineteenth.

But by the nineteenth century, major transformations in the nature of the paint used by artists were under way. A revolution in the synthesizing and manufacture of coloured pigments had begun in the late eighteenth century in tandem with theoretical, philosophical, scientific and industrial developments, with the result that by the time colour was 'emancipated' by the Romantics and the Impressionists, many pigments were no longer derived from natural sources or artisanally produced. Prussian blue – a deep, cold blue pigment that was much cheaper than ultramarine blue – was the first chemically synthetized pigment. Many new and cheap colour compounds quickly followed, such as synthetic ultramarine and cerulean blue, chrome orange and cadmium yellow.

Synthetic colours radically altered the nature of the artist's relationship to their materials. Colour was turned into a product that could be selected from within a pre-organized commercial context, and as a result, artists were inevitably drawn into the modern world of production and consumption. Similarly, the manufacture of oil paint in tubes, which dates from 1841, meant that the consistency of paint was now standardized according to industrial norms. The tube also made paint easy to carry around and was thus an innovation on which Impressionist *plein air* painting greatly depended. 'Earth colours, the colours of crushed sea animals, and the metallic colours which are the basis of painting's brilliance, were supplemented for the Impressionists by industrial colours, of no recognizable origin in the natural world or the age of iron,' writes the artist and critic Jeremy Gilbert-Rolfe,

> The Impressionists, doctrinally committed to reconstituting the brightness of daylight, were obliged to the inventiveness of the German petro-chemical industry, which gave them alizarin crimson, viridian, and other colours necessary to the task of simulating the natural which are in themselves unnatural in every obvious sense except that they do indeed exist in nature.[8]

So, while the blue of the Mediterranean sky, or 'azure', was central to Yves Klein's monochrome aesthetics, it wasn't necessary for him go to the same complicated and time-consuming lengths as a fifteenth-century artist, who had to follow a recipe or rely on a rich patron to stump up for ultramarine pigment. In fact, while Klein chose a shade similar to ultramarine blue as his preferred hue, the pigment he sourced was synthetic – and not from Afghanistan – and therefore considerably cheaper. But Klein wanted this pigment to be extremely intense and at first was unable to find what he needed. Eventually he succeeded in identifying an obscure acrylic paint product named Rhodopas M60A, which consists of synthetic ultramarine pigment powder mixed with a special resin binder composed of ethyl alcohol, ethyl acetate and vinyl chloride resin. This mixture has the important practical effect of preserving the maximum possible intensity of the blue pigment when the paint dries. It is also highly toxic. Working with a Paris art supplier, Klein developed a variant on this product and had it shipped to him ready-to-use. He christened it International Klein Blue (IKB) – although he never patented it.

But Klein wasn't just interested in covering a surface with a beautiful blue. As we have seen, he claimed that to focus on a single colour entailed a fundamental challenge to the prevailing cultural hierarchy. In his vision of a battle between line and colour, Klein was alluding to the fact that despite colour's centrality to making art, its status was routinely denigrated, and his notion of a contest takes its place within a long history. Since the High Renaissance a distinction had customarily been made between the partisans of colour, or 'painterly' artists, such as the Venetians, Correggio, Rubens and Rembrandt, and the 'linear' artists in the Raphaelesque tradition. In French art, these two 'camps' had coalesced by the nineteenth century around the terms 'Romantic' (colour) and 'classical' (line). This was the more specific context for Klein's hyperbolic argument, and in his opinion, the tide in the battle had definitively turned. Colour was now gaining victory:

> Last outburst and attempt to defend the line in the debate between Ingres and Delacroix: 'Color,' said Ingres, 'adds ornament to painting, but it is only the lady-in-waiting.'
>
> But Delacroix jotted down some observations in his journal that had struck him: 'Colors are music for the eyes . . . Certain harmonies of color produce sensations that music by itself cannot achieve.'[9]

The course of painting in the nineteenth century certainly provided Klein with solid grounds for this bold assertion. In fact, the evolution of modern art can be understood as the systematic inversion of the hierarchy that placed line above colour, the immutable above the fugitive. 'When you go out to paint, try to forget what objects you have before you, a tree, a house, a field, or whatever,' wrote the Impressionist Claude Monet. 'Merely think here is a little square of blue, here an oblong of pink, here a streak of yellow, and paint it just as it looks to you, the exact colour and shape, until it gives your own naive impression of the scene before you.'[10] A painting was becoming an all-over mosaic of shifting chromatic relations that were intended to replicate the effect of light upon surfaces and within empty space. But at the same time, an Impressionist painting also drew the eye towards the material roughness of the surface, to the physicality of the paint itself. The use of dynamic brushstrokes defined a surface, which is homogeneous and two-dimensional.

For Vincent van Gogh the autonomy of the brightly coloured paint mark, or *tache*, as it is called in French, was even more important. 'A painter does better to start from the colours on his palette than from the colours in nature,' he wrote in a letter to his brother Theo. 'I retain from nature a certain sequence and a certain correctness in placing tones, I study nature, so as not to do foolish things, to remain reasonable – however, I don't mind so much whether my colour corresponds exactly, as long as it looks beautiful on my canvas, as beautiful as it looks in nature.'[11] For Van Gogh, colour was independent of any representational function, and was recast as an autonomous pictorial element.

Writing in 1899, the Neo-Impressionist painter Paul Signac summarized the phases in the liberation of colour – which, like Klein, he saw as initiated by Delacroix, developed by the Impressionists and consolidated by the Neo-Impressionists – as aiming to 'maximize the brilliance of colour'.[12] Painters felt compelled to abandon the task of representing the visible world as they strove to do away with 'a battle horse, a nude model, or some anecdote', as the Symbolist artist Maurice Denis famously put it.[13] The result was an unprecedented schematization or purification of the medium, as artists sought concentration and condensation. Form and colour were now the whole subject or content, as well as the object of art, which henceforth was supposed to arise only from within painting's own resources. The idea of autonomous 'form', based on specificity, purity and autonomy, became the principal regulative idea within the avant-garde. By 1908 Henri Matisse would capture the spirit of the new chromatic painting by declaring: 'I put down my colours without preconceived plan. To paint an autumn landscape I will not try to remember what colours suit this season, I will be inspired only by the sensation that the season gives me.'[14]

In embracing colour, painting also moved closer to music, which was considered the most expressive and the most perfect of the arts, as it is deeper and more comprehensive than any coded language. Music is untranslatable and yet at the same time also directly comprehensible. The fact that music is both autonomous and seemingly transparent in meaning would become the model for a new kind of painting, and it was towards achieving this end that colour was nominated as the most important visual ingredient. Colour's status as a self-determining structure increasingly seemed more important than any role it might play within a code used to describe objects in the external world. As Paul Gauguin declared:

> Like music, [painting] acts on the soul through the intermediary of the senses: harmonious colors correspond to the harmonies of sounds. But in painting a unity is obtained which is not possible in music, where the accords follow one another, so that the judgment experiences a continuous fatigue if it wants to reunite the end with the beginning. The ear is actually a sense inferior to the eye. The hearing can only grasp a single sound at a time, whereas the sight takes in everything and simultaneously simplifies it at will.[15]

BUT JUST WHAT *is* colour?

First of all, colour vision is by no means a universal attribute of animals. Indeed, most other mammals do not have colour vision.[16] The human visual system comprises broadly two kinds of photoreceptive cells – cones and rods. Cone cells are clustered in a small area of the central part of the retina and make it possible to change fixation four or five times a second (called 'saccades'), building up a detailed and informative picture of the world. These cones help to concentrate attention on specific aspects of the visual field one at a time, thereby delivering fine-grained vision, enhanced shape clarity and colour awareness. Rod-shaped cells, meanwhile, are distributed throughout the periphery of the eye and give coarser-grained vision; they lack colour receptors but make it possible to see in dim light and to detect movement in the wider visual field, and to perceive the whole simultaneously.

When we look at a monochrome – one by Yves Klein, say – our senses will convince us that we are seeing a blue colour that names something out there on the canvas. But science shows that colour perception is really a response to the visual dimension of light caused by electromagnetic radiation. Light in itself is not coloured, and only when radiation vibrates within a frequency that can be picked up by our retina will we actually *see* colour. Seeing in colour is therefore the result of four interrelated factors: wavelengths of reflected light, lighting conditions, the colour cones in the retina which absorb light of long, medium and short wavelengths, and the neural circuitry connected to these cones. Light is reflected off an object and enters the eye, activating the cones in the retina. Our brain then unconsciously determines the wavelength composition of that light, taking into account both the surface reflectance of the object and the wavelength composition of the light illuminating the scene.

The colour we see is therefore not independent of the body and brain that is perceiving it, but it is also wrong to say it is purely a mental projection. More accurately, colour is created by interaction. It is a brain-produced chromatic constancy, rather than a property of a given surface or object. As a result, it is also inherently perceptually unstable. The light in which we see the Klein – the daylight of a sunny or gloomy day, or the tungsten or fluorescent lighting of a gallery – will generate different light wavelengths, and its colour will constantly change as a result. But our brains will not register such changes, and we will automatically and unconsciously compensate for such variations in the light source. We will always see the same blue colour in Klein's painting.

Colour is usually classified in terms of hue, value and tone. The hue of Klein's painting is the blue colour itself. Its value is this colour's relative lightness or darkness; tint is when the value of a colour is mixed with white, which increases lightness, while shade is the mixture with black, which reduces lightness. A tone is produced either by the mixture of a colour with grey, or by tinting and shading. Klein's particular blue is a hue that appears undiluted by value or tone. We further organize colour in terms of the three primaries, red, yellow and blue, which are considered pure and indivisible, and cannot be made through mixing, and the three secondary colours – green, orange and purple – which are also known as 'complementary' colours because they tend to work well together through optically intensifying their respective chromatic properties. However, for Leon Battista Alberti, writing in the fifteenth century, colour was divided in four *genera* which corresponded to the four elements: 'There is fire-colour which they call red, and the colour of air which is said to be blue-grey, and the green of water, and the earth is ash-coloured.'[17] Alberti did not consider black and white to be true colours but rather 'moderators' of colour.[18] This was a recent idea, and is often assumed to be the case today, but from ancient times black and white were routinely considered true colours, and this is still the consensus in cultures beyond the modern West.

We construe colours as being intrinsically different – red is different from green, and green is different from violet. But when we say that Klein's painting is 'blue', we are really describing a potentially infinite number of different hues. Broadly speaking, there is a 'central' blue, which is the result of the maximal neural response to light frequencies, and increasingly peripheral blues, shading towards hues of a more purplish-blue or greenish-blue (and so forth) on the colour wheel. We can assume that the particular ultramarine blue that Klein adopted was chosen in order to express the maximum possible experience of archetypal 'blueness', unmixed with other hues. Colours never exist in total isolation, however, and they are inherently interactive and relational. If you place the blue of Klein's painting next to its complementary – its opposite on the colour wheel, which is orange – the blue will seem to be more vividly 'blue', and vice versa. If you stare directly at the blue, and then look at the white wall upon which Klein's painting hangs, you will see an orange afterglow – its complementary.[19] Colour also produces the optical illusion of spatial depth. A blue seems to recede before the eye, while a red jumps forward. In general, 'warm' colours move towards us; a green, meanwhile, will sit somewhere in between and is therefore one of the most stable hues. 'Warm' colours also appear larger to the eye than 'cool' colours like blue. These optical effects explain why we talk of 'warm' colours that optically advance as potentially 'aggressive', and of 'cool' ones that are recessive as 'calming', a metaphorical transferral of language from the perceptual to the affective, which is a common role played by colour.

While colour is a natural phenomenon, it is, as Michel Pastoureau emphasizes, also 'a complex cultural construct that resists generalizations and, indeed, analysis itself.'[20] The naming of a specific colour, and its containment within a coded linguistic system, is closely related not only to belief systems, but to utility and social and economic value, and all these factors render colour a thoroughly social phenomenon. The words for specific colours stand in meaningful relationship to other words for other colours. But we must be careful not to project our own conceptions and definitions of colour onto the past. How a name is put to qualitative chromatic nuances is dependent on both social conditioning and the structure of the language being used by a culture. Some colours may not be 'seen' in the sense familiar within Western language groups, that is, with a specific word given to them. But that does not mean that the people cannot physically see the colour.[21] In antiquity, blue wasn't considered a true colour – with the exception of ancient Egypt, the first culture to have a word for blue, probably because it was in the Nile delta that a method was first developed for producing a synthetic blue dye.[22] In the nineteenth century it was realized that blue may not have been recognized as a distinct hue by the ancient Greeks – in Homer's *Odyssey*, the sea is described as 'wine-dark'.[23] The problem in assessing colour perception is that it was not, as was initially assumed, that the Greeks could not actually *see* blue, only that it seems they did not possess the vocabulary to distinguish between blue, grey and green. Recently, however, a psychologist working with the Himba people from Namibia in southwest Africa tested to see whether the fact that the Himba had no word for blue really meant they couldn't actually see the hue. As a report in *Science Alert* relates, members of the tribe were shown 'a circle with 11 green squares and one painfully obvious blue square. Well, obvious to us, at least.' The test revealed that the members of the tribe were unable to tell any difference between the coloured squares.[24]

We perceive colours purposively. In order for blue to mean something it must cease to be simply something we feel, and become something that represents. The ubiquity of colours in the world has meant that they are enlisted in all cultures to serve as symbols, and various meanings are associated with each one. Colour is routinely used in religious and cultural rituals to symbolize significant aspects of belief. Such usage often has its roots in the appearance of colour within nature and within bodily experience. White is the colour of snow, and so denotes 'snow', but it also seems to be commonly linked to ideas of eternity, heaven, virtue, innocence, purity, light, reverence, birth, simplicity, cleanliness, peace, humility, precision, youth, winter, sterility, the cold and the clinical. Black denoted 'night' and connotes remorse, unhappiness, murder, anger, evil, fear, sin and devils, impurity, hell, darkness, death and the underworld, but also depth, power, sexuality, sophistication, formality, elegance, wealth, mystery, anonymity and so on. Red is very often associated with excitement, energy, love, desire, speed, strength, power, heat, aggression, danger, fire, blood, war, violence and all things intense and passionate, while green is associated with good luck, renewal, youth, vigour, spring, generosity, fertility, eternity, family, harmony, health, peace and prosperity. Blue is closely allied in many cultures with the notion of infinity. The French word for 'heaven' and 'sky' are the same – *le ciel*; and in Chinese the written character for 'heaven' is also used for 'sky'.

But the actual *experience* of colour remains fundamentally enigmatic. The visual system is connected to other systems within the brain that are involved with affect and feeling and generating emotion, and the effect colour has on the emotions is mainly involuntary, tied to stimuli that are direct and pre-conscious, while also partly dependent on learned associations. Colour arouses emotions, generating a powerful affective field. 'People experience a great delight in colour, generally,' noted Johann Wolfgang von Goethe in his pioneering study *Theory of Colours* (1810). 'The eye requires it as much as it requires light. We have only to remember the refreshing sensation we experience, if on a cloudy day the sun illumines a simple portion of the scene before us and displays its colours.'[25] Colours also have a direct impact on alertness, bringing about physiological changes in relation to brain activity, blood pressure, respiration rates and other processes, and also enhance the awareness of sensory access to the world. Through generating a pulsing and nebulous sensation of space, colour encourages the sensory activities of looking and feeling rather than those of intellectual reflection and thought. Unlike the latter, in which some thing or event must first be understood in order to be known, the experience of colour does not require the engagement of our conscious understanding to be 'known' in all its enigmatic beauty.

Colour is fundamentally ambiguous in experience, and is a pre-cognitive, pre-linguistic force. The fact that colour is neither purely objective nor purely subjective – that it is semi-independent of the body and the brain that perceives it – explains its powerful affective potential. We respond to colours not only as visual and expressive events but on levels that encompass the intellectual, conscious, unconscious and subconscious. But there is still considerable disagreement about the nature of colour and its relationship to the human brain. In relation to art, it remains unclear exactly which sensual and cognitive mechanisms in the brain are specifically involved in creating the capacity for colour to function so powerfully as an expressive dimension.[26]

4

GROUND

They were pictures of nothing.[1]
William Hazlitt (1816)

When we look at J.M.W. Turner's painting *Norham Castle, Sunrise* (1845) we see only vaguely outlined and subtly distinct coloured patches that spread out across the rectangular surface, even seeming to continue beyond the physical frame of the painting itself. In terms of the work's representational logic, what is 'closest' to us – the viewer – has been painted in the same way as what is 'far away'. A contemporary of Turner's, William Hazlitt, wrote that Turner seemed to make paintings that 'go back to the first chaos of the world . . . "All is without form and void"'.[2] Forms seem to have been eroded or absorbed back into a homogeneous ground, and as a result Turner's painting almost resists decoding as an image. Its status as a recognizable view across a lake, past a grazing cow and towards a castle on a rocky outcrop is in serious jeopardy, and its credentials as a representation of a specific castle in Northumberland, England, are wholly unobtainable on the evidence of the work itself, depending instead on access to the title. In short, *Norham Castle,*

Sunrise seems to be heading towards what today we would call a monochrome.

Hazlitt noted that his contemporaries attributed to Turner's work a fundamental lack of meaning. 'Someone said of his landscapes that they were *pictures of nothing, and very like*,' he wrote.[3] Instead of fulfilling the obligation to make a representation of something, Turner seems to want to draw attention to the materials used to make his painting – the paint on the surface, and the fact that it is a framed, two-dimensional, geometrically shaped surface. Contemporaries such as Hazlitt were made uncomfortably aware that they were looking at a two-dimensional, geometrically framed area with a clearly defined limit or boundary, covered in subtly differentiated coloured and textured marks. By contrast, in the more familiar conventions of painting, the surface is only latently present and has no intrinsic value or meaning. What we are invited to see is the illusion of a three-dimensional space. The surface is only the substrate for the communication of the content. But Turner makes the framed-off surface of the canvas actively manifest.

A work like this exposes the fact that traditionally, the capacity of a painting to function as a meaning-bearing surface depends mostly on a specific organization of that surface, on its division into zones of attention and inattention using the bounding line to describe forms and variations in colour which are comparable to the colours of objects in the world. Within this convention, some aspects of what we see are understood to possess coded meaning, while other aspects are ignored and go uncoded. A traditionally representational picture is essentially organized into two zones: a 'figure' or 'positive space', and 'ground' or 'negative space'. The former is what carries meaning or tells a story, while the latter is just the container or envelope for this meaning or story.

This opposition between and hierarchization of the 'figure' and the 'ground' closely duplicates the organizing principle of vision in general. Human high-focus vision is the most pronounced of all primate vision, and resolution is about one hundred times that at the periphery of the visual field. But this focused vision is only about 1 degree across, while the part of the visual field brought to resolution is no more than 3 degrees across. This acuity at the centre corresponds to a pronounced lack in peripheral vision, in contradistinction to animals such as deer and other herbivores, who possess a much wider perceptual field, so the fundamental division of vision into the focused and peripheral yields a small area of clearly seen space and simultaneously a nebulous field of unconscious peripheral awareness.[4] The optic nerves arrayed at the centre of the human eye which furnish high-focus vision provide essential data for the establishing of clear, finite and distinct readings of space. By contrast, peripheral vision draws attention to the ground. While focused vision puts the world at a distance, peripheral vision is immersive, and envelops us in the world. But most of the time we are completely unaware of the periphery's importance. Focused vision is always a kind of 'reading', while the periphery is in some senses a more truthful or authentic experience, because it unconsciously communicates one's awareness of the unbalanced configuration of space. But this field can never be 'captured' in conscious attention.

As a matter of survival the brain seeks equilibrium, and so the human visual system is organized to discover patterns. Some aspects of the perceptual field rather than others become the focus of attention. This grouping and binding into graspable and stable patterns is driven by the need for focused attention on the gratification of needs. We strive for wholeness where we sense lack, and for understanding where something is unclear. Normal modulations within the brain include the production of general, universal schemata that order the perceptual field in terms of contoured patterns, intersections, and zones of attention and inattention, schemata that can be applied to all objects and scenes, offering rules that construct the visual world so that more or less the same essential information is extracted from the environment by the visual system. We automatically dichotomize sight, elevating for attention a figure or a form, consigning the rest – the ground – to unconsciousness. 'It is necessary to put the surroundings in abeyance the better to see the object, and to lose in ground what one gains in focal figure,' writes the philosopher Maurice Merleau-Ponty, 'because to look at the object is to plunge oneself into it, and because objects form a system in which one cannot show itself without concealing others.'[5] In other words, in order to see a 'figure' it is necessary to abandon the 'ground', which slips into unconscious vagueness. The neuroscientist V. S. Ramachandran and the philosopher William Hirstein provide a scientific description of how this assignment occurs:

> Given the limited attentional resources in the brain and limited neural space for competing representations, at every stage in processing there is generated a 'Look here, there is a clue to something potentially object-like' signal that produces limbic activation and draws your attention to that region (or feature), thereby facilitating the processing of those regions or features at earlier stages. Furthermore, partial 'solutions' or conjectures to perceptual problems are fed back from every level in the hierarchy to every earlier module to impose a small bias in processing and the final percept emerges from such progressive 'bootstrapping'.[6]

Contours or edges – where we perceive a more or less abrupt change in visual stimulus – define an outline and produce a figure/ground assignment. These configurational cues are hard-wired components of human perception that are pre-conscious and pre-linguistic in nature. As psychologists have shown, a 'figure' will always seem more present than the 'ground' and will also appear to be in front of it. The boundary between a 'figure' and a 'ground' will always belong to the 'figure', and all shapes belonging to the 'ground' plane tend to be seen as part of a continuous backdrop, which will be unformed and lack a dynamic of its own.[7]

In other words, perception requires a choice, which is unconsciously made. When I look at something, the computer in front of me, say, it automatically becomes the 'figure', and I consign the rest of the visual field – the books around the computer, the table, the lamp, the half-drunk cup of coffee – to the 'ground', which goes unnoticed until I turn to look at the open book to the left of my computer in order to read, or take a sip of coffee; then these things become 'figure' and the computer temporarily merges with the 'ground'. This shifting between figure and ground can be both voluntary and involuntary and occurs not just within the visual modality but with the other senses too. When I hear the magpie cackling outside, this sound becomes the 'figure', and involuntarily banishes from my mind my computer screen. But once the magpie stops, the world outside recedes and becomes the 'ground' again, and so I now voluntarily return to my previous 'figure', my computer screen.

The establishment of a stable and coherent visual field reduces potentially dangerous ambiguity by constructing a sense of security, thereby providing a sound basis for practical decision-making and action. But familiar configurations generally win out over novel ones, because cognitive value lies in repeatability and reliability. So the mind is predisposed to accept a 'readymade' gestalt – that is, a whole organized so that it is perceived as more than the sum of its parts.

This tendency is especially significant because the same model of dual assignment also conditions the organization of the *cognitive* field. We favour precision, detail, linearity and states of closure, which then encourage mental states characterized by focus, individuation, detachment, objectivity, abstraction and analysis. As the cultural theorist Paul Virilio writes: 'Unconsciously we repeat the typologies of apprehension. From the initial separation of the figure from the ground – the detachment between the line of the earth and the sky, between the shoreline and the primordial ocean – to the elaboration of scientific perspective.'[8] A horizon of meaning surrounds each situation, and this is what allows us to adopt a perspective. But it is also what prohibits us from being open to change. In fact, it is possible to become so locked into understanding something in one particular way (locked onto the 'figure' and never the 'ground') that we will not be able to comprehend any other point of view.

What this dichotomizing organization of perception and thought demonstrates is that we do not experience the actual world but rather a mental re-creation, or an interactive experience of the world. An intrinsic aspect of this re-creation is duality or difference. But at the same time, our neural architecture undergoes continuous changes and disruptions. 'Gestalt shifts' take place. So-called 'ambiguous figures', such as the face/goblet Rubin vase or Necker cube optical illusions, demonstrate the extent to which figure/ground assignment is cognitively metamorphic rather than an inherent aspect of a scene. In the case of the face/goblet, for example, it is possible to flip back and forth between readings – between the faces as figure and the goblet as ground, and vice versa. But assignments are also vulnerable in more usual settings, as when ambient lighting conditions do not bring high visual contrast. High contrast means visual 'noise' is low, and a figure will thus stand out clearly from the ground, but without radiant and ambient light the amount of 'noise' increases, and this limits the capacity to detect shape, contour and colour differences, and as a result it is no longer so easy to establish and grasp hold of stable patterns. In the low ambient light of a darkened room, or at twilight, focused vision loosens its firm grip over consciousness. Without sufficient perceptual cues, we engage in cognitive filling-in, compensating for the visual deficit by acts of imaginative extrapolation. When there are no visible contours, or no overall contrasts, an undifferentiated perceptual expanse is perceived, and this induces a kind of blindness, such as happens in situations of perceptual deprivation like a sea mist or fog. Changes in perception result in changes in cognition. When the brain is cut off from sensory input altogether, what is called 'deafferentation' occurs, and as the philosopher Thomas Metzinger describes it, instead of turning outwards towards the world, the brain turns inwards to focus on itself as pure 'mind.' There is a growing body of research to suggest that the various meditation practices developed within different cultures organize and direct the processes through which, as Metzinger writes, 'human beings can sometimes turn the global background into the gestalt, the dominating feature of consciousness itself', and as a result achieve heightened awareness of wholeness and well-being.[9]

At such moments we get closer to the experience of perception at a pre-conscious level, when the visual field is experienced as an undifferentiated flow, a continuum of solids, liquids, gases and minerals, characterized by voids and currents rather than coherent forms – rather like Turner's painting, in fact. This means that what we call conscious 'reality' is the result of a series of predictive hypotheses about a fundamentally ambiguous and indeterminate environment, and therefore is only tenuously related to the actual flow of the undifferentiated continuum within which we exist.

IN TURNER'S PAINTING, the familiar duality of figure/ground assignment has dissolved, and it is now the spatial continuum that is made radiantly present. The prioritizing of the 'figure' has been abandoned, and with it any sense that what we see within the framed-off space is contained by the work's physical boundaries. In fact, the rectangular canvas has now itself become a kind of figure, which is set against the indeterminate ground of the wall upon which the painting itself hangs. Turner's work flies in the face of normal, or normative, visual perception, and also in the face of the protocols of painting established with the invention of fixed-point perspective in the fifteenth century in Italy, which grounded Western art in a logical system based on the detached analysis of an abstract grid.

It was Leonardo da Vinci who first systematically challenged and extended what was then the still new visualizing system, and like Turner, Leonardo did so by narrowing and erasing the clear polarities that organized the pictorial code based on the ratio of line. Most obviously, Leonardo actively encouraged indeterminacy and ambiguity in his work through *chiaroscuro* (light-dark) and *sfumato* (smokiness), which replaced sharp contours with soft transitions, with the result that his works were imbued with a new kind of intangible or 'poetic' mood. Through softening, confusing and displacing readings of figure and ground, Leonardo's paintings bring to attention the latent forces organizing the visual field and conditioning thought; by the time of the Baroque, the emptiness of the ground has begun to compete actively with the fullness of the figure, eating away at the visible. In the paintings of Rembrandt and Caravaggio, for example, dark and indistinct areas of compositions become spaces where the imagination can get to work, and the numinous is evoked. Later, in the work of the Romantics such as Turner, the horizon completely disappears, while the ground expands to absorb the figure and is used to evoke the 'ground of being' itself. In Turner's painting of Norham Castle the loss of a firm and credible relationship to any external reference is compensated for by an increased interest in what is happening on the surface of the painting itself.

This preoccupation with surface texture becomes ever more pronounced within Impressionism. Coloured brushstrokes are vigorously applied across the whole surface of canvases, irrespective of what they describe, and seem to involve the manipulation of paint for its own sake. The coloured daubs smooth and dismantle forms, blur boundaries and bathe the eye in a luminous ambience. Such heightened interest in surface shifted attention away from retinal sensations to the haptic, which engages two bodily functions – the tactile and the kinaesthetic. The tactile brings direct physical contact, providing information about location, surface, vibration and temperature, while the kinaesthetic is involved in knowledge about position, orientation and force. While sight facilitates a general conceptual knowledge through offering spatial detachment from what is perceived, touch verifies and brings conviction by providing specific knowledge revealed intimately through close contact. Although the accumulation of knowledge gained through touch is slower than through visual perception, the sense of touch is more difficult to deceive. The haptic therefore helps to build stronger and more authentic awareness of a three-dimensional and temporal world than the sense of sight. Making sense of physical contact with an object through the haptic sense means gaining clarification – touching confirms and demystifies, and enhances awareness of body movements, of stimuli relating to position, posture and equilibrium that come from a more immersive engagement. While a predominantly retinal response to a painting necessitates viewing from a distance, emphasis on the haptic by an artist encourages engagement at close range, as the figure and the ground lie in the same place on the surface, equally close to each other and to the viewer.[10] In the haptic mode, frontal or close viewing is essential, and as a result a closer link is made between the eye and the hand, because perception is linked to the tactility of the work's surface. Viewing slows down and becomes more intimate, as the eyes move across a work's surface taking in the nuances produced by brushstroke and paint application.

As a result of this new emphasis on the material surface in nineteenth-century painting, the activity of seeing becomes radically bifurcated into two distinct phases, which also had the effect of transforming the viewer into a much more active partner in the making of meaning. At least for those who were prepared to see an Impressionist work in the way the artist had intended, the marks were transformed into a representation. But rather than the blending of colour occurring on the palette or the canvas, the generation of a representation takes place during the active process of perceiving the work. A viewer is obliged to combine the colours optically into what is a simulacrum of the fleeting effects of light in the real world. On the one hand they perceive a tactile surface area, while on the other, they read the marks within that area as constituting an image. But, as a spoof about an Impressionist exhibition in the magazine *Le Charivari* suggested in 1874, for the uninitiated an Impressionist painting such as one by Monet inevitably seemed to be nothing more than 'palette-scrapings placed uniformly on a dirty canvas' that possessed 'neither head nor tail, top nor bottom, front nor back'.[11]

For many artists this very bifurcation also entailed making a monumental choice. After an encounter with a composition by Monet depicting a haystack, Wassily Kandinsky remarked in 1895 that it made him realize that painting's role as an imitator of the visible world had lost all significance:

> It was the catalogue that told me that that was a haystack. I numbly felt that the object was missing in this picture. Painting received a fabulous power and magnificence. Unconsciously the object was also discredited as the inevitable element of the picture.[12]

Modern art as a whole amounts to a multifaceted assault on the illusion fabricated by fixed-point perspective, but also any 'trick' that sought to disguise or conceal the two-dimensional plane in the service of production of an image. Artists would encourage mobile, concrete and qualitative apprehensions of space. They attend to both positive and negative space, treating the ground as the location of 'negative' shapes. Cubist collage, for example, subverts codes based on ratio and logic so that it is often unclear whether one fragment is on top of another or behind it, or whether the two coexist in the same shallow space. In fact, as James Elkins writes, modernist painting 'begins with the rejection of the concept of background – that is, an ontologically and naturalistically subsidiary surrounding or setting for the figure', and in its place set about the 'instating of ground'. It was now understood to be 'ontologically equal and co-dependent with the figure'.[13]

The substantiation of the ground in painting introduced both emptiness, or the absence of content, and fullness, the presence of the surface, as major themes in modern art. But the value given by a particular artist to the ground they reveal will largely depend on their beliefs regarding its apprehension. For some, the emphasis on the 'ground' will suggest that painting has at last achieved specificity and literalness, has become a new kind of 'realism' based on the repudiation of illusion. But for others, the 'ground' will take on profound spiritual or psychological significance. It is, indeed, analogous to the very 'ground of being' itself.

'I have overcome the lining of the coloured sky, torn it down and into the bag thus formed, put colour, tying it up with a knot. Swim in the white free abyss, infinity is before you,' declared Kazimir Malevich in 1919 as he obliterated the material surface at the moment of declaring that it is the ground.[14] *'Every plane is a plane and there is to be no representation,'* announced another Russian, Aleksandr Rodchenko, commenting on what in 1921 were certainly the most uncompromisingly reductive paintings ever produced – his triptych of primary colours, *Pure Red Colour, Pure Yellow Colour, Pure Blue Colour* (1921).[15] In deliberate contrast to Malevich, Rodchenko claims that by reducing his painting to the self-evident fact of a two-dimensional surface plane in one colour he is showing that it is no more than a literal surface, and that through this action he is announcing the death of painting as a whole.

5

SPIRITUAL

This formless form is beautiful as form.[1]

Plotinus (3rd century CE)

At the dawn of the modern age, the Romantic movement of which Delacroix and Turner were part sought to transfer the energies and aspirations traditionally associated with religious creeds and devotional images into the newly emancipated aesthetic domain of art. The German Romantic notion of *Bildung*, or self-cultivation, signalled a desire to transform art into a sphere within which to examine basic ontological questions of being and belonging. This was to be an art dedicated to what the art historian Robert Rosenblum calls 'art for *life's* sake', rather than the 'art for art's sake' promulgated by the Impressionists and embraced in the early twentieth century by School of Paris artists like Henri Matisse.[2] What amounted to an alternative 'tradition' gained renewed influence in the late nineteenth century through Symbolism, and in its turn Symbolism greatly influenced the genesis of abstract art in the early twentieth century.

To work within an artistic tradition dedicated to the 'spiritual' means that in one way or another an artist will aim to encourage the human capacity for *ekstasis* (ecstasy) – the capacity to transcend situations, and the limits imposed by convention on time and space, through an emphasis on the relationship of humanity to the ineffable and immaterial. Artists committed to this notion of the spiritual in art explored their own mind, imagination, inner consciousness or 'soul', in the belief that these faculties possess autonomous and immaterial agency. The 'spiritually' inclined artist considers that refined feelings, emotions and intuitions are more important than reflection and rationality. They strive to create works of art that are concerned with the beauty or the value of the mind rather than the beauty of the physical world.

One of the most important textual justifications for the then embryonic abstract or 'objectless' art, that is, an art without representational subject-matter, is Wassily Kandinsky's book *Über das Geistige in der Kunst* (1911). Translated in English as *Concerning the Spiritual in Art*, its title therefore refers not to supernatural beings or some specific theological dogma, but rather to a new kind of art that is concerned above all with the faculties of memory and imagination as they are involved in recalling and representing a non-sensory reality withdrawn from or existing independently of the conscious perception of the material world.[3] And so it would be that the monochrome becomes both a symbol for the ground of being, and 'an invitation to be united with that ground'.[4]

IT IS A universal characteristic of all religious traditions to believe, as Aldous Huxley writes in *The Perennial Philosophy* (1945), that 'the divine Ground of all existence is a spiritual Absolute, ineffable in terms of discursive thought, but (in certain circumstances) susceptible of being directly experienced and realized in the human being.'[5] But Western culture is especially pervaded by a specific variation on this insight: the 'divine ground' is of a fundamentally different nature to the world perceived via the senses and which conforms to the laws of time and three-dimensional space. Philosophically, this belief was justified in terms of the separation of reality into two realms, the phenomenal and the noumenal, or by the division between what appears to the senses and what presents itself to consciousness but exists independently of the sense perceptions of the phenomenal world and is therefore beyond comprehension and articulation in language.

Plato's name is especially associated with a tradition in which the material realm of the 'Many' is understood to conceal the immaterial but ultimate reality of 'One', the 'Good' or the 'True'. In the *Timaeus* Plato refers to what he calls the *khōra*, a space or receptacle which, as it has no inherent qualities of its own, is unnameable and unrepresentable, and yet is also the very ground of all existence.[6] It is towards this intangible *khōra*, Plato argued, that the soul naturally cleaves. Following in a tradition that stretches back to Pythagoras, Plato also saw the divine harmony expressed in proportion, geometry and music. Numbers, forming the basis for music and geometry, have sacred significance, because these abstract signs, conceived within the mind, are purified and essentialized residues of the phenomenal world.

But the Platonic or Neoplatonic tradition also emphasizes that the ability to apprehend the correlation between numbers, geometry, music and the 'divine ground' is possible only for those who are capable of recognizing that the seemingly tangible and practical forms we see are merely visual prompts aiding in the recall of the essential One. Responses to the material world in this worldview therefore occur on potentially three levels, which also constitute a hierarchy. On the first, which is available to the senses and therefore to all, a phenomenon's existence as a tangible and specific object is recognized. On the second and more refined level, a connection to an intangible ideal – the non-sensory level that lies behind specific manifestations – is apprehended by the soul. On the third, which is accessible only to the initiated, an archetypal meaning is grasped that recognizes the status of all phenomena as being grounded in an intangible universal process or dynamic pattern wholly independent of specific structures or material forms.[7]

Dedication to the 'spiritual' in art as it is construed within the Platonist or Neoplatonist worldview therefore means seeking to evoke the 'divine ground' through a process of reduction, elimination and subtraction. This process of subtraction necessitated a 'contemplative' attitude, in the sense of an inwardness or a concentration on sustained reflective thought, with the aim of drawing closer to an awareness of the sacredness of life – the ground of being. But the role of the artist within such a worldview is inevitably ambiguous. Plato famously banished artists from his fictional Republic because they work only on the first level, of mere appearances. But in this tradition it was also argued that the refined and spiritually aware artist could potentially play an indispensable role if their work somehow participated in the 'One' and brought the 'divine ground' to awareness so that it could be contemplated. The artist could embody through their work the One and the Good, while such principles were in and of themselves inherently beyond representation, beyond thought or imagination. The artist committed to the 'spiritual' within this tradition is obliged to find a visual equivalence for what is fundamentally *beyond* the visible. They are credited with the potential capacity to have profound insight into the divine One, but only when they themselves and their work are purified of the signs of the Many. 'Nothing visible is to be conceived, or at once we descend from beauty to what but bears the name in virtue of some faint participation,' wrote the third century CE Neoplatonist Plotinus: 'This formless form is beautiful as form, beautiful in proportion as we strip away all shape.'[8]

Medieval Christianity assimilated aspects of Neoplatonism, conjoining it with Judaism's strict prohibition on idolatry. Within Christianity, the status of the sacred image has been subject to continuous questioning and controversy. Does an image merely represent the sacred or somehow participate in it? In an attempt to answer this question, medieval theology conceived of three ways of understanding an image. The first and least important was the literal meaning of the image, in which it functions in relation to sensory perception. Beyond this literal meaning lay a second: the moral significance of the image. This engaged the mind and resonated in the soul, or with psychological truth. Third, there was the mystical or spiritual aspect of an image, which placed it in relation to the most spiritually elevated strivings of consciousness, and goes beyond the limits of individual consciousness. This highest level, in which the divine ground is directly intuited, could be construed in two ways – allegorically, whereby the hidden meaning was revealed through reflection and analysis via the mediation of symbol and metaphor, and anagogically, whereby the ground was directly felt or intuited.[9]

For the Christian mystic, God could only ever be encountered within what an anonymous fourteenth-century Christian treatise called 'the cloud of unknowing'. God's complete otherness – his ineffability – demanded the recognition that nothing visible to the eye or accessible to the senses can embody him. The goal must therefore be to remove two obstacles – the outer appearance of phenomena and the conscious self who clings to such appearances.

An apophatic method of contemplation (from the Greek *apophemi*, to deny), also known as negative theology or *via negativa* (negative way), was forged within the mystical Christian tradition. One common practice was known as *aphaeresis*, in which the particular qualities of a given phenomenon were abstracted or subtracted to make an empty or negative space within which God could be sensed through his absence. 'It is evident that the faith is a dark night of the soul and it is thus that it gives light; the more it darkens the soul the more does it enlighten it. It is by darkening that it gives light,' wrote the sixteenth-century Spanish friar St John of the Cross.[10] What was revealed was the *Ungrund* (unground), as the Protestant theologian Jakob Böhme (1575–1624) described it. Like Plato's *khōra*, the *Ungrund* was the negation of the tangible, physical ground, an ineffable source from which all things arise.

Within such a radically 'negative' theology of the image, a painting must become a site of non-reference or non-meaning, of an intrinsic negativity. In this sense, the painting is merely instrumental, a means to an end. It is perhaps not so surprising that from one of the more esoteric corners of this culture of mysticism a curious instance of proto-monochromy would be created. In a seventeenth-century occult treatise by Robert Fludd, strongly influenced by Neoplatonism, Christian mysticism, alchemy and proto-scientific research, there is an etching of a black square with the phrase 'et sic in infinitum' (and so on to infinity) written along all four axes.[11] Compositional emptiness, produced by the substitution of a simple square in a single colour where we would normally expect to see a representational image, is used to symbolize infinity or the divine ground. In the tradition embraced by Fludd, a simple geometric form in a single colour takes on immense metaphysical implications.

THE 'SPIRITUAL' IMPULSE proved to be especially strong in early twentieth-century Russian culture, where the avant-garde commingled speculative theosophical teachings, utopian political aspiration, and fascination for the latest revelations in science in their debates concerning 'cosmic consciousness', the 'fourth dimension' and the future of art. The Russian avant-garde avidly read and debated the writings of contemporary thinkers who sought to unite Eastern and Western spiritual traditions with the latest theories in science – thinkers such as Madame Blavatsky, who promoted Theosophy, the movement she had co-founded; Rudolf Steiner, who broke with the Theosophists to create his own Anthroposophical movement; and, for Kazimir Malevich in particular, Pyotr Ouspensky, who forged a philosophy inspired by his spiritual teacher George Gurdjieff. 'The phenomenal world is merely a means for the artist – just as colours are for the painter, and sounds for the musician – a means for the understanding of the noumenal and for the expression of that understanding,' wrote Ouspensky in *Tertium Organum* (1912), reflecting his deep immersion in both Neoplatonism and Eastern thought and foreshadowing Malevich's own future justification for his Suprematism.[12]

The spiritual potency of colour and form, once they were removed from their customary representational roles, played a central role in the visualizing practices of these esoteric systems. In theosophy, for example, it was argued that 'thought forms' and 'auras' were perceptible as colours, at least to the initiated. The quality of thought determined the colour of the thought-form emanation, while the form revealed the nature of the thought. An elaborate colour code visualizing spiritual evolution was presented, in which colour was organized in a hierarchy from earthy, sensual reds to the ethereal blues and whites of spiritual enlightenment.[13] In his contemporaneous psychological research Carl Jung also drew attention to the links between colour, form and mystical experience, discussing Hindu and Buddhist mandalas and Western alchemy, and arguing that mandalas were ideograms of unconscious elements within the psyche, and that the alchemical quest was ultimately bound to the life of the mind and the desire for self-transcendence.[14]

Pursuing the 'spiritual' within modern art inevitably forced a confrontation with the same fundamental paradox faced by the medieval mystic. It obliged artists to find ways to represent the unrepresentable, to use their materials to evoke the immaterial. Much of the ambiguous potency behind the will to monochromism lies in this ambivalence. In this sense, the monochrome emerged from loosely linked traditions within which the role of art is to serve as a visual correspondence to an invisible reality, one that can be sensed or intuited in the mind but never directly perceived or rationally grasped.

The mystical-spiritual sensibility of the Russian modernists was especially closely connected to Byzantine Orthodox Christian tradition within which the sacred icon plays a central role. Within the secular context of the early twentieth-century Russian avant-garde, the Orthodox belief in an immaterial prototype was still deeply embedded, and would become a powerful justification for the new 'objectless' painting. In this context, the reductive geometry that is such a pronounced characteristic of the Russian avant-garde can be seen to have its roots in the Orthodox icon, which in its turn derived the belief in the mystical power of number and geometry from ancient Greek philosophy.[15] As the art historian and critic Nikolai Punin argued at the time, it was in fact precisely the influence of Orthodox Christianity upon the Russian avant-garde's conception of art that, in his opinion, distinguished the new Russian art from that of the School of Paris.[16]

Within this Byzantine tradition, a different relationship between the image and the sacred content it represents was envisaged in comparison to Western Christianity. At the Second Council of Nicaea in 787, Roman Catholicism had achieved a compromise concerning the status of the image by decreeing that the rejection and destruction of religious images must be condemned, but so too must the idolatrous worship of images. Images were sanctioned and revered, but were not considered to 'participate' directly in the invisible divine reality. By contrast, in the eighth and ninth centuries in the Orthodox Christian world, a crisis called the 'struggle over images' erupted, which involved heated debates between iconoclasts (those who wished to ban religious images) and iconodules (those who believed in the efficacy of religious images as real presences) over the correct use of the icon. The problem, as the art historian Moshe Barasch writes, was that 'there was no independent criteria to fall back on when you had to decide about the truthfulness of an image. The god who was portrayed in the icon had no known form, and you did not know its external appearance from your own personal experience. In these conditions, what sense does it make to ask whether an image is true or false?'[17] The iconodules, who finally triumphed over the iconoclasts, solved the problem by an appeal to Neoplatonism, claiming that an icon directly partook of or participated in the intangible, and could therefore be said to be a true resemblance or real presence.[18] But the presence of the divine could only be intuitively grasped. 'Instead of being an illusionistic "window" onto some preconceived sensory reality, the icon was therefore defined as a physical materialization of an intangible reality – a direct "presentation" of it,' writes the art historian Maria Taroutina.[19] But the resemblance to inner spiritual reality could only be understood within an allegorical or anagogical frame of mind, as it was necessarily extrasensory and therefore beyond conscious reflection and analysis. Rather than any relationship to phenomena that were copied from the visible world, the new Russian avant-garde's 'objectless' art was therefore said to present or participate, like an icon, in a transcendent spiritual prototype through having a resemblance to an intangible reality, mediated through pure form and colour.

But to the Russian avant-garde it also seemed that the premises of this metaphysical-religious tradition were being confirmed by the most dramatic scientific discoveries of the period. The new physics clearly suggested that reality was no longer something to be visualized according to Euclidian coordinates, and was certainly not amenable to the senses.[20] In Einstein's special theory of relativity and quantum mechanics, for example, reality was revealed as wholly abstract. Furthermore, evidence of the great benefits of adopting a detached, analytic model of thought, which is central to the scientific method, were plentiful, and this also became an exemplar for the attitude adopted by practitioners of the new art.

Kandinsky laid out the new role of painting in *Concerning the Spiritual in Art*. The content of painting was no longer to be related to the representation of an external material object, but rather was now derived from the meditative practice of visualizing an inner, 'spiritual' or mental reality. The goal was to discover the visual correlation for an experience that lies outside the confines of the phenomenal world and that connects the individual directly to the universal. This was not 'abstract' art in the sense of being based on the reduction or simplification of the image. Rather, it was an independent form of art that was dedicated to the evocation of a non-sensory reality.

Within this new definition of painting, coloured paint pigment was an especially complex property, one that was highly prized but which also had to be tamed. Colour had to be purified of associations; paint must be freed from entrapment by the objects it is customarily used to describe, but also freed from the lower, sensory experiences it provokes. The immateriality of colour allowed painting to work more directly on the soul, touching the universal, like music, but as we have seen, colour is also the most sensual aspect of the medium of painting, the one that encourages dynamic, sensory responses rather than an inward-facing, contemplative relationship to refined thoughts and feelings. Kandinsky therefore argued that it was necessary to cleanse colour of its traditional role as mere sensual decoration.

A dual status of colour was established on clearly Platonist lines. At one point, Kandinsky imagined the application of the colour red to paintings of the sky, flowers, a garment, a face, a tree and a horse. The sequence is one in which the naturalistic association between the colour and an object becomes increasingly tenuous, so that when we arrive at the red horse, 'the very words put us in another atmosphere,' as Kandinsky writes. 'It is possible that this combination of colour and form will appeal as a freak, a purely superficial and non-artistic appeal – or as a hint of a fairy story – once more a non-artistic appeal.'[21] At this point, Kandinsky is imagining the red horse within an otherwise naturalistically coloured scene, and in order to fully embrace the expressive potential of pure colour it was therefore necessary to turn inwards so as to ensure that 'the inner value of a picture should remain unified whatever the variations or contrasts of outward form or colour. The elements of the new art are to be found, therefore, in the inner and not the outer qualities of nature.'[22] Red had to be separated from the horse. There were therefore two ways to experience colour, Kandinsky declared. The first involved '*a purely physical impression*, one of pleasure and contentment at the varied and beautiful colours'. The second, by contrast, was more refined, and available only to 'a more sensitive soul'. Then, 'the effect of colours is deeper and intensely moving', producing the 'psychic effect' of colours, that is, when colours 'produce a corresponding spiritual vibration'.[23] As Kandinsky concluded: 'It is only as a step towards this spiritual vibration that the elementary physical impression is of importance.'[24]

A far more rigorous divestment of both the expressive function and reference to the natural world through colour and shape was implied in the work of Kazimir Malevich (1879–1935), who pursued a level of reductiveness that will open the way to the monochrome that Kandinsky never painted. Malevich saw his work as a pure diagram of a non-visual but real world. He wanted to convey as directly as possible his conviction in the absoluteness of the work of art, its status as embodying a higher reality independent of merely subjective responses. He conjoined what he considered objective analysis with a conviction in the superiority of a non-material reality. This reality was one that could only be revealed by intuition, and never by reason, and what he overtly called his 'objectless' paintings were meant to be tools for contemplation used only by the initiated.[25]

In this sense, Malevich inverted the procedures of the scientific method, which were detoured into an exploration of 'spiritual' rather than empirical reality. Like the scientist, Malevich said he sought 'reality', and not mere appearances. But this was a reality that, like the mystic's, was without weight, measure, time or place and could never become a fixed form. Malevich announced that he had finally achieved a form of art that embodied a higher state of consciousness – what he called 'pure feeling' – which was accessible only through intuition. He declared that 'the phenomena of the object world per se have no meaning. Only the feeling per se is substantive, totally independent of the environment in which it was elicited.'[26] The issue was not 'the comprehension and cognition of the world', as it was for the scientist, 'but feeling and sensing it'.[27] Malevich believed that he had finally rid painting of all that impeded access to such pure feeling, and thereby that this art objectively revealed the truth of ultimate reality; 'And thus Art comes to objectless depiction – to Suprematism,' he declared in 1927 – the new art of purified geometric form and colour that was the culmination of the art of the past, and the only art suited to the present.[28] For a work of art to achieve the exalted status that Malevich claimed for it, he believed it was necessary for painting to become a site of no-reference, of no-meaning in relation to phenomena, one that challenges the compulsion to seek within the visual for familiar meaning and significance.

It was for this reason that Malevich developed in his Suprematist style a technique that deliberately minimized the signs of expressive and bodily engagement with materials. He crafted a formal language characterized by the non-autographic mark, the non-expressive application of paint, and neutral geometric forms and colours. His brushstrokes were methodical and repetitive, his colours non-naturalistic, non-descriptive and non-expressive. His was a technique intended to create the maximum distance between himself and the work that was produced, a distance that conveyed a stance of absolute detachment, neutrality and anonymity.

Malevich casts the monochrome as the limit or threshold, a limit beyond which painting ceases to be painting. Through giving visual form to such a liminal, boundary situation, he hoped to open painting towards an ineffable and intangible totality that could only be experienced directly and never put into language. But he stressed that the void-like space was 'not the end of Art, as people think, but the beginning of actual existence'.[29] Malevich described his monochromatic *Black Square* (1915) as 'a desert where there is nothing but the sensation of desert'.[30] He declared that the colour black was 'pure feeling', that is, feeling freed from attachment to the material realm, while the white field was the void beyond feeling: 'The white margins are not margins framing a black square, but merely the sensation of desert, the sensation of non-existence, in which the square form is the first objectless element of sensation.'[31]

The reference to the desert was meant to suggest a limiting and empty condition, the absence of any objects whatsoever; Malevich drew on a natural phenomenon characterized by a solid and lifeless earth and a cloudless sky, stretching in all directions, which evokes a state of lifelessness. But Malevich also stressed the aerial dimension to his Suprematism, emphasizing the influence of aerial photography and aviation on his work. In this context, his paintings can be seen to involve a reorientation of the picture plane from the vertical axis of the perspectival window to the horizontal one that characterizes the aerial point of view. Indeed, in *White on White* the reference to the desert has been replaced by an overtly aerial one. A gaseous cloud or fog seems to obscure the tilted square that has been painted within the square shape of the canvas support. By reducing visual contrast to a minimum, Malevich emphasized more overtly than in *Black Square* the experience of an enveloping and unbroken ground, one that is in the process of absorbing or negating the figure. Malevich was now exploring the limits of the visible, testing the eye's capacity to make distinctions according to contour and differences in colour.

For the Last Futurist Exhibition of Painting, titled '0,10' and held in Petrograd from December 1915 to January 1916, Malevich hung his *Black Square* high up across a corner of the gallery, surrounded by other more visually complex but equally geometric Suprematist works. This location self-consciously replicated the position of a religious icon in a Russian home. Later, when Malevich's body lay in repose in his Leningrad apartment after his death in 1935, another painting of a black square on a white ground was suspended above his head. Malevich consciously recognized his debt to the Orthodox tradition. In an autobiographical note written two years before his death, he wrote:

> My acquaintance with icon painting convinced me that the point is not the study of anatomy and perspective, nor in depicting the truth of nature, but in sensing art and artistic reality through the emotions. In other words, I saw that reality or subject matter is something to be transformed into an ideal form away from the depths of aesthetics.[32]

Malevich's vision of the monochrome was ultimately premised on an unflinching faith in the possibility of a kind of modern art that could have universal relevance once the audience was initiated into its new language, and when the old habits of perception and conception which separate and alienate them from contact with the universal are abandoned. As the art historian Myroslava M.

Mudrak notes, the motif of the black square was intended to signal 'the communal value of transcendence' and was 'the ultimate symbol of inclusiveness'.[33] Malevich was committed to the belief that art must serve to unite people through creating a higher sense of community based on the principle of redemption.[34] Inevitably, he felt drawn to the ideals of the October Revolution that in 1917 swept away the old Tzarist system and, with it, the Russian Orthodox Church's official role within the state. Malevich, like other members of the Russian avant-garde, shared in the general frustration felt by Russian intellectuals at the beginning of the twentieth century when they compared the backwardness of their country to the apparently economically sophisticated and successful Western European powers like Germany and Great Britain. In this sense, Malevich shared the conviction that change must come through revolutionary action. But through proposing a 'spiritual' awakening in art, and adopting the role of secular priest, Malevich was clearly at odds with the materialistic ideology and pragmatic goals of the Bolsheviks as they forged the new 'classless' society. His utopian commitments went far beyond communism, and would soon be exposed as fundamentally contrary to the Bolsheviks' vision. Malevich placed his faith in a perpetual process of transformation that will never attain its goal and never solidifies into a system. He believed that art serves to keep open a passageway through which pure potentiality can flow from life into art, and from art into life.

6

INDEFINABLE

This inexpressible poetic moment.[1]
Yves Klein (1960)

Several decades after Malevich painted his *Black Square* and *White on White*, the Frenchman Yves Klein would also seek through the medium of the monochrome to explore a 'spiritual' space that lies beyond structures, beyond representation. But as we saw, for Klein it was the liberation of colour from the constraints imposed on painting by line that was to be the most vital goal of the new monochrome painting. Only colour, Klein declared, possessed the necessary properties for freeing art from its dreary incarceration within the symbolic, pushing it towards zones of intense feeling and expression based in the powers of intuition and imagination. 'For me, colours are living beings, highly evolved individuals that integrate themselves with us, as with everything,' Klein wrote.

> Colours are the true inhabitants of space. The line merely travels across, passes through space . . . Each nuance originates from the base colour but clearly possesses its own autonomous existence,

> which immediately signals that the fact of painting in a unique colour is not limited; there are myriad nuances for all colours, each of which possesses its individual and particular worth.[2]

For Klein, colour functioned as the visual correlate for a fundamental ontological choice: health over disease.[3] But it is important to stress that colour was not really important in its own right; rather, its value lay in what it facilitated. To this end, colour had to undergo purification, and this is why he elected to paint in a single colour. 'As soon as there are two colours in a painting, combat begins,' Klein wrote. 'The permanent spectacle of this battle of two colours may give the onlooker a subtle psychological and emotional pleasure, that is nonetheless morbid from a purely human, philosophical point of view.'[4]

In fact, Klein exaggerated for rhetorical effect the extent to which the domination of line brought painting wholly under the control of reason and suppressed the 'inexpressible poetic moment'. As we have seen, the system of linear fixed-point perspective had actually been challenged almost from the beginning from within its own codes. As James Elkins notes, marks can '*exfoliate*' or have 'deliquescence', and such metamorphic qualities will bring to attention the ontological instability of painting as a picturing code.[5] One moment an image may seem solid and clearly defined, while at the next appear to operate at the limit of resolution of the eye. The transitory nature of such perception confuses the boundary that the line seeks to impose, and so, 'barely perceptible forms are another universal mode for graphic marking. Their indistinctness is not always meant to be resolved . . . it is part of their way of accepting and declining determinate meaning.'[6]

In the fluid, multiple contours that traverse Renaissance sketches, and in Leonardo's hazy *sfumato*, the 'indefinable' holds sway. In Leonardo's work, writes Dario Gamboni, 'imaginative perception' is accorded 'a central place in the most advanced theory and practice of painting. We can see that, without formally challenging the doctrine of imitation, Leonardo's approach extends it well beyond the "visible" and the foreseeable.'[7] Colour was also enlisted to similar ends by other artists. In Fra Angelico's chromatically suffused sacred spaces and in the Venetian colourists' substitution of the luminously coloured ambience for linear outline, the linear grid is engulfed and softened by the nebulousness of chroma. Indeed, by the Baroque period, erosions of the established sense of pictorial order had introduced a destabilizing subjectivity into the very heart of picture-making.[8]

It was above all within the genre of landscape painting that the experiences of uncertainty and unreliability were most assiduously explored, and it is to landscape that we can look for another of the origins of the monochrome. In order to paint a perspectival rendering of a scene it is necessary to faithfully reproduce optical indeterminacy and fugitive effects. In a perspectival projection the foreground of a depicted landscape requires an accumulation of detail, simulating the effect of optical focus on phenomena close to a viewer, but the further a landscape recedes, the more vague and diffuse the phenomena become. Leonardo and other artists established a repertoire of pictorial signs for the depiction of such deep and visually vague spatial recession, as well as other aspects of nature that, by their inherent character, cannot be forced into the geometric structure of perspective. The meteorological characteristics of the distant horizon – of light scattering at a distance – challenged artists to find the stylistic means to simulate perceptual indistinctness. Leonardo, for example, listed four such characteristics of the technique of atmospheric (or aerial) perspective he developed: diminution of clarity of form; diminution of tonal contrast; change of hue; and diminution of saturation with distance.[9]

The depiction of clouds, a natural phenomenon with neither form nor consistency, also exposed the limits of a system of painting dominated by ratio and line. The clouds that populate the sky within landscape paintings effectively 'connoted the closure of the system, revealing its limitations by operating at its margins', as the art historian and philosopher Hubert Damisch writes. By incorporating clouds into their compositions, artists were able to find ways to address the intangible and invisible, 'at the meeting point of what was depictable and what was not'.[10]

In these ways, openings on to visual experiences that surpass the limits of the visible were being tested. The loosening and blurring of contours, the evocation of infinite depth, the collapsing of the figure/ground relation and the adoption of techniques that seemed deliberately to lack 'finish' encouraged an emotional rather than rational involvement with the painting, inviting a viewer to engage imaginatively with a depiction and to thereby 'complete' it. The genre of landscape thereby became a site for the testing of boundaries and limits. As the philosopher François Jullien writes:

> In taking its distance from the perceptual logic of a sensation that can be passively organized by reason, landscape painting uncovered the immediate, invasive power of the impression and, in so doing, led the more primordial consciousness of a being-in-the-world to outstrip the visual object. In addition, in shattering the self-sufficiency of those paintings whose meaning was

> conferred entirely by history, landscape painting makes the beholder dream of vague, far-off places, including him in its reverie through its indeterminations.[11]

In Romantic art, a distinction was made between the 'beautiful' and a new category borrowed from the classical era, the 'sublime'. While a beautiful work of art generates a sense of comfort and security through the perception of clearly defined forms and balanced colours, the indeterminacy evoked by awe-inspiring natural phenomena, such as mountains or a stormy sea, provokes the sublime experience. In pictorial terms the experience of indeterminacy and ambiguity was communicated by a deliberate rejection of stable contrasts between forms, by a heightened emphasis on colour at the expense of line and by the blurring of the horizon, so that the boundaries between figure and ground become confused. As we saw earlier, colour, once freed from the constraints of contour, made space homogeneous and unbroken, and as a result a deeper sense of compositional unity and wholeness was evoked as the undifferentiated ground became a primary pictorial characteristic. Furthermore, the linear compositional framework supplied by geometric perspective now forms a limiting condition to be overcome, and the rectangular framing edge of the canvas was no longer a firm and finite boundary uniting the forms within, but an arbitrary line of demarcation that must be breached.

In the late nineteenth century, the Symbolists furthered the goals of Romanticism, actively encouraging imaginative flights inwards and conjuring chimeras, poetic moods and the mysteriously equivocal. The French artist Odilon Redon praised Leonardo as the initiator of a new concept of art that was reaching fruition, one that Redon said consisted in the 'irradiation of things'.[12]

The indeterminate and ambiguous were valued more than anything lifelike produced through the stabilization of perceptual forms and the coherent reading of content. Redon postulated the idea of a 'suggestive art', an art that was 'like an illumination of things from dreams, toward which thought also is directed'.[13]

The 'spiritual' benefits of the indeterminate, the ambiguous and of occluded vision, and its importance for the development of abstract art, was made explicit in Kandinsky's account of an encounter one night in his own studio with what he called a 'mysterious picture':

> It was the hour when dusk draws in. I returned home with my painting box having finished a study still dreaming and absorbed in the work I had completed, and suddenly saw an indescribably beautiful picture, pervaded by an inner glow. At first, I stopped short and then quickly approached this mysterious picture, on which I could discern only forms and colours and whose contents was incomprehensible. At once, I discovered the key to the puzzle: it was a picture I had painted, standing on its side against the wall. The next day, I tried to re-create my impression of the picture from the previous evening by daylight. I only half-succeeded, however; even on its side, I constantly recognized objects, and the fine bloom of dusk was missing. Now I could see clearly that objects harmed my pictures.[14]

YVES KLEIN'S FAVOURITE quotation, which he used in several of his texts, came from the journals of Eugène Delacroix: 'The merit of painting is the indefinable.'[15] In 'The Monochrome Adventure' (1960), for example, Klein writes:

> From the voiceless conversation that ensues between these states of things and myself, an impalpable affinity is born, 'indefinable,' as Delacroix would say. It is this 'indefinable,' this inexpressible poetic moment, that I desire to fix on my canvas since my mode of being . . . is to make paintings. And so I paint the pictorial moment that is born of an illumination by impregnation in life itself.[16]

An especially important influence on Klein was the philosopher Gaston Bachelard (1884–1962). In his phenomenological account of art, Bachelard argued that the imagination is the pre-eminent faculty:

> If there is no change, or unexpected fusion of images, there is no imagination; there is no *imaginative act*. If the image that is *present* does not make us think of one that is *absent*, if an image does not determine an abundance – an explosion – of unusual images, then there is no imagination. There is only perception, the memory of a perception, a familiar memory, an habitual way of viewing form and colour . . . Thanks to the *imaginary*, imagination is essentially open and elusive. It is the human psyche's experience of openness and novelty.[17]

In terms that greatly influenced Klein, Bachelard also wrote: 'We always think of the imagination as the faculty that *forms* images. But on the contrary, it deforms what we perceive; it is, above all, the faculty that frees us from immediate images and *changes* them.'[18] The imaginary is by necessity without clear limits, and works on the level of subconscious formations. For Klein the imagination shows that consciousness is pervaded by diffuseness, immateriality and evanescence. It is environmental, like an all-enveloping sky. But we diminish the power of the imagination by segregating the world using lines, allocating some of what we perceive to the category of figure and the rest to ground. By becoming fixated on the former and wholly forgetting about the latter, we diminish the power of the imagination.

In one of his own texts, Klein quotes Bachelard directly on the colour blue and its association with the sky, and its relationship to specific emotional states:

> The blue of the sky, if we were to examine its many values, would require a long study in which we would see all the types of material imagination being determined according to the basic elements of water, fire, earth, and air. In other words, we could divide poets into our classifications by their response to the single themes of celestial blue;
>
> Those who see in an immobile sky a flowing liquid that comes to life with the smallest cloud.
>
> Those who experience the blue sky as though it were an enormous flame 'searing' blue, as the Comtesse de Noailles [Anna de Noailles (1876–1933), poet and novelist] described it.
>
> Those who contemplate the sky as if it were a solidified blue, a painted vault – 'compact and hard azure.' As the Comtesse de Noailles says.
>
> Finally those who can truly participate in the aerial nature of celestial blue.
>
> . . .
>
> Moreover, if we are truly willing to live, with Éluard [Paul Éluard (1895–1952), Surrealist poet], by imagination and for imagination, these hours of pure vision in front of the tender and delicate blue

> of a sky from which all objects have been banished, we will be able to understand that the aerial kind of imagination offered a domain in which the values of the dream and of the representational are interchangeable on the most basic level. Other matters harden objects. Also, in the realm of blue air more than elsewhere, we feel that the world may be permeated by the most indeterminate reverie. This is when reverie really has depth. The blue sky opens up in depth beneath the dream. Then dreams are not limited to one-dimensional images.[19]

As Bachelard added in his *Air and Dreams* (1943), the text from which Klein quoted:

> It is by following the scale of *dematerialization* of celestial blue that we can see aerial reverie at work. Then we will understand that it is an aerial *Einfühlung* [empathy]: the fusion of a dreamer with as undifferentiated a universe as possible, one that is blue and gentle, infinite and formless, with a *minimum of substance*.[20]

Klein seems to have identified fully with the 'aerial' in the sense described by Bachelard, thinking of himself as a true aeronautical 'participant'. For Klein, the limpid gaseousness of the blue sky would come to serve as the strongest possible environmental image for the most indefinable of all experiences – infinity. Born in 1928 in Nice, in the south of France, and to artist parents, Klein was exposed at an early age to the vast pellucid dome of the Mediterranean sky. The experience of such an intense and pure azure expanse must have contrasted strongly with the pallid grey skies he also experienced between 1930 and 1939, when, from the ages of two to eleven, Klein lived with his parents in Paris –

a contrast continually reinforced because Klein usually spent the summer months in the care of his aunt in Nice, during his parents' painting expeditions elsewhere on the Côte d'Azur. As Klein wrote: 'As an adolescent, I wrote my name on the back of the sky in a fantastic realistico-imaginary journey, stretched out on a beach one day in Nice . . . I have hated birds ever since for trying to make holes in my greatest and most beautiful work! Away with birds!'[21] Klein also recalled how he and his friends were on a beach in Nice when they decided to divide the universe among themselves, as the Greek gods Zeus, Poseidon and Hades had done. One friend, the future artist Arman, was given the animal realm; another, who became a poet, was allotted the plants; and Klein himself took command of the mineral world and the blue expanse of the sky.[22]

For Klein, the blue monochrome would come to signal the physical threshold to a reality that was released not just from the constraints of language but from the entire phenomenal world. In 1955 he exhibited his blue monochromes for the first time, in Paris, which was soon followed by another exhibition in Paris, 'Yves: Propositions Monochromes', in early 1956. Through limiting himself to blue, Klein believed he gained access to the ineffable and intangible, giving it visible form. Like Malevich before him, and for similar reasons, he also adopted a neutral painting style, one that mimicked the anonymous and detached procedures typical of not only sacred art but the scientist. As Klein later recounted, he showed in 'Yves: Propositions Monochromes', ten paintings 'in dark ultramarine blue, all of them rigorously similar in tone, intensity, proportions, and dimensions'. But despite the fact that they were more or less identical, Klein stressed that 'each of the blue propositions . . . were perceived by the public as clearly distinct from each other.'[23] As he explained:

> For the creative act to succeed, the immaterialization of the invisible and intangible canvas must act upon the sensuous vehicle or bodies of the gallery visitors with much more efficiency than ordinary, physical, representational paintings. The latter, if they are of good quality, are also endowed with this special pictorial essence and affective presence, that is, with sensibility, but it is transmitted by the suggestion of every physical and psychological appearance of the painting, by its lines, contours, forms, composition, juxtaposition of colours, etc. These intermediaries are now no longer needed: one is literally impregnated with the pictorial sensibility, refined and stabilized beforehand by the painter in a given space. It is a direct and immediate perception and assimilation without other effects, without gadgets or hoaxes.[24]

Klein also priced each of his seemingly identically painted monochrome works differently, a strategy, so he said, that demonstrated that 'the pictorial quality of each painting was perceptible by something other than the material and physical appearance' and that 'those who made their choice recognized that state to which I refer as "Pictorial Sensibility."'[25] A monochrome by Klein was therefore 'pure' only when it reflected purity of spirit or 'sensibility'. In fact, as he wrote: 'Painting no longer appeared to me to be functionally related to the eye when in my blue monochrome period of 1957 I became acquainted with what I have termed the pictorial sensibility.'[26] His painting had 'nothing to do with the five senses, with the domain of feeling or even with the purely and fundamentally emotional'.[27] Rather, 'pure pictorial sensibility' was somehow injected into the artwork, and was there to be intuited by the sensitive viewer.[28]

Klein directly invoked the fruits of scientific endeavour, but only to argue for an entirely different understanding of reality:

> It is not with rockets, Sputniks, or missiles that modern man will achieve the conquest of space. That's the dream of present-day scientists who live in a romantic and sentimental state of mind that belongs to the 19th century. It is through the terrific peaceful force of sensibility that man will inhabit space. It is through the impregnation with the human sensibility that the ardently desired conquest of this space will be achieved. For human sensibility is capable of anything in immaterial reality; it can even read in nature's memory about the past, the present, and the future. It is our potential of effective extradimensional action.[29]

But this goal was greatly aided by the ritual processes within which he persistently contextualized his work. Klein was a devout Roman Catholic, a follower of St Rita of Cascia (the patron saint of lost causes), and a Knight of the Order of St Sebastian (in whose ceremonial robes he enjoyed dressing, and was married). But Klein was also deeply influenced by Christian mystical traditions, alchemy and Rosicrucianism – an esoteric manifestation of Platonism and Neoplatonism that fused Hermeticism, Jewish mysticism and Gnosticism.[30] To this heady mix, Klein added the influence of the martial art of Judo (which he taught, and about which he wrote a book), and he was also deeply interested in East Asian philosophy and religion, especially Zen Buddhism (a theme to which I return in Chapter Nine).[31]

Ritual was in fact central to Klein's entire conception of art. For 'The Void', the exhibition held in Paris in 1958, Klein hired

Republican Guards for the opening. For his *Anthropométries* series (1960), he wore a tuxedo as a group of naked models rolled in blue paint, performing as human 'paintbrushes' while he conducted an orchestra playing his 'Monotone Silence Symphony'. 'Yves Klein was the first artist of the avant-garde to mythologize the material with which he worked,' the artist Anish Kapoor later noted. 'He made it clear through his life and work that artists don't just make objects, they make mythologies. Through this he was able to bring the religious into the realm of the avant-garde.'[32]

KLEIN'S VISION FOR art was shared by many other artists at mid-century. As he himself noted: 'Young painters, BURRI, TAPIÈS, MACK, DAWING, IONESCO, PIENE, MANZONI, MUBIN, and others still that I do not know, have now come to paint in an almost monochrome manner. But this is not a grave matter to me, quite the contrary. It is not important "who first composed a monochrome painting."'[33]

The Zero group explicitly cast the monochrome in terms encouraged by Klein.[34] An artist associated with Zero, Lucio Fontana, for example, described in language very close to Klein's own his practice of cutting directly into monochromatic canvas with a knife:

> The discovery of the cosmos is a new dimension, it is infinity, so I make a hole in this canvas, which was at the basis of all the arts and I have created an infinite dimension . . . the idea is precisely that, it is a new dimension corresponding to the cosmos . . . The hole is, precisely, creating this void behind there . . . Einstein's discovery of the cosmos is the infinite dimension, without end. And so here we have: foreground, middle-ground

> and background . . . to go farther what do I have to do? . . . I make holes, infinity passes through them, light passes through them, there is no need to paint.[35]

But Klein himself seems to have recognized that his vision of the 'indefinable' monochrome was based on a fundamental contradiction, and artists like Fontana and members of Zero also seemed to oscillate between claiming that they evoked an immaterial realm while producing works that seem especially to affirm their status as concrete realities. How was something ineffable supposed to be evoked through the most material aspect of painting: colour? For, as Yve-Alain Bois writes: 'Klein reached his dream of having the colour alone, without mediation, at maximum intensity – so that it could be experienced in the moment only, in the inarticulate moment of the sensation – through a mystical logic that seemed to be in complete opposition to his affirmation of colour.'[36]

The Italian artist Piero Manzoni (1933–1963), who was also greatly influenced by Klein, and like Fontana showed with artists associated with Zero, saw the essential problem. While Klein had chosen blue, Manzoni focused exclusively on painting white pictures – what he called his 'Achromes'. In a typical work from this series, *Achrome* (1958), a painting of 1 metre square, Manzoni built up the work's surface with sections of cut canvas and overlaid them with kaolin, a china clay used in the making of porcelain. The result is an unyielding material presence. White, Manzoni insisted, was chosen because of its neutrality. 'White is not a polar landscape,' he declared, 'not a material in evolution or a beautiful material, not a sensation or a symbol or anything else: just a white surface that is simply a white surface and nothing else (a colourless surface that is just a colourless surface).'[37] What was important, Manzoni announced, was that the viewer attend to the formal nature of white – what they perceived before them in the here and now, and not to reach after some metaphysical or imaginative addition – our 'mental scenography' as he called it.[38]

> All problems of colour and all questions of chromatic relationships are . . . useless, even if one is only dealing with tonal modulations. We can only utilize a single colour, or, rather, utilize a single uninterrupted and continuous surface from which anything superfluous and all interpretative possibilities are excluded. It is not a question of 'painting' blue on blue or white on white either in the sense of composing or in the sense of expressing oneself. In fact, it is quite the contrary. The question for me is that of creating integrally white surfaces (yes, integrally colourless, neutral), which is completely unrelated to any pictorial phenomenon or to any element extraneous to the value of the surface.[39]

In retrospect, the attempt to use a painted surface to embrace the indefinable does seem fundamentally paradoxical. As long as colour remains physically applied to a material plane, and bound to the limitations imposed by the geometric contour or edge of the support, the ineffable can never be fully expressed. Klein himself would seek to solve this problem by going beyond painting. He saw the ultimate purpose of the monochrome as a way of demonstrating that the artist who had made them was committed to 'total freedom'. 'When there is imprisonment in whatever manner,' Klein wrote, 'liberty is restrained and life is diminished in relation to the degree of imprisonment.'[40] A monochrome painting was therefore ultimately of little formal importance for Klein. It was valuable only because it was the material point before art took flight, or was released from the mundane world. 'My works are the ashes of my art,' Klein declared on more than one occasion.[41] His exhibition 'The Void', which consisted of a gallery completely devoid of objects, was nevertheless, so he declared, full of a 'pictorial sensibility' wholly independent of any material support and was not manifested visually. In this context, the medium of the monochrome leads us to the threshold at which art takes a leap into pure invisibility. At the limits of material form, the monochrome is making way for a wholly intangible work of art.

7

NOTHINGNESS

the immense number of nihilations.[1]
Arthur Danto (1991)

Gaps, aporias, lapses and voids within the established system of the language of art allow emptiness to be recognized as a constitutive aspect of its meaning. 'To see emptiness means to place into a percept something that belongs there but is absent and to notice its absence as a property of the present,' notes the psychologist and visual theorist Rudolf Arnheim. 'The stimulus material can be perceived as the ground for an absent figure.'[2] In the seascape by the German Romantic painter Caspar David Friedrich *Monk by the Sea* (*c.* 1808–10), which is arguably the first monochromatic painting in the West, the artist has emptied out the compositional structure in order to make his work the ground for the invisible and transcendent God. Friedrich's painting shows a tiny figure standing on a desolate shore, contemplating a vast and ominous sea and sky. Compositionally, the work consists of three horizontal divisions, only one of which – the seashore – is sufficiently contrasted with its neighbour to stand out clearly from what, from a normal viewing distance, might seem to be an almost completely undifferentiated gloom. Friedrich inverts the normal meaning-bearing syntax of the language of painting so that it is the 'negative' space that is the focus of attention, rather than the 'positive' figure. His painting generates the feeling that something ineffable is being brought into the light through the negation of the familiar compositional scaffold that usually organizes the visible within a painting.

In the process, Friedrich had effectively forged a new pictorial language, one motivated by strong religious belief. For him, the loss of firm structural distinctions within a painted composition was intended to signal the fact that the faithful were drawing closer to God within a nothingness in which divinity is sensed as a numinous power, as the 'wholly other'.[3] Friedrich was a devout Protestant, and believed as a fundamental principle in the impossibility of representing the divine. The visible was a deceptive screen, and so we must be vigilant against the perpetual danger of succumbing to idolatry, to mistaking the visible for the real. During the Reformation, iconoclasm had become an especially encouraged form of sacred purification among Protestants. This regime of purging involved the reduction of visual images to the material status of non-symbolic objects: countless cult images were destroyed or defaced to prove their powerlessness, and as a result a clear distinction was made between the profane, material realm of representation and the immaterial realm of the sacred.[4] But Friedrich also inherited a conception of the artist as someone potentially capable of seeing beyond the material world in order to evoke the ineffable. In this sense, Friedrich's work can be seen as a continuation of the apophatic tradition of mystical art discussed earlier. The goal, Friedrich declared, was to 'blind' the sensory and active eye in order to make way for the higher and more spiritual and contemplative vision of the 'inner' eye. 'Close your physical eye, so that you may see your picture first with the spiritual eye,' Friedrich advised, 'Then bring what you saw in the dark into the light, so that it may have an effect on others, shining inwards from outside.'[5]

IN AN OBVIOUS way, the overt blankness of a painting like Friedrich's invites a meditation on nothingness. Through emptying the canvas of its usual content, the notion of the void is turned to account and made to mean something. This would also be the case with the monochrome. When Malevich declared that his *Black Square* created a 'desert' beyond form – a wasteland of paint – he was indicating that the monochrome was equivalent to the end of the world, while at the same time proposing that his iconoclastic act was also one of purification that prepared the ground for a new beginning. For Yves Klein, the void expressed through the colour blue was meant to signal emancipation from the prison-house of daily life.

But as the twentieth century unfolded the experience of nothingness came to hold more ominous implications, reflecting a deep-seated anxiety over the meaning and value of life. Starting in the seventeenth century, the spirit of scientific rationalism central to the Enlightenment had brought great benefits to Western society, especially in the form of technological innovation and social emancipation, but by the late nineteenth century it had become increasingly clear that the Enlightenment's goal of systematic 'disenchantment' through the application of critical reason to all dimensions of human existence also left many estranged from religious doctrine and simultaneously suspicious of the increasingly cult-like status of reason and science. If there was no social hierarchy justified by an all-powerful God, humans were simply part of nature and, far from being able to gain mastery over it, must instead recognize that their values and meanings are invented to conceal nature's essential indifference to humanity's fate. A new and gnawing sense of inner emptiness was being precipitated, the psychic equivalent of what entropy is on the level of physical processes – the recognition of the inevitability of increasing disorder and uncertainty.

For Friedrich Nietzsche (1844–1900), to be modern meant being thrown into a nihilistic darkness. In response, an ascetic ideal and a stoic will to power were required, driven by 'that hatred against everything human, even more, against everything animal, everything material, this disgust with the senses, with reason itself, this fear of happiness and beauty, this desire to get away from all semblance, change, becoming, death, wish, desire itself'. Behind the quintessentially modern attitude, Nietzsche continued, there must lie 'a *will* to *nothingness*, a will running counter to life, a revolt against the most fundamental presuppositions of life; yet it is and remains a *will*! And, to repeat at the end what I said at the beginning: rather than want nothing, man even wants *nothingness*.'[6]

A heightened awareness of a meaningless existential void felt by increasing numbers in the modern West was further deepened by plentiful evidence that society was very far from embodying the noble ideals praised by Christianity and humanism. In the shadow of the mechanized butchery in the trenches between 1914 and 1918, the rise of totalitarianism, the application of instrumental reason to achieve the goals of the Holocaust and the use of science to create the atomic bombs detonated over Hiroshima and Nagasaki, it was increasingly difficult to ignore the fact that culture was inextricably entwined with barbarism, that the highest of human aspirations were wedded to the lowest degradations. As George Steiner writes: 'The spheres of Auschwitz-Birkenau and of the Beethoven recital, of the torture-cellar and the great library, were contiguous in space and time. Men could come home from their day's butchery and falsehood to weep over Rilke or play Schubert.'[7] In such circumstances it seemed evident to many that, as the German Jewish philosopher Theodor Adorno wrote in 1966: 'if thinking is to be true – if it is to be true today, in any case – it must be a thinking against itself. If thought is not measured by the extremity that eludes the concept, it is from the outset in the nature of the musical accompaniment with which the ss liked to drown out the screams of its victims.'[8]

To this awareness of the polluting proximity of culture and violence was added the increasing awareness that the burgeoning consumerism of the period, in which the technologies of the mass media such as the newspaper, magazine, advertising, radio, cinema and, from the 1950s, television, was engineering a society glutted on visual spectacle, and required a concerted response. As Walter Benjamin noted in 'The Work of Art in the Age of Mechanical Reproduction' (1935), traditional notions of 'authenticity' and the 'aura' or transcendent value of art were jeopardized by the ease and rapidity of technological reproducibility.[9] For many artists, these transformations required that they assiduously resist the fetishism which assumes all too easily that the image is an adequate agent of representation.

In this broad social context, the monochrome becomes an especially uncompromising form of painting 'against itself'. The inevitable tendency of art to function as a language of positive meanings, simply because it exists in a complicit relationship to the status quo of society, needed to be radically deconstructed. Art had to become a force of negation.

It is in this context that the work of Ad Reinhardt, and his statements like the following, can be interpreted:

> A square (*neutral, shapeless*) canvas, five feet wide, five feet high, as high as a man, as wide as a man's outstretched arms (*not large, not small, sizeless*), trisected (*no composition*), one horizontal form negating one vertical form (*formless, no top, no bottom, directionless*), three (*more or less*) dark (*lightless*) no-contrasting (*colourless*) colours, brushwork brushed out to remove brushwork, a matte, flat, free-hand painted surface (*glossless, non-linear, no hard-edge, no soft-edge*) which does not reflect its surroundings – a pure, abstract, non-objective, timeless, spaceless, changeless, relationless, disinterested painting – an object that is self-conscious (*no unconsciousness*) ideal, transcendent, aware of no thing but art (*absolutely no anti-art*).[10]

His practice involved a process of negation-as-affirmation through which repetitive acts of cancellation, erasure and withdrawal were meant to lead to a purification and strengthening of art. As he recognized, to practise art from within an iconoclastic worldview means finding ways to make a visual sign allude to what necessarily lies beyond signs. 'Even if Reinhardt's canvases were completely monochrome,' writes Arthur Danto, 'they would have as their substance the immense number of nihilations of everything Reinhardt was convinced was not essential to art. Their richness would be a function of the totality of those denials, and to experience them as art would require grasping this as an objective fact.'[11] From a logical point of view, Reinhardt's repetition of the act of negation is clearly contradictory, a rational impossibility that claims to abolish the object he makes in the process of making it. But Reinhardt postulates the possibility of an empty object without a concept, a painting existing in a (non-)space both beyond and within language.

In the course of discussing Reinhardt, Danto refers to the German philosopher Martin Heidegger's notion of 'nothingness nothinging', a similarly paradoxical use of language that aims to negotiate the very limits of what can be conceived and put into words.[12] Heidegger used the phrase in order to argue that awareness of nothingness should serve as the foundation stone of authentic existence. Since everything is finite, nothingness lies at the very heart of being and determines its nature. Mindless involvement in the social world can repress the fear of oblivion, but this essential anxiety can never fully be expunged because death is inevitable. At moments of existential anxiety, or in great works of art, we sense it, thereby grasping the true implications of the utter unknowability of death.

In his essay 'The Origin of the Work of Art' (1950), Heidegger discusses Vincent van Gogh's painting *A Pair of Shoes* (1886), in which a murky monochromatic space surrounds a pair of old, battered peasant boots. The emptiness of this ground functions for Heidegger as the precondition for the representation of something deeply imbued with an aura that lifts the shoes above the status of mere object. He wrote: 'There is nothing surrounding this pair of peasant shoes in or to which they might belong – only an indefinite space.' But this 'indefinite space' is not simply an empty space without meaning; it is precisely through the monochromatic field that Van Gogh is able to create the boundary around the shoes that allows them to be more present through opening up a web of relations beyond their finite objecthood.[13] The painted void is thereby a ground allowing the figure to appear more fully, to stand forth, to radiate in relationship to the finitude of death.

Reinhardt was from Russo-German Protestant immigrant stock and seems to have naturally adopted a puritanical aesthetic attitude grounded in a contemplative approach that is imbued with a strong iconophobic impulse. In 1957 he offered a small black monochrome to the writer on spirituality Thomas Merton, a friend from Reinhardt's days at Columbia University who had become a Trappist monk. Merton hung it in his austere cell in the monastery of Gethsemani, Kentucky. 'It is a most recollected small painting,' he wrote to Reinhardt. 'It thinks that only one thing is necessary & this is time. But this one thing is by no means apparent to one who will not take the trouble to look. It is a most religious, devout, and latreutic [conducive to worship] small painting.'[14] Merton recognized in Reinhardt's aesthetic parsimony what amounted to a modern-day version of the Christian mystic's *via negativa.* To this extent Reinhardt was in effect a secular exponent of the apophatic – the tradition of approaching the sacred via negation. Indeed Reinhardt's writings about his own work, or at least those that were not meant for immediate public airing, often seem to confirm Merton's assessment. In one unpublished note, for example, he observes:

> Shadow of the spiritual, the one, the good
> (Sign, image, universe of sense only) purest, most equivocal
> Movement beyond itself toward its idea
> Intensified, purified, exalted, awesome nearness of centre
> Purgative, illuminative, unitive most secret working
> Innermost essence, perfection inner concentration.[15]

Reinhardt was indeed rather like a medieval mystic in many ways – his notebooks are full of quotations from St John of the Cross, Meister Eckhart, among others. He inherited a well-established contemplative tradition that involves withdrawal from the active life in order to savour life's essence, but with an important and crucial difference. Merton – who, against the grain of modernity, had chosen to become a Catholic monk – still interpreted this tradition as having a religious colouring. Reinhardt, by contrast, had no faith at all – except in art.

As was the case for many Western artists, the Christian tradition at best seemed marginal and at worst was a travesty of modern reality. But as we will see in Chapter Nine, one possible way to connect his artistic practice to traditional forms of spiritual practice remained alive, and meant embracing a non-Western religious tradition, one far removed from the overt dogmatism, ritual and moral repressiveness of Christianity: Zen Buddhism, a tradition for which the concept of void is absolutely central.

EMPTINESS AND NOTHINGNESS are also central to the experience of the paintings of Mark Rothko (1903–1970), but unlike Reinhardt's work, in ways that powerfully evoke emotional responses from the viewer – responses that the artist himself often termed 'tragic'.

Born to Jewish parents in Dvinsk, Russia, Rothko emigrated with his family to Portland, Oregon, at ten years old. This biographical context places him between two deep religious traditions, Judaism and Puritan Christianity, which converge in their shared suspicion of the sign, of conventional carriers of information. A cultural background in which iconophobia is central was now reinforced by Rothko's awareness of the crushing banalization of the visual brought about by the impact of the mass media in the United States. As a result, he concluded, as he wrote in 1947, that 'the familiar identity of things' had to be 'pulverized in order to destroy the finite associations with which society enshrouds every aspect of our environment'.[16]

When he wrote the above, Rothko was on the threshold of the breakthrough to his mature painting style. In the early 1940s, his paintings were heavily influenced by Surrealism; glyph- or hieroglyph-like forms populate flat chromatic fields, and the decisive moment came in the late 1940s when he effectively omitted or buried these forms, leaving as the 'content' of his work the loose structure of coloured rectangles that previously served as a kind of stage, setting or ground. The large scale of these new paintings, which typically consist of horizontal layers of floating, coloured, loosely contoured rectilinear forms, was a vital dimension of their directly experiential impact. But as Rothko explained: 'My paintings are intimate and intense, and are the opposite of what is decorative, and have been painted in a scale of normal human living rather than an institutional scale.'[17] He vehemently rejected the rationalism of geometric abstraction, as well as Surrealism's emphasis on generating imagery from the unconscious. He also denied any connection between his work and Henri Matisse and the School of Paris, a link that was often made on account of his apparently sensuous use of colour. For Rothko, the creative act must be involved with the perennial existential questions of finitude, suffering, nothingness and the yearning for transcendence, and as such he perpetuates the Romantic-Symbolist tradition that proposes that great art is concerned not with art-for-art's sake exploration of form, but with approaching the expression of the ineffable and intangible.

Rothko aimed to create an intangible and benevolent void that necessarily lies beyond the capacities of figurative representation. What at first seems to be simply a coloured canvas can, after sustained attention, become pregnant with limitless depth. But perhaps in response to the misunderstandings concerning the significance of the aesthetically pleasing colour arrangements he orchestrated in his work, around 1954 Rothko shifted to a much darker palette. 'Technically speaking, Rothko was essentially a "night" painter, such as, perhaps, Odilon Redon, but on a sublime scale,' as his friend the Abstract Expressionist painter Robert Motherwell observed astutely.[18] The way forward, Rothko had decided, lay in the exploration of the Romantic concept of the sublime.

In his seminal *A Philosophical Enquiry into the Origin of Our Ideas of the Sublime and Beautiful* (1757), the statesman and philosopher Edmund Burke defined the sublime thus:

> anything which elevates the mind is sublime, and elevation of mind is produced by the contemplation of greatness of any kind . . . Sublimity is, therefore, only another word for the effect of greatness upon the feelings – greatness, whether of matter, space, power, virtue, or beauty: and there is perhaps no desirable quality of a work of art, which, in its perfection, is not, in some way or degree, sublime.[19]

The experience of grandeur is inevitably overwhelming, testing the boundaries of the self, and the 'effect of greatness upon the feelings' is therefore also necessarily potentially terrorizing. But Burke considered that this terror was ultimately strengthening for those willing to endure it, because through the thrill of being brought to the threshold, to a point close to annihilation, the true limits of our reasoning powers are revealed. Furthermore, as Burke observed, when the sublime is represented in art – as in Friedrich's work – it is safely mediated, captured and tamed within the framed-off space of painting, and so becomes something it is possible to contemplate.

In his *Critique of Judgement* (1790) the philosopher Immanuel Kant also addressed the sublime as a primary sign of existential and intellectual limits. But he shifted attention away from external sources of the experience – the response to natural phenomena – to consider the Sublime's ultimate origins within the labyrinth of the human mind itself. Kant argued that while certain awe-inspiring phenomena in the natural world – the infinitesimally large or small, for instance – may indeed be experienced as 'sublime', this situation *in extremis* could also be provoked within the realm of thought. For Kant, the presentation of a mental construct so complex that the mind fails to gain a clear understanding of it may lead to a profound and humbling awareness of the difference between the idea itself and any ability we may have to encompass or think about it. In the sublime experience, Kant declared, we are therefore made aware of an ontological threshold, and, like Burke, he believed that it was precisely through this forced awareness of limits that it was possible to better understand the true character of human existence.[20]

Under the sway of the concept of the sublime, Romantic landscape painting as practised by artists such as Friedrich and J.M.W. Turner explored a more fluid and deregulated relationship with the world, making painting an arena within which to evoke infinity and emptiness. America would prove an especially conducive environment within which to prolong the tradition of the Sublime, and in the vast wilderness spaces of New England, artists such as Albert Bierstadt and Frederic Edwin Church found an 'abundance of

1 Yves Klein, *Blue Monochrome*, 1961, dry pigment in polyvinyl acetate on cotton over plywood. Perhaps the archetypal 'monochrome', by an artist who called himself 'Yves le Monochrome'.

2 Ad Reinhardt, *Abstract Painting 1960–1965*, oil on canvas. Although at first this painting may seem to be a single black square, closer inspection reveals it is comprised of nine slightly differently coloured squares. The artist claimed that works like this were painting reduced to its essence.

3 Kazimir Malevich, *Black Square*, 1915, oil on canvas. This is the painting that is generally considered to be the first monochrome. Malevich declared it was 'a desert where there is nothing but the sensation of desert'. The cracking of the surface began soon after he finished the painting, inadvertently revealing the ghostly outlines of an earlier work beneath.

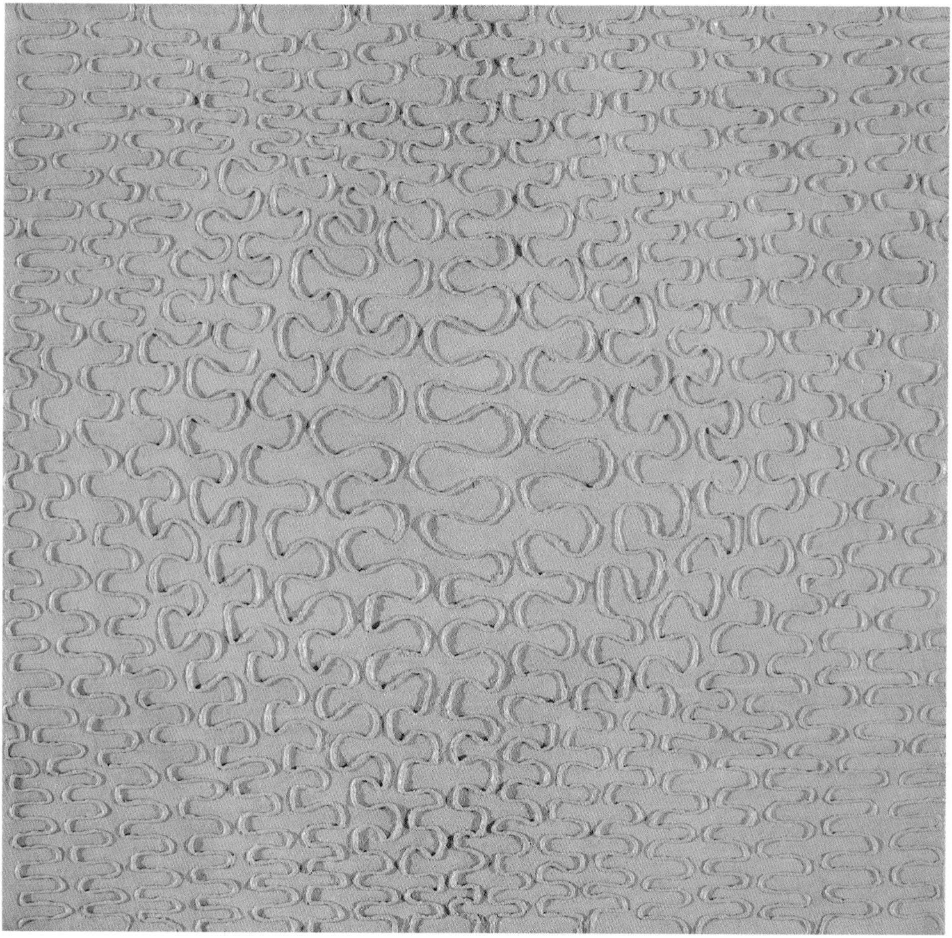

4 Władysław Strzemiński, *Unistic Composition 13*, 1934, oil on canvas. Working in the relative isolation of Poland between the wars Strzemiński developed a rigorous theory of the monochrome as a new form of literalist realism.

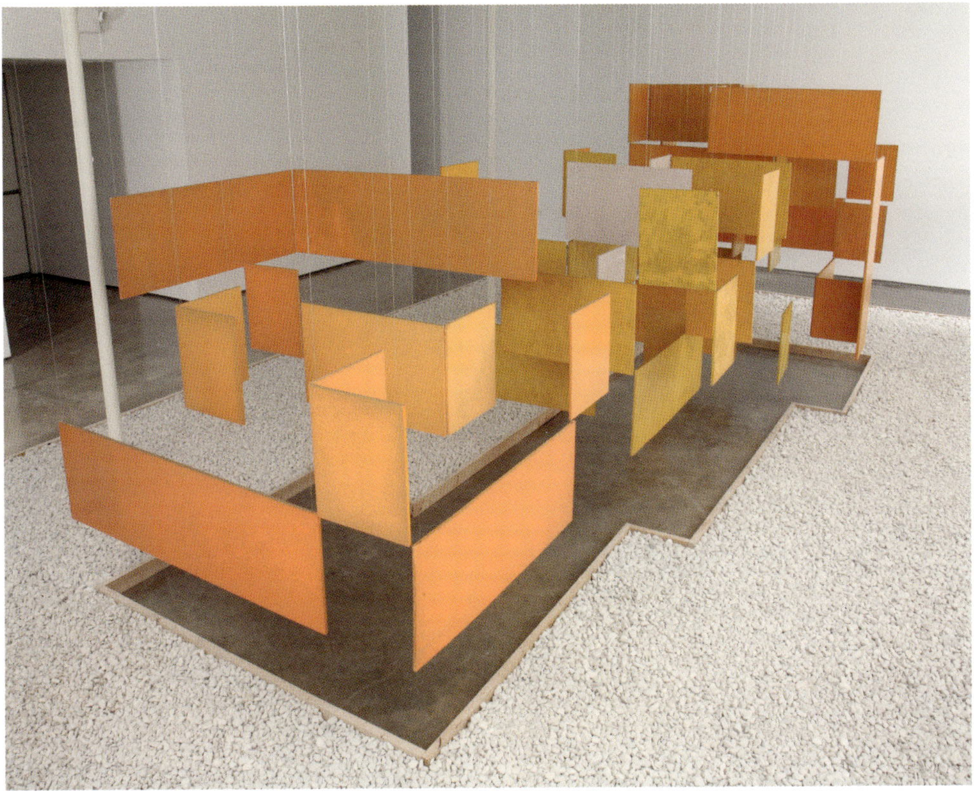

5 Hélio Oiticica, *Grande núcleo composto por NC3, NC4 e NC6* (Grand nucleus, comprising NC3, NC4 and NC6), 1960–66, oil on wood. By moving off the wall, the Brazilian artist extends the possibilities of the monochrome into three-dimensional and interactive space.

6 Agnes Martin, *Untitled No. 12*, 1977, India ink, graphite and gesso on canvas. This painting juxtaposes two seemingly incompatible visual experiences – of a wall-like surface and of infinite depth, thereby actively engaging the viewer in different readings of the work.

7 Park Seo-bo, *Ecriture (描法) No. 14–79*, 1979, pencil and oil on hemp cloth. This Korean artist brings the Western monochrome into fruitful dialogue with East Asian traditions concerning the void, or 'full emptiness', and the performative dimensions of calligraphy.

Overleaf:

8 and 9 David Batchelor, *Found Monochrome 126, Bilbrook, Wolverhampton 16.05.04*, 2004, and *Found Monochrome 481, Higinoplous, São Paulo, 13.11.11*, 2011. Two photographs from an ongoing series in which the artist finds 'ready-made' monochromes on the city streets.

10 Olafur Eliasson, *Room for One Colour*, 1997, monofrequency lamps, Moderna Museet, Stockholm, 2015. Through to the manipulation of artificial light, everything and everybody within the space seems to be immersed in the same colour.

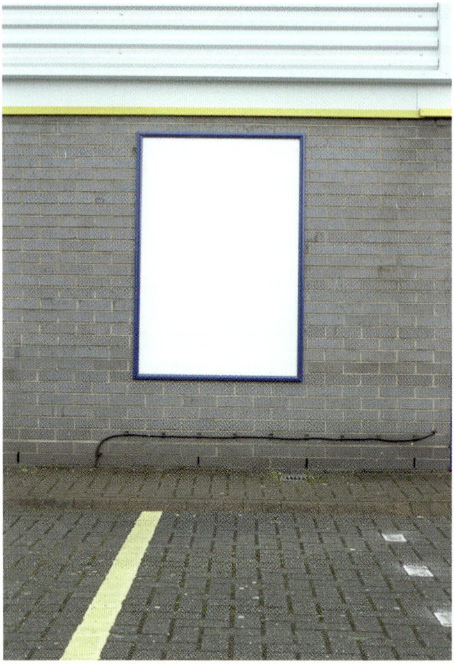

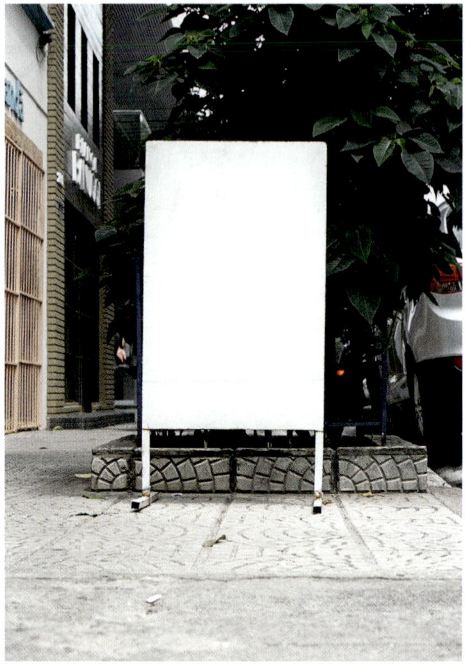

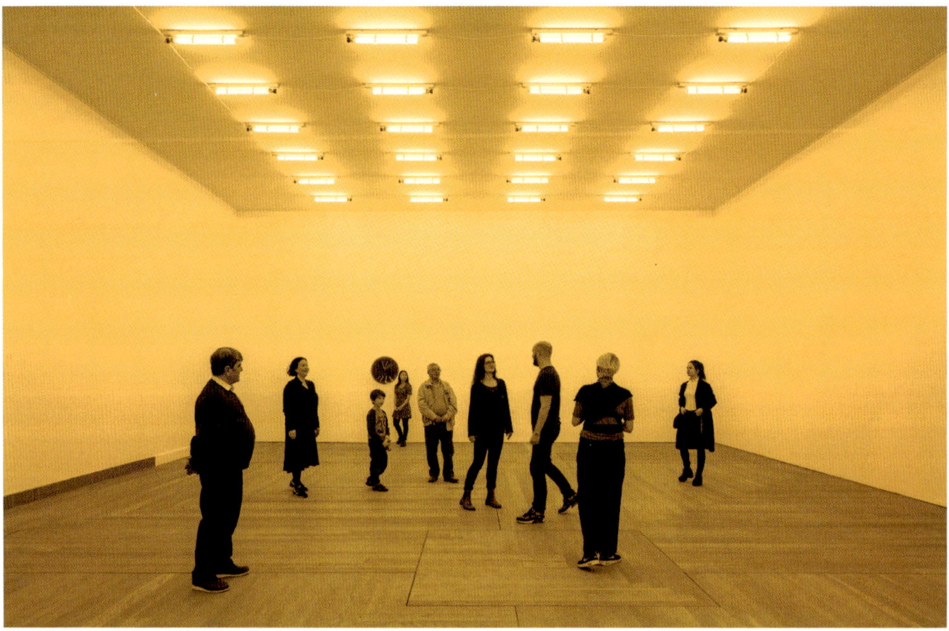

sublimities'.[21] But by the mid-twentieth century the concept of the sublime was increasingly explored beyond landscape painting, becoming what the art historian Robert Rosenblum terms the 'abstract sublime'.[22] As Rosenblum writes in *Modern Painting and the Northern Romantic Tradition* (1975):

> By 1950 Rothko had reached that stark format he was to explore, with variations, for the remaining two decades of his life, an image that . . . locates the beholder at the brink of a resonant void from which any palpable form is banned. Instead, there are metaphorical suggestions of an elemental nature: horizontal divisions evoking the primordial separation of earth or sea from cloud and sky, and luminous fields of dense, quietly lambent colour that seem to generate the primal energies of natural light. Rothko's pursuit of the most irreducible image pertains not only to his rejection of matter in favour of an impalpable void that wavers, imaginatively, between extremes of an awesome, mysterious presence or its complete negation, but also to his equally elementary structure, which . . . is of a numbing symmetry that fixes these luminous expanses in an emblem of iconic permanence.[23]

Rothko's move towards increasing sublime monochromatic effects culminates in two suites of paintings: the *Seagram Murals* (1958–9) and the cycle of paintings for the Rothko Chapel (1964–70), a specially designed non-denominational chapel in Houston, Texas. The *Seagram Murals* were painted in closely related quasi-monotonal hues in a tonal range of maroon, wine-red, reddish-black, blue-black, deep golden red and purplish-blue.[24] On occasion, Rothko also departed from his by then standard format of stacked rectangles, and some of the paintings have the appearance of entrances, being reminiscent of doorways or windows. *Sketch for 'Mural No. 6'* (or *Black on Maroon*, 1958), for example, suggests a window, and is also uncannily like the afterimage created if one stares through a brightly lit opening and then closes one's eyes. The monochromatic colour and anti-relational compositions of the Chapel paintings, however, are even more overt. At a distance, the similarity of the dark red-brown and black tones within a single work makes it difficult to distinguish contour, and unlike in Rothko's earlier paintings, on closer inspection the bounding edges are more hard-edged and unyielding. The works seem to function as brooding, monumental planar forms, and when seen as an installation suggest a sealed-off, even claustrophobic reality.

When looking at Rothko's most overtly monochromatic works a viewer is unable to clearly distinguish edges, and relationships between figure and ground become transitory. Uncertain visibility breeds a sense of emptiness. As a result, we sense that we are being obliged to consider not only an optical indeterminacy but a mental state in which the usual cognitive distinctions are rendered vulnerable. 'Rothko's work is retrogressive. It returns us to a moment of looking we have always skipped, to an effort to establish boundaries that a certain economy in human evolution may have succeeded in sparing us,' write Leo Bersani and Ulysse Dutoit in their study of the artist. 'What we have been spared, however, is the very work of being, the renewed possibility that presence might not take place.'[25] In this sense, Rothko's mature paintings embody 'not the end of difference – the unpresentable, in any case – but rather the drama of individuation, the tracing and erasing of those boundaries without which there would be no phenomenal world, no individual life.'[26]

This 'drama' signals Rothko's desire to communicate psychic fluidity through his work, opening the viewer up to the experience of the expansive and limitless void that, as we have seen, is familiar from accounts of mystical experiences. But how can we understand such experiences from within a secular worldview? Sigmund Freud addressed this question through his discussion of what he called 'oceanic' feeling or state, which derives from a powerfully visual metaphor drawn from the experience of the limitlessness of nature.[27] For Freud, the oceanic feeling – a sense of the boundlessness of the self which is often closely associated with mystical enlightenment – was construed as a dangerous re-enacting of the memory of a less differentiated stage of ego development. He related this stage to the 'Nirvana principle', a choice of terminology which indicates that within Eastern cultures this boundary-breaching experience is most especially valued and analysed.[28] For Freud, the Nirvana principle defined the tendency within life processes to seek the removal of tensions and conflict and to reach a dedifferentiated state of zero tension or total stability, which is equivalent to the inorganic state.

In other words, the 'oceanic feeling' signalled the closeness of the death drive. In contemporary psychoanalytic terms, however, the experience that 'oceanic' is understood to address not only speaks of a dangerous submission to the death drive, but potentially of a deep-seated desire for 'the intimate union of the Ego and the surrounding world, experienced as an absolute certitude of satisfaction and security', as the philosopher and psychoanalyst Julia Kristeva puts it.[29] In this state, a feeling of the boundlessness of the self signals a postive regression to a level 'at the limits of primal repression', one where 'consciousness has not assumed its rights and transformed into signifiers those fluid demarcations of yet unstable territories where an "I" that is taking shape is ceaselessly straying'.[30] This experience, as Kristeva writes in an essay on the soft chromatic ambience which is such a striking characteristic of the paintings of Venetian Renaissance artist Giovanni Bellini, can be described as a space 'beyond discourse, beyond narrative, beyond psychology, beyond lived experience and biography – in short, beyond representation'.[31]

Seen within this context, the empty chromatic fields created by Rothko can be understood as liminal zones where boundaries are loosened and structures are no longer firmly established. They evoke the feeling of the intimate union of the ego with the surrounding world.

But Rothko's later works veer perilously close to being simply grey and inert blanks, and as such they can seem to reflect Rothko's growing ambivalence towards the experience of such a boundary-breaking union. In Rothko's hands, the monochrome can suggest an analogy both with the womb and with the tomb. It becomes the pictorial equivalent of joyful fusion with the undifferentiated whole, but also of a depressing inner void that is dangerously allied with the death drive. It is as if Rothko induces a kind of blindness with his monochromes. Bersani and Dutoit describe the Chapel paintings as communicating an overwhelming sensation of 'maimed sight'. In this sense, 'the peace of the undifferentiated is also a deathlike stillness.'[32]

8

EXPERIENTIAL

The observer makes the painting.[1]
Agnes Martin (1971)

In 1949 Barnett Newman (1905–1970) took a trip to southwest Ohio, where he visited some Native American burial mounds. They provoked a kind of epiphany. 'Here is the self-evident nature of the artistic act, its utter simplicity,' Newman declared soon afterwards. 'There are no subjects – nothing that can be shown in a museum or even photographed: [the earthwork is] a work of art that cannot even be seen, so it is something that must be experienced there on the spot: The feeling [is] that here is the space.'[2] Newman believed that this heightened and unmediated experience of being fully present in the here and now had been made possible through the manner in which the finite forms of the earthwork made the unlimited remainder of space more manifest. In other words, the 'figure' of the earthwork had somehow engendered the surrounding 'ground', opening experience on to an expanded field. This exhilarating experience, Newman later declared, could be summed up by the idea that through this special organization of space he was made aware in an unprecedented way that 'Man is Present'.[3]

In seeking to then respond creatively to his intense experience, Newman made several far-reaching decisions in relation to his own practice. He began to look for a way to bring about greater immersion in the presentness of the pure moment of a work of art, one divested of the unnecessary clutter of memory and associations. He hoped thereby to nurture a state of mind characterized by temporal deceleration, stasis or timelessness, in which the usual sense of duration is replaced by permanence or awareness of the eternal. Spatio-temporal limitations are temporarily overcome or suspended, and a kind of stretched time and space experienced – a heightened experience of the now.

Newman furthered this goal through two technical innovations. The first was to increase the size of his canvases to make them more 'environmental'. Like the paintings of several other Americans of the period, such as Jackson Pollock, Clyfford Still and Mark Rothko, Newman's work was characterized by a new, monumental sense of scale. These artists were no longer interested in making easel paintings to be hung over the mantelpiece. Newman rejected the convention in which a painting depicted a miniaturized world seen as if through a window. But nor was he aiming to make grandiose works in the tradition of European church, court or academic art. Rather, like Rothko, Newman argued that his work had to be big in order to have a literal relationship to the human body, instead of merely a metaphorical one as it did in European art. His work was deliberately scaled to the human encounter.

But unlike his fellow Abstract Expressionists, including his friend Rothko, Newman adopted a second innovation. He developed a much more reductive attitude to colour and gesture, adopting a style that would be characterized by large fields of flatly painted and unmodulated colour. His breakthrough painting, *Onement, I* (1948), is tall and narrow in shape, and painted in a flatly applied layer of sanguine brownish-red. This even chromatic field is bisected through the middle by an orange vertical line, or 'zip' as Newman preferred to call it, which in contrast to the smoothness of the ground is roughly and unevenly painted. In a work with a pronounced horizontal orientation from two years later, *Cathedra* (1951), the size has been augmented considerably. A huge area of deep blue ground (the work is 5.5 metres/18 feet long) is bisected by a white zip near the middle, taped and therefore straight-edged, and a wobbly hand-painted zip, which is much less prominent, towards the far right.[4] For Newman, the presence of these vertical zips was essential because they served both to divide and to unite the flat field of colour, charging it with dynamic tension and enhancing the experience of 'now'.

The profound implications of Newman's belief in the potential of his highly reductive visual language found perhaps its most clear demonstration in what are also his most overtly monochromatic paintings – the series made between 1958 and 1966 called *The Stations of the Cross: Lema Sabachtani*.[5] The subtitle refers to the words 'Why have you forsaken me?', one of Christ's sayings on the cross, and Newman saw his *Stations* as consciously evoking the Christian ritual, and considered them to be generating a secular 'sacred' space, that is, a space freed from specific religious dogma, but alluding to the same deep existential questions that religions have traditionally addressed. As he said in an interview in 1965: 'I hope that my painting has the impact of giving someone, as it did me, the feeling of his own totality, of his separateness, of his own individuality, and at the same time, of his connection to others who are also separate.'[6]

Newman recognized the potential of abstract art to elicit directly experiential responses, the likes of which traditionally it was the purpose of sacred art to encourage. Here, however, was the opportunity to do so without recourse to familiar religious iconography and shorn of metaphysical justification.

RESPONSES TO ABSTRACT art are derived from its ability to decentre, traverse and supplement our normal awareness of time and space, by directly bringing to attention our connectedness and inter-animated relationship with the world. For the secular modern individual who was severed from traditional religious values, this transformative experience was now to be found in relationships to art. Through its own internal resources, Newman believed art could directly engage with and enhance our perceptual experience of the world, and thereby transform our relationship to that world. Within a social context that is densely populated with visually complex artefacts, an encounter with an 'empty' framed chromatic field can elicit specific new experiences, bringing to attention the overlooked nuances and fine distinctions that lie within the perceptual world. These 'micro-perceptions' relate to attenuated levels of representation – ignored, unnoticed, obscure, subtle or suppressed dimensions within the world of perception, such as the ground, the periphery and various modes of diminished, in-between, impaired and 'visionless' experiences of space. Becoming aware of these nuances or micro-perceptions constitutes a refinement of perception, a removal of impurities or unwanted elements and the making of small adjustments.

On a formal and performative level, such micro-perceptions can include becoming aware of the consistency and weight of paint, the varieties of ways in which paint, brush and surface meet, and variations in the texture of the canvas through brushmarks. They also include the apprehension of minuscule differences between colours, and how colour perceptions are subtly relative and change according to ambient light conditions. In this sense, such highly nuanced perception narrows the distance between the ostensibly 'ideal' monochrome and the 'monochromatic' work, because what might at first seem to be an example of the former often turns out to be the latter.

The black paintings of Ad Reinhardt are a good example of how these shifts can occur. As we noted, from a distance, Reinhardt's *Abstract Painting 1960–1965* (illus. 2) looks like a homogeneous black square – a geometric 'figure' seen against the 'ground' of the wall upon which it hangs. But as we move to the viewing position normally associated with looking at a painting, this perceptual effect is transformed into something akin to an indistinct black fog or a slowly shifting haze. We have the optical sensation that the painting's surface is slowly pulsing, and that an indeterminate spatiality is dissolving the material planarity of the surface. But if we move in even closer, this optically generated effect suddenly disappears. The dark, dense planarity takes over, and we are confronted by a smooth, matt surface. This effect is not purely subjective, because it is generated retinally as a response to direct sensory stimulation (which means that the assailant at Christie's mentioned in Chapter Two would also have experienced it – if he bothered to look long enough). Furthermore, it cannot be reproduced in a photograph.

Reinhardt exploited the physiological limits imposed on vision when confronted by a lack of visual contrast. His works thereby confuse the norms of visual perception in relation to painting. This optical instability suggests, as Rosalind Krauss puts it, that Reinhardt aimed to open up 'some kind of back door in the mind, an expanding, pulsing awareness of the visual process itself'.[7] As a result, Reinhardt also enhances the role played by time within the encounter with a painting. He encourages a more intimate experience of time, the heightening of our awareness of temporal sequence and duration, order and precedence. In generating a subtly stochastic visual effect in this way, Reinhardt's work effectively flies in the face of the formalism espoused by Clement Greenberg at the time, which intended to banish illusion through an emphasis on the material surface of the picture perceived in a moment in time.

Even something as seemingly uninteresting as a field of a single colour can provoke unstable and differential spatial readings, and bring to the fore awareness of the mobility of forms, the ambiguity of locations and the fluidity of contours. As noted earlier, the experience of a monochrome can also incorporate more than just the visual sense, engaging the haptic – the sense of touch – as well as foregrounding the intimate relationship between seeing and thinking, absence and presence, and the role of time within perception. In all these ways, a monochrome can engage directly with the instabilities of perception in the here and now. The contemplation of a single coloured rectangle can make us aware of latent characteristics of our perceptual and cognitive apparatus, thereby demonstrating how we actively constitute our world.

In Rothko's work, for example, stable optical boundaries are undermined. Instead of the clear structure delivered by linear contour, Rothko builds his paintings using vague chromatic fields, using colour rather than line. He explores fugitive light vibrations, which confuse distinctions between inside and outside space and generate an illusion of indeterminate spatiality. He also examined the unstable nature of the mark, examining the way a brushmark can be vague and indeterminate rather than serving to define a clear edge or transition. The chromatic shapes within Rothko's compositions are loosely suggested and seem to exist within a 'ground' that is always potentially enveloping them, and so they are never consciously perceived as distinct forms, which, as we have seen, has significant psychological implications.

Physiologically speaking, the late works of Rothko, like the black paintings of Reinhardt, are primarily perceived through the rod-shaped cells that exist at the periphery of the retina. The optical effects generated by these artists' works are a direct consequence of the eye's limited ability to process stimuli in what are termed 'low' spatial frequency channels, which calibrate coarse- or fine-grained vision. These spatial frequencies are a property of the retina rather than 'out there' in the world. As you read this page of text you are using predominantly 'high' spatial frequency channels that allow you to discriminate the printed letters. If you look at this page in dim light, you will be using low spatial frequencies, and high spatial frequency information will be lost. As a consequence, the letters will seem blurred and will coalesce into vague, irregular shapes organized in dark grey fuzzy lines. Generally, however, we perceive the visual field at medium or intermediate frequencies, which is what generates coherent, viewpoint-specific representations.[8]

As in everyday life, when we look at a painting more of our brain's capacity is dedicated to the cone cells, because these supply the most important practical data, bringing the in-depth, clear and detailed vision necessary for the organization of random stimuli into stable patterns. It is this level of medium-grained vision that representational art aims to replicate, but even abstract art depends on clear ambient light for the perception of its formal arrangements, which supplies optimal viewing conditions and is nowadays virtually guaranteed by the 'white cube' space of the gallery or museum, brightly illuminated by electric lighting rigs.

Rothko, however, was especially hostile to such conditions: 'He liked to paint, even in the daytime, with incandescent electric light, and publicly exhibited his pictures with an extraordinarily low degree of illumination,' recalled Robert Motherwell. 'I remember a huge studio of his on the Bowery, a former storage space, I think, that had no windows at all, which gave one the sense of being inside the scenes on a darkened movie set.'[9] Rothko also wanted viewers to see his works in lower than normal ambient lighting conditions in order to encourage a less lucid, rationalizing form of cognition. Like Reinhardt, Rothko actively directs the viewer's sustained attention to a perceptual experience rarely addressed within painting – one that, furthermore, is rigorously suppressed in the environment typical of a museum or gallery. In looking at the internal properties of their paintings we become attuned to the subtly altered consciousness that is produced when light reaching the retina is insufficient to distinguish spatial relations. We can no longer use only the disembodied eye of foveal vision, and the encounter becomes somatic as well as optical. As a result, we gain greater awareness of the holistic continuum of space, or how vision is dependent on movement in time and ambient conditions.

ANOTHER AMERICAN ARTIST of the period, Agnes Martin (1912–2004), also explored the inherent instability of the indeterminate perceptual field as it functions in relation to time. Her work does not invite the adoption of an 'ideal' viewing position and instead engages the viewer in a more mobile and animated, yet contemplative, response. Indeed, as Martin herself wrote, 'The observer makes the painting.'[10]

Normally, we assume that there is only one 'ideal' viewing position in relation to a painting's surface, and this is derived from the viewing distance at which we most effectively organize what is seen in real-life situations into a stable schema based on figure/ground segregation. The assumption that is intrinsic to the success of fixed-point perspective as a convincing illusion is that such a static, unmoving position is adopted, with the further result that all but one viewing position will deliver a distortion of the protected virtual space.

From about 6 metres (20 ft) away, Martin's *Untitled No. 12* (1981) (illus. 6) for example, looks like a pale grey square. From this viewing position, it functions as a whole – a unified, symmetrical, total and harmonious field – and this produces a clear and stable gestalt, delivering a relatively uncomplicated experience of a simple geometric construction located within the canvas field. If we move in closer, however, the surface of Martin's painting begins to pulse slightly. We perceive a vaguely defined grid of lines, made by running a pencil along a straight-edge. Because they traverse a textured canvas, the traces of graphite are uneven and slightly wobbly; it is a very tentative structure, but a structure nevertheless. If we move in more closely to get a better look at the grid lines, the visual experience seems to compress any lingering illusionism out of the surface, rendering the painting factual, planar and unitary. The repetitiveness of the grid, and the persistent straightness of the lines, suggest concentrated and rhythmic effort, or focused action over time, thereby serving as an indexical sign leading us to an awareness of the active bodily engagement of the artist. And though we are back with the potential for figure/ground segregation, this time it is internal or compositional, with the lines coalescing into forms and standing out from the ground. Because the lines are so feeble and are part of a grid-like continuum, however, they never attain a securely assigned figure status and instead remain provisional.

Martin, like Rothko and Reinhardt, obliges us to perceive her work using areas of the visual spectrum that are typically engaged in the environmental conditions of twilight or at the periphery of the visual field, but are distinctly abnormal in an art gallery. She exploits ambiguous figure/ground relations in order to undermine stable readings of space. This, in its turn, suggests analogies with consciousness itself. As in Rothko and Reinhardt's work, a close correlation seems to be made between the structure of consciousness and the homogenous, monochromatic structure of painting. In Martin's words, 'Joy is *Perception*. Perception, reception and response are all the same . . . It is all awareness of reality.'[11]

9

ZEN

Where emptiness is possible / Everything is possible[1]
Nāgārjuna, *Mūlamadhyamakakārikā* (*c*. 2nd century CE)

In response to a question about her influences, Agnes Martin said: 'My greatest spiritual inspiration came from the Chinese spiritual teachers, especially Lao Tzu . . . My next strongest influence is the Sixth Patriarch Hui Neng . . . I have also read and been inspired by the sutras of the other . . . Buddhist masters, and Chuang Tzu . . . who was very wise and amusing.'[2] In one cryptic note about her own work, Martin wrote: '"Free and easy wandering" – Chuang Tzu / In free and easy wandering there is only freshness and adventure. It is really awareness of perfection within the mind.'[3] But when Martin declared more generally that 'These paintings are about freedom from the cares of this world,' it seems fairly explicit that what she perceived was the wisdom of a worldview in which detachment from worldly concerns is understood to be a primary goal of the artist.[4] Like many other Westerners in the mid-twentieth century, Martin's quest for a life and art more attuned to a benevolent sense of the holistic integration of mind and body was greatly inspired by her study of non-Western traditions, and like several other artists, this interest would propel her towards monochromy.

Around the period when Ad Reinhardt sent the small black monochrome painting to Thomas Merton to display in his monastic cell, Merton himself was exploring the links between Christian mysticism and Eastern traditions in the hope of finding viable cultural models that could aid in the process of spiritual renewal in the West. He saw parallels especially between Zen Buddhist meditation techniques and those of the Christian Desert Fathers and considered that, despite obvious doctrinal differences, the early Christian mystic and the Zen Buddhist monk shared essentially the same desire: to overcome the limited boundaries of the conventional self and to expand consciousness in order to merge with a larger, undivided whole.

Merton was interested in the Buddhist concept of *śūnyatā*, which can mean 'voidness', 'hollowness', 'emptiness' or 'groundlessness'. The term refers to the belief that the foundation of all phenomena, both material and immaterial, is characterized by nothingness, which is their true nature and the basic principle of all existence. Merton studied how such concepts were manifested in the painting of mandalas – geometrically composed images with pronounced symmetry that are intended to aid meditation. He wrote:

> Everything I think or do enters into the construction of a mandala. It is the balancing of experience over the void, not the censorship of experience. And no duality of experience – void. Experience is full because it is inexhaustible void. It is uninterrupted exchange . . . The self is merely a locus in which the dance of the universe is aware of itself as complete from beginning to end – and returning to the void.[5]

Reinhardt's paintings have often been likened to mandalas, even by the artist himself.[6] Like Merton, Reinhardt was deeply interested in Eastern thought, and in Zen Buddhism in particular. In one unpublished text, for example, he wrote:

> Primary, unique, underivable from anything else
> Aweful 'absolute unapproachability' ←
> Supra-rational
> Ideogram for what is beyond utterance, 'unutterableness'
> Chain of negations, Buddhist 'theology of negation' ← [7]

Reinhardt attended the New York lectures of D. T. Suzuki, the Zen scholar and priest who was one of the most important vessels for intercultural dialogue on Buddhism and Zen in the 1940s and '50s, and he also travelled extensively in Asia and the Middle East, being especially impressed, for example, by Japan's most famous Zen temples in Kyoto. While Reinhardt steered clear of making religious references in public statements about his work, preferring an austerely empirical and pragmatic discourse, his private notebooks were full of transcriptions from Hindu and Buddhist texts and quotations from the *Tao Te Ching*, a primary text of Taoist philosophy and religion probably written in the fourth century BCE.[8]

THE DRAMATIC TRANSFORMATIONS in the meaning of modern art inaugurated by abstraction in the second decade of the twentieth century were to a considerable degree a direct consequence of a growing awareness of non-Western spiritual and philosophical traditions. Eastern thought is much more sympathetic to the idea that the purpose of a work of art is not to produce a representation but rather to embody a state of mind. Furthermore, the possibility that a field of a single colour might be a significant focus of sustained attention – a novel or marginal idea in the West before the early twentieth century – had long ago been recognized within contemplative practices in the East as a useful tool. For example, the earliest examples of one-colour paintings akin to the modern monochrome are seventeenth-century Hindu and Buddhist Tantric *yantras* (similar to mandalas) consisting of a one-coloured square. They were not intended for aesthetic purposes but rather used as meditation devices to help draw the mind towards *samadhi*, or 'pure consciousness', a state of mind in which a sense of absolute unity is grasped. It is therefore unsurprising that in the 1950s and '60s, the monochrome would become especially closely associated with Western interest in Eastern religious traditions and their connection to image-making.

Zen in particular was welcomed in the West as an experientially based spiritual practice directed at emotional integration and well-being, one that was associated with a distant and radically different culture untainted by what were seen by many to be the reactionary oppressiveness and increasingly outdated teachings of Christianity. In the art that would be produced in the West that was ostensibly in Zen's spirit, non-conceptual, visual and practical thinking were highly valued. Emphasis was laid on spontaneous process rather than on the making of fixed, finite forms or the articulation of an essence or idea. The suspension of analysis and prioritizing of non-conceptual knowing that were central to the mid-century styles of Art Informel, Tachisme, Abstract Expressionism, Neo-Dada, nouveau réalisme, Happenings, Zero and Fluxus were often derived directly or indirectly from Zen.

These tendencies all shared the belief that art should express a direct experience of the here and now, thereby placing emphasis on ontological impermanence and the ephemeral, and supplanting notions of symbolic reference and formal analysis. Performative procedures based on gesturalism and dynamism were important consequences, but so too were more measured practices founded in repetition and seriality, which directed artists towards reflective and contemplative goals.[9] The spirit of Zen encouraged the exploration of such themes as the unrepresentable, void, negation and nothingness, but 'emptiness' is a privileged term. Zen placed vital significance on the experience of unity of the phenomenal and the absolute, and on the desire to encourage the non-intellectual and spontaneous, and this lent itself particularly well to the elaboration of an art aesthetic in which the dominant characteristic is wholeness or oneness, a lack of division or internal relation. In other words, artists found the ideas and aims of Zen to be conducive to the concept of a correlation between a field of a single colour and important spiritual insight.

Broadly speaking, the Japanese word 'Zen' refers to meditation practice, and developed from Chinese Chan Buddhism, a cultural fusion of indigenous Taoism and Indian Mahayana Buddhism. Chan arrived in Japan from China in the twelfth century via Korea (where it is known as Seon). As it disseminated, Zen developed characteristics of the local cultures, while still recognizably belonging to a distinctive denomination of Mahayana Buddhist thought and practice. Zen was particularly influenced by the *Tao Te Ching*. Here, emphasis is placed on the primal force of *qi* (or *ch'i*) – 'breath' or 'energy' – which is understood to freely circulate, connecting and bringing consistency to reality. Everything is suffused with and open to this circulating energy, this invisible 'breath' of life, and as a consequence everything is recognized to be radically impermanent. Taoism describes this all-pervasive energy as being composed of the non-dualistic intertwining of the principles of *yin* and *yang,* and while it is fundamentally rather misleading to set them in strict opposition to each other, broadly speaking, *yin* is negative, dark and feminine, while *yang* is positive, bright and masculine. The sky is *yang* and the earth is *yin. Yang* is active and *yin* is restful. But it is their perpetual interaction that influences all creatures and things, and they can never be dichotomized into separate forces.

Taoism had little difficulty absorbing the Buddhist concept of *śūnyatā,* and evolving into Chan (Zen). Buddhism also teaches that everything in the world realizes itself and its relationship with other things within the unity of nothingness, and that the self is just a phase within a continual process of transformation within the void. As the twentieth-century Japanese philosopher Nishitani Keiji, who endeavoured to link Zen with modern tendencies in Western philosophy, writes

> In the locus of emptiness, beyond the human standpoint, a world of 'dependent origination' is opened up in which everything is related to everything else. Seen in this light, there is nothing in the world that arises from 'self-power' and yet all 'self-powered' workings arise from the world. Existence at each instant . . . the humanization in which the self becomes human – all these can be said to arise ceaselessly as new accommodations from a locus of emptiness that absolutely negates the human standpoint.[10]

Ultimately, experiencing void in this sense means going beyond the normal tendency to make distinctions between something and nothing, and in this sense the goal of Zen is to privilege neither fullness nor emptiness but instead to seek to express a world in process, an omnipresent reality permeating and underlying all phenomena, both material and mental. A central symbol of this experience in Mahayana Buddhism is that of Indra's net, an infinitely large net that stretches out in all directions. Within it, faceted jewels multiply the structure endlessly. Indra's net thereby visualizes the deep truth of infinitely repeated interdependency of all things in the universe.

Buddhism teaches that what the habitual mind conceals from consciousness is the fact that the universe is impermanent and indivisible, and that all phenomena arise due to the coexistence or contingent arising of various causes. It is only when we recognize this that we can achieve 'Buddha-nature'. Everyone is already in possession of this Buddha-nature – that is, everyone has innate knowledge of ultimate reality. 'Mind' in this context is understood as not being limited to the reflexive experience of the individual and thinking self but rather is seen to be fully embodied and includes affect, feeling and emotion, while also extending beyond the physical body into the wider environmental network. If we cling only to the reality revealed to the ego-based self, achieving an absolute state of freedom of consciousness will be impossible.

Like Mahayana Buddhism, Zen posits the existence of an 'original self' or 'Buddha-nature' (or 'Buddha mind') revealed when one has relinquished habitual attachments. But the most innovative teaching of Zen in particular is the importance given to achieving a direct, experiential and embodied realization of Buddhist awakening to 'emptiness'. In Zen, 'freeing the mind' is not dependent on truths revealed through study and learning, which are considered impediments. Instead it must be an intuitive or immediate insight. As mentioned, one of the most important interpreters of Zen for Westerners in the middle of the twentieth century was the Japanese scholar D. T. Suzuki, whose understanding of Zen reflected not only his immersion in his native culture but his deep knowledge of Western philosophy and culture. In 1934 he wrote in *An Introduction to Zen Buddhism* that Zen is fundamentally illogical, non-cognitive and irrational and that it is 'primarily and ultimately a discipline and an experience, which is dependent on no explanation'.[11] Intellectual discourse can never satisfactorily explain an ultimate reality which cannot be analysed or dissected, only experienced. As a result, a characteristic technique in Zen is that when questions arise about the nature of reality, Zen masters reply in unexpected and seemingly irrational ways. 'If you have been in the habit of thinking logically according to the rules of dualism,' Suzuki advised, 'rid yourself of it.'[12] Zen is therefore an experiential rather than an intellectual practice. Zen, Suzuki declared, strives to catch 'life as it flows'.[13]

The reason Zen was especially valued in the West was that it is a worldly practical philosophy that questions fundamental oppositions, such as that between soul and body, the immaterial and material, without dependence on a complex set of religious principles and practices. Interest in Zen spirituality was part of a much wider spiritual tendency that has been called 'immediatism', which refers to 'a religious assertion of spontaneous, direct, unmediated spiritual insight into reality (typically with little or no prior training)'.[14] This impulse gathered strength within Romanticism during the nineteenth century, gradually absorbing aspects of Western and Eastern spirituality to create a loose and ever-evolving union of intuition with spirituality that was intended to counter the stultifying influence of traditional religion and the high rationalism and intellectualism of modern society. Zen thus became a central part of an ad hoc movement for liberation from what was perceived as the 'prison' of materialistic life under consumer capitalism, and it subsequently bore fruit in the hippie phenomenon of the 1960s and '70s.

Traditionally in Zen-inspired art, an image is produced with the knowledge that it must somehow capture a reality that is perpetually coming into existence, developing, decaying and going out of existence. In fourteenth-century Japanese *haboku*, or 'broken' or 'flung-ink' painting, which was greatly influenced by Zen, for example, the fundamental fluidity, permeability and boundlessness of reality is expressed through a dynamic formal technique, giving rise to works characterized by a pronounced dynamism, spontaneity, ease and directness. The goal was to use the simplest and most direct means of expression. But while the execution of a work was usually spontaneous, considerable preparation went into achieving the correct state of mind. Artists inspired by the spirit of Zen deliberately sought a means through which to remove the obstacle of the habitual self from their practice. A work of art imbued with the spirit of Zen is typically characterized by 'an elemental sense of unadorned simplicity, artlessness, objectiveness and purity; a feeling for unforced naturalness, forceful directness and a deep respect for nature'.[15] Emphasis was placed on the general aesthetic principle of *wabi-sabi*, which invited the prolonged meditation on impermanence and imperfection.[16] While the execution of a work was spontaneous and natural, considerable preparation nevertheless went into achieving the correct state of mind, known as *te* (or *de*), a concept drawn from Taoism that signifies the qualities of nature bestowed by the Tao ('the Way'), manifest within humanity as moral character, grace, rightness or virtue.

ONE OF THE first Western artists to overtly cite Zen as an influence on his move towards monochromatic non-representational art was the much-travelled American Mark Tobey (1890–1976).[17] In 1934 Tobey stayed in a Zen monastery in Kyoto in order to further his studies in East Asian calligraphy, and Zen thinking manifested itself in Tobey's interest in the all-over calligraphic mark, which came to fruition in his monochromatic 'white writing' paintings, such as *White Journey* (1956), a non-hierarchical composition made up of an intricate web of interweaving dynamic brushstrokes and lines that extend across the whole surface of the work.

But by the late 1940s, Zen was being used as inspiration for, and invoked to supply the interpretative framework of, much more radically reductive monochrome works. Robert Rauschenberg, in discussing his pure white monochromes from the early 1950s, used terms pervaded by a mix of Christian mysticism and the spirit of Zen:

> They are large white (one white as one God) canvases organized and selected with the experience of time and presented with the innocence of a virgin. Dealing with the suspense and excitement and body of an organic silence, the restriction and freedom of absence, the plastic fullness of nothing, the point where a circle begins and ends.[18]

Rauschenberg's reference to the circle alludes to the famous Ox-herding cycle of ten Zen poems and paintings, of which the eighth image is of a simple calligraphic circle. The circle was used to symbolize the moment when the duality of self and reality is overcome and enlightenment achieved.[19]

Rauschenberg's friend the composer John Cage had, like Ad Reinhardt, attended Suzuki's lectures in New York in the 1950s and later commented that 'the taste of Zen for me comes from the admixture of humour, intransigence, and detachment.'[20] With reference to Rauschenberg's paintings Cage wrote that for him they were 'airports for the lights, shadows, particles' and said he valued the potential of their blankness to serve as a bulwark against the insidious 'noise' of culture – its endless circulation of intentions, words, associations and agendas.[21] In a litany that evokes the apophatic tradition of mysticism, Cage drew attention to all that Rauschenberg's monochrome left behind:

> To Whom
> No subject
> No image
> No taste
> No object
> No beauty
> No message
> No talent
> No technique (no why)
> No idea
> No intention
> No art
> No object
> No feeling
> No black
> No white (no *and*)[22]

Cage casts Rauschenberg's paintings as the embodiment of a willed withdrawal of meaning – the 'idea-less' condition central to Zen. They were the result of an elevated form of nonchalance or indifference that Cage saw as equivalent to Zen detachment. Citing a celebrated statement by Rauschenberg, Cage wrote:

> Do you understand this idea?: *Painting relates to both art and life. Neither can be made. (I try to act in that gap between the two.)* The nothingness in between is where for no reason at all every practical thing that one actually takes the time to do so stirs up the dregs that they're no longer sitting as we thought on the bottom. All you need to do is stretch canvas, make markings, and join.[23]

Cage's own response to the revelation of Rauschenberg's work was the now famous composition *4'33"* (1952), in which a pianist sits at a piano or with some musical instrument without touching it for four minutes and thirty-three seconds. As a result, the ambient sounds pervading the real environment become the content of the work.

Across the Atlantic, in France, Yves Klein was also pursuing the monochrome under the influence of Zen. Between 1952 and 1953 Klein actually lived in Japan, where he studied and became proficient in judo. As we have seen, Klein asserted that the true essence of a work of art was something wholly intangible, and he equated his notion of invisible 'sensibility' with the invisibility of *qi* energy. 'What is sensibility?' Klein asked, while going on to answer the question in the spirit of Zen:

> It is what exists beyond our being yet belongs to us always. Life itself does not belong to us. It is with our sensibility that we can purchase life. Sensibility is the currency of the universe, of space, of Nature. It allows us to purchase life in the first material state.

> Imagination is the vehicle of sensibility. Transported by imagination we attain life, life itself, which is absolute art.[24]

Zen provided Klein with a rationale for transcending the limits of the ego-based mind, which, as we saw, meant for him in formal artistic terms the domination of line over colour. Art, even abstract art, Klein believed, was always implicated in conflict because it consisted of dualities – line and colour, form and content, thought and feeling. As Klein declared: 'This is a situation of the psyche, of the senses, of the emotions, which perpetuates a sort of reign of cruelty.'[25] But once art had been freed from such agonistic confrontations by entering fully into the undifferentiated totality of immaterial reality, it would be possible to gain insight or enlightenment. In this sense, Zen also provided the justification for the complete overcoming of painting.

But there were limits to such transcultural exchange. In retrospect, the geographically located cultural characteristics that underpinned Western interest in Zen during the 1950s and '60s were as much a way of addressing hidden, underexplored or suppressed aspects of Western culture as they were about understanding a school of Buddhist teaching. The Western essentialist versions of 'Zen' greatly simplified and distorted understanding. During the 'Zen boom' of these decades, Zen was essentially cast as a unified body of teachings and the ultimate global religion, while in fact the teachings portrayed as timeless wisdom were a reflection of more contingent geopolitical, intellectual and spiritual factors that had been informing discussions of 'East' and 'West' on both sides of the world since the nineteenth century.

Furthermore, Zen was often misinterpreted according to deep-seated Western principles and beliefs. The limitations inherent in a cultural perspective inevitably mean that the contents of a different worldview are significantly transformed. Mark Tobey, for example, belonged to the Bahá'í Faith, which was founded in Persia in the late nineteenth century in an attempt to create a world religion suited to the modern age, and like Buddhism, placed special emphasis on the unity of ultimate reality. But Bahá'í is essentially 'Western' in its spiritual orientation. It emphasizes dualism – a fundamental division between godlike man and nature – and is based on a hierarchy, with humankind aspiring to the spiritual and immaterial through an escape from the bonds of nature. 'Man, because he is endowed with intellect, reason, and spiritual powers, can probe the mysteries of nature, control natural law and even deviate from it,' writes the art historian William C. Seitz in his discussion of Tobey's work. 'He is therefore not part of nature but its ruler.'[26]

Agnes Martin and Ad Reinhardt's interest in Taoism and Buddhism would also inevitably be filtered through a worldview in which dualism remains a central theme. In fact, Martin defined her position in clearly dualistic terms when she described herself as a 'classicist', writing, for example:

> Just follow what Plato has to say
> Classicists are people that look out with their back to the world.
> It represents something that isn't possible in the world
> More perfection than is possible in the world[27]

In fact, one can argue that the austere philosophy of life shared by Martin and Reinhardt invites comparison less with Buddhism than with what can broadly be termed 'Stoicism' and Protestant Christianity. The Stoic philosophy of life evolved in the Hellenistic period, and subsequently came to pervade Western culture.[28] The ultimate goal within the Stoic vision is to live in harmony with the underlying rational order that nature obscures. It advocates setting oneself apart from nature and the communal ties of society. It seeks to guarantee tranquillity through the reduction of the influence of the passions over life. Self-cultivation is premised on making a distinction between affects that are unhealthy and those that are healthy, and suppressing the former. Serene detachment is achieved through extirpation, that is, removing from consciousness the sources of unhealthy emotional ties. The emphasis of Martin and Reinhardt on negation, their focus on denying the body its pleasures, their emphasis on the smallness and insignificance of human life in relation to the vastness of the cosmos (Martin wrote: 'The wiggle of a worm as important as the assassination of a president'), and their advocacy of an 'apathetic' vision of the equal value of all things, seem to give voice to a very Stoic-like *amor fati* (love of fate).[29] And while Stoicism might seem to share similarities with Buddhist or Taoist ideals of detachment, it is actually fundamentally different. The ideal of detachment in Taoism and Buddhism is related to resilience, or the capacity to overcome rather than suppress the passions, and emotional ties and relationships. Taoism and Zen therefore involve not so much a denial of feeling but rather the heightened awareness of existing within a larger perspective that recognizes the interdependence of all things.[30]

The general suspicion of the carnal and of the natural world that is central to Stoicism is also especially to be found within the Puritan tradition of North American Protestant Christianity within which Reinhardt and Martin grew up. The strong tone of moral piety in their writings, and their tendency to adopt the rhetorical form of the sermon and the parable (especially in the case of Martin) reflect the influence of this background culture. In Protestantism, too, the human struggle is dramatized as one between the pathological (evil) emotions associated with the body, and the non-pathological (good) emotions that characterize the human soul. The self is therefore understood to be vulnerably located between incompatible and antagonistic forces, and in need of redemption. Within Protestant visual culture, one consequence of this dualism was the tendency towards iconoclasm. Images were judged to be false, deceptive surface illusions that encourage idolatry, and inherently lead away from closeness to God.

Despite his passionate interest in judo and Zen, Yves Klein's thinking and practice were firmly grounded in the Roman Catholic religiosity of his culture, which was melded with dualistic Western esoteric mystical traditions like alchemy and Rosicrucianism. The evolution of Klein's art, as it moved from monochrome painting to the complete dematerialization of his practice – to the 'leap in the void' – reflects how a Zen concept was transformed by the artist's immersion in Western traditions rooted in a metaphysics that, like Tobey's, rigorously opposes the material and the immaterial. Klein himself noted: 'As I continued to paint monochromes, I almost automatically reached the immaterial, which made me understand that I was clearly a product of Western civilization, a true Christian who rightly believes in "the resurrection of bodies, in the resurrection of the flesh."' But a few lines later in the same text, in terms close to the Zen aesthetic, Klein declared, 'what was revealed is separate from form, becomes immediate experience. "The mark of the immediate."'[31] In Klein's universe there is a correlation between 'pure sensibility', derived from the Zen concept of enlightenment, and Klein's own 'pictorial sensibility', which is pure energy destined for the soul. Klein juxtaposed the transcendental perspective of

Western metaphysics with the immanentist position of the East. Because the immaterial is incapable of being adequately represented in words or images, in the model of thought and practice Klein inherited, it is also judged to be of a wholly different order to the life of the senses. This idea compelled him to push further and further towards the immaterial – away from the body.

Klein's interest in Eugène Delacroix's eulogy to the indefinable, for example, can be seen as being premised on an ontological opposition that is fundamentally at odds with the spirit of Zen, and Eastern thought in general. Deriving his ideas from a philosophical position that has been dominant in the West at least since Plato, Delacroix had affirmed the necessity of an opposition between the visible and the invisible, rigorously defying the former in order to better 'receive' the mysteriously invisible 'ground'. Klein formalized and essentialized this within painting as an opposition between line and colour. Furthermore, while he aimed to assimilate the Western idea of soul and 'pure sensibility' to the notion of *qi* energy, he seemed to ignore the fundamental difference between the two concepts.[32] In this sense, Klein effectively isolated pure awareness of the essential openness or intangibility of reality, turning it into a cult of pure 'sensibility'. In Zen, however, purity and impurity (or colour and line, figure and ground) are understood to be mutually dependent. While the dominant tendency within Western thought is to believe that what cannot be adequately represented in words or images is incommensurable with the world that is revealed to the ordinary mind, by contrast, although Zen Buddhism stresses ultimate reality is beyond the grasp of concepts or language, it is also recognized that this reality is only ever encountered within the here and now. The 'void' may be beyond the visible, but it is not definitively separated from it in another dimension; rather, it is understood to be an extension of the visible, one that is inevitably characterized by indistinctness, evanescence and unintelligibility.

IN JAPAN, WHERE Zen is indigenous and deeply rooted, artists associated with the Gutai group of the post-war period also explored the monochrome, but in ways that reflect their ability to be deeply permeated by the spirit of Zen. Furthermore, the cultural background of these Gutai artists was one already familiar with the convention of all-over, one-colour painting, and with the idea that art should be directed towards evoking the intangible as part and parcel of the totality of experience in the here and now. Their background culture would now converge with the influence of Western modernism to produce a distinctly non-Western form of monochrome art.

These artists approached their practices in ways that related to the Western avant-garde but which were also informed by personal and indigenous cultural priorities. Gutai means 'concreteness', and artists drawn to the group engaged in performance, installation and theatrical events as well as painting and sculpture. Their works, in diverse materials, have pronounced tactile properties and emphasize the performative over the detached perception of colour relations. Ultimately, Gutai was dedicated to transforming Western individualism and the cult of the new to bring it into line with the specific Japanese cultural context.[33]

In the Western artistic tradition, the support used for painting is usually propped on an upright easel, and the surface is worked with the artist standing or sitting perpendicular to it. In traditional East Asian art practice, by contrast, an artist works a surface while sitting on the ground, and with the surface laid horizontally. This orientation creates a very different relationship to the image: marks on a surface perpendicular to the ground will naturally be read as possessing depth, while a horizontally oriented surface will be seen as more obdurately two-dimensional. Furthermore, these orientations imply distinct relationships between the surface and the body, with the former placing the artist away from and outside what they represent, and the latter providing a much greater sense of being in the midst of things. Traditionally, East Asian artists have also used different kinds of supports, usually paper or silk rather than canvas or wood, as well as different types of paint – black ink or water-based colour as opposed to tempera or oil. These conventions, in their turn, led to specific biases within both practice and theory. For example, because of the physiological constraints imposed on sight, the Western convention led to a focus on the creation of an illusionistic space. Laying a surface flat and working it from above, on the other hand, led to a greater preoccupation with the graphic organization of two-dimensional space. By engaging the body of the artist to a far greater extent than in the Western model, the performative dimension also became much more manifest in Eastern practice.

Gutai artists brought these contrasting traditions into fruitful contact. Informed by traditional ideas originating from Zen concerning the value of spontaneous process in relation to the liberation of the mind, they especially explored the freedom of the instinctual as opposed to reflection and the order of the intellect. They sought to balance destruction and creation via ritualized performance, and emphasized the 'unmade', or what already exists before conscious intervention, but not in the sense meant by Marcel Duchamp when he invented the readymade. Rather, for

Gutai artists, the unmade signalled the value of void, what remains 'untouched' and therefore beyond the grasping controlling mind. They aimed to reveal the void through the non-intentional, and focused on the materiality of the painted surface rather than on compositional relations – with the goal of generating a more visceral physical encounter.

In works such as *Holes* (1954), for example, Gutai's co-founder Shōzō Shimamoto (1928–2013) built up a tactile surface out of layers of newspaper, which were vigorously painted over in white and pierced to expose the underlying layers. The paintings of Chiyū Uemae (1920–2018) involved building up multiple layers of paint into a rough terrain, and he also laboriously stitched works to create intricately articulated monochromatic surfaces. Toshio Yoshida (1928–1997), in his *Sakuhin* series of the mid-1950s, produced quasi-monochrome canvases featuring deeply encrusted terrains of paint reminiscent of geological formations. Atsuko Tanaka (1932–2005), who joined the Gutai group in 1955, experimented heavily with the use of everyday materials; in the piece *Work (Yellow Cloth)* (1955), for example, she took seven sheets of yellow cotton factory-made cloth and hung them directly on the gallery wall, as 'paintings'. The cloth edges were scored and re-glued in places, but this constituted Tanaka's only artistic intervention.

IN 1957, AS YVES KLEIN was exhibiting his first blue monochromes, the young Japanese artist Yayoi Kusama (b. 1929) left Japan for America, moving first to Seattle and then in 1958 to New York. She quickly gained a critical reputation, exhibiting both in the United States and with Zero artists in Europe. Kusama would remain in New York until 1972, whereupon she returned to Japan. Kusama brought her native Zen aesthetic with her to the United States, finding novel ways to fuse it with the minimalistic modernism she encountered in New York. Although Kusama emphasized that her work cannot be limited to an interpretative framework limited to a specific philosophical or religious system, it is clearly and consciously pervaded by Zen.[34] For example, in relation to her *Infinity Nets* works, such as *No. F* (1959), in which she covered an entire canvas with an intricate meshwork of off-white impastoed paint over a dark ground, producing an effect reminiscent of a roughly woven net, she declared:

> Everything – I, others, the entire universe – would be obliterated by white nets of nothingness connecting astronomical accumulations of dots. White nets are enveloping the black dots of silent death against a pitch-dark background of nothingness.[35]

Kusama sought through the use of monochrome to evoke the experience of void central to the culture within which her worldview was formed. She had begun using the dots and a repetitive procedure when she was still a child, finding that compulsive mark-making offered her a way of coping with her unstable mental health – she suffers from audio-visual hallucinations, and voluntarily committed herself to a psychiatric hospital in Tokyo in 1977, where she has continued to work prolifically from a studio in the grounds of the hospital. For Kusama, there was therefore a consciously therapeutic goal, involving the transformation of an experience of 'infinity' from the horror of self-annihilation to one of a benign sense of freedom and plenitude. This personal motivation was combined with her background culture's spirit of Zen, and when applied within the context of the formal concerns of modernist monochrome painting tilted her work towards the performative, ritualized and experiential rather than formal and intellectual – towards an art that aims to grasp reality as encountered in immediate experience rather than as the embodiment of an idea. What is important are the psychological states produced through the repetitious, ritualized process of making, which are fundamentally idea-less. To this extent Kusama's *Infinity Nets* can be described as neither full nor empty. Her monochromes seek to express complementary relations that function within a dynamic and unfolding continuum, via the body acting in the here and now.

By contrast, Klein's conception of void, while it was deeply indebted to Eastern ideas, essentially remained tied to a model of thinking that proceeds in oppositional and hierarchic terms – line/colour, body/spirit, visible/invisible, fullness/void, material/immaterial, tangible/intangible. Klein only managed to invert these polarities, celebrating colour, spirit and the immaterial while denigrating line, the body and materiality. In practice, then, Klein, like other Western artists, seemed to vacillate between the belief that in order to embrace the immaterial it is necessary to transcend the body, and the Zen spirit that sees enlightenment as coming only through the body's engagement with a world that is understood to be inherently ineffable.

10

MATERIAL

What you see is what you get.[1]
Frank Stella (1966)

In the early 1920s the Russian artist Aleksandr Rodchenko (1891–1956) would take the monochrome in a direction very different to those explored by the artists discussed so far. According to Rodchenko, the increased importance given to autonomous colour within the art of the late nineteenth and early twentieth centuries had had the effect of binding painting to the senses and the material world, rather than to anything that could be called intangible, ineffable, spiritual, expressive or psychological. As such, Rodchenko's work of this period marks the beginning of another important strand in our narrative: what we might call the 'literal' monochrome. This is an idea grounded in the belief that in order for art to be truly modern it must have no truck with illusion, which in formal terms means the rejection of any illusionism produced not only via representational images but by abstract forms and colours on a flat surface. But furthermore, Rodchenko also aimed to assault the very foundations of art in general as a form of expression, emotional or spiritual.

Rodchenko premises his work on the idea that by reducing a painting to a single unbroken ground, one inevitably draws attention to the concrete tangibility of the medium. Colour, for example, which is produced from powdered pigment mixed with a binder, coats a work's surface and is therefore the most material property possessed by painting. Furthermore, colour makes an obvious appeal to the eye and the senses. Talk of the 'infinite' or the 'ground of being' as employed by Kazimir Malevich in relation to his Suprematism was nothing more than a rhetorical flourish. No contemplative metaphysics was attached to Rodchenko's triptych *Pure Red Colour, Pure Yellow Colour, Pure Blue Colour* (1921), which was intended as a direct riposte to what he saw as the misplaced metaphysics of Malevich.

Rodchenko's vision of the material and literal monochrome, one that was designed to be concrete and real, brought to fruition a tendency that is central to modernism. In the nineteenth century, as we saw, the surface of a painting increasingly became like a site for the depositing of paint, rather than a space of representation. In other words, a painting's content was now found within the plastic resources of a painting, not outside them. Art, for Rodchenko, was logically reduced to questions of materials. Drawing on the prestige of the scientific model of technological progress, Rodchenko announced in his 'Slogans' and 'Organizational Programme' of 1920 that 'art is a branch of mathematics, like all the sciences. Construction is the modern requirement for organization and utilitarian use of material.'[2]

These principles were also closely allied to social utility. In order to connect the artist to the forces of production within the new communist society in which Russian artists were now living it was necessary to put emphasis not on expression of the self but on expression of social structures, which would have the effect of drawing art more closely to the true conditions of everyday life, which Rodchenko understood in terms of the citizen's productive capabilities. Henceforth, the function of art, as Rodchenko's colleague Aleks Gan declared in 1922, was

> not to reflect, not to represent and not to interpret reality, but to really build and express the systematic tasks of the new class, the proletariat . . . The master of colour and line, the builder of space-volume forms and the organizer of mass productions – must all become constructors in the general work of arming and moving the many-millioned human masses.[3]

In this alternative vision of what was called 'Constructivism', the artist's studio is recast as a workshop in which to conduct experiments. The basis for this in practice was what Rodchenko called *faktura*, which he defined as 'material consciously worked and expediently used'.[4] He wrote that these new concerns would be displayed as follows:

> 1. In the field of colour
> 2. In the field of form
> 3. Following the laws of construction
> 4. Studying the treatment of the surface layers of materials, i.e. their preparation.[5]

For Rodchenko, then, the monochrome was intended to be a terminus, the end of art. Any idea of continuing to make any more of them after his 1921 triptych was for him patently absurd. The deeper purpose in making a triptych of primary colours was much more radical than simply a declaration about a work of art's status as a material fact. Rodchenko was using the monochrome to pass what he saw as a death sentence on bourgeois painting in general. Execution was necessary because within the newly founded Soviet Union the traditional role of the artist and the status of the work of art were no longer valid. The revolution required sacrifices. The monochrome was therefore a polemical object that, through a literal act of material purification, rid painting of its parasitic dependence on the bourgeois sensibility. But of course, Rodchenko's monochrome triptych did not bring about the end of art – nor even the end of the monochrome work of art. Instead, Rodchenko became the originator of a new kind of art.

The lesson was quickly learned. Taking the practical advice while ignoring the utilitarian political implications of Soviet Constructivism, the Polish artist Władysław Strzemiński (1893–1952) and his sculptor wife Katarzyna Kobro (1898–1951) developed a new conception of art, one in which the monochrome became a dominant concern. Both had in fact studied with Malevich in Moscow, but when they returned to their native Poland they effectively redirected the metaphysical intentions of their teacher towards the more concrete and material ends explored by Rodchenko, and as a result gave birth to the first 'literal' or 'realist' monochromes – or what they called Unism.

The purpose of art, Strzemiński and Kobro argued, was to transform society in an incremental fashion by embodying within the microcosm of art's own resources the practical demonstration of the pure, uncompromised properties necessary for the establishment of an egalitarian and rational society. They therefore developed a conception of art in which their own paintings and sculptures were declared the culmination of the journey towards a more empirical kind of realism, one firmly grounded in the tactile properties of *faktura*. Until the twentieth century, they argued, Western painting had been composed of two different dimensions: a surface (including the support and the paint applied to the support), which is physically made and materially present, and a dimension that is materially absent – the virtual dimension, a site for imaginative transformations and subjective expression. A conventional representational painting is therefore both an artefact and a fiction: a material object made from paint covering a flat support, and a receptive surface for the image that then sets in train a cluster of memories, associations, reveries and psychological projections. However, Strzemiński and Kobro noted that much of the newly emergent abstract art was still much too closely wedded to this virtual dimension. It continued to function within an associational and relational field generated by the artist and the viewer, generating extra-pictorial associations and expressive intentions. Therefore, most artworks were what Strzemiński and Kobro called 'baroque'. As Yve-Alain Bois explains:

> a work of art is 'baroque' (that is, 'arbitrary') when its formal configuration is not completely justified by its material conditions (dimensions, materials, etc.) but originates instead in an a priori system, in a preexisting vision. In what Strzemiński and Kobro call the 'pictorial baroque,' 'the idea, alien to painting, stands in the way and bars the understanding that a picture is not an illusion of a phenomenon seen elsewhere or even calculated right away and transported to a picture, but that it is itself, in itself, and for itself.'[6]

To establish an art that 'is itself, in itself, and for itself', Strzemiński and Kobro saw that it was necessary to work against not only mimetic representation but the idea of the pictorial composition as an organized, meaning-bearing device. The pure elements of art were synonymous with absolute truth, and therefore only finite material qualities were credible. A Unist work was therefore premised on the complete absence of associations and of any requirement to express the subjectivity of the artist. Instead, it was directed towards the production of an essential and concrete reality. Strzemiński systematically examined the procedural processes involved in painting, proposing to reduce it to the unequivocal level of material fact. 'A work of plastic art does not express anything,' he declared. 'A work of plastic art is not a sign of anything. It is (exists) in itself.'[7] He was especially set on banishing 'divisions' from painting, noting,

> where we have a line, we will have a division and instead of a single painting, we will have separated parts. line divides – the aim must not be the division of painting, but its unity, presented in a direct way: optically.
>
> in consequence it is necessary to renounce line. it is necessary to renounce rhythm, because it only exists in the relations between independent parts. it is necessary to renounce opposites and contrast. because only separated forms can create opposition and contrasts. it is necessary to renounce division, because it gives concentration and the greatest intensity to forms in proximity to outline – and cuts the painting into sections, containing concentrated forms and weak forms.[8]

In practice, Strzemiński would explore four dimensions of painting: flatness, colour, the 'deduction of forms from the shape of the frame' and the 'abolition of the figure/ground opposition'.[9] As he also recognized, by using a single field of colour, the integrity or unity of the surface plane could be more rigorously maintained. Once colours are set in relationship to each other, they interact, losing their autonomy, and spatial illusion is generated. The goal, therefore, was to ensure that a colour would remain self-sufficient. It needed to be alone and undiluted by chromatic relationships. In order to suppress non-optical associations further, Strzemiński composed space within the picture plane so that it mirrors, repeats or is deduced from the shape of the support itself, thereby forcing out any possibility of illusionistic depth. The use of the grid also supplied a pre-given formal structure through which to flatten and reduce the plane to a unified field.[10] What these strategies share is a commitment to a non-hierarchic compositional structure achieved through an emphasis on bilateral symmetry – the balanced distribution of duplicate parts.

Strzemiński's *Unistic Composition 13* (1934) (illus. 4), for example, is an entirely yellow painting whose surface is covered in rhythmic lines that have been built into a terrain of low relief and which ripple across the surface following the orientation of the vertical edges. Kobro's work, meanwhile, such as *Spatial Sculpture 1* (1925), in white-painted steel, developed Unist ideas in the direction of the three-dimensional form. She produced planar geometric structures painted in flat, monochromatic white or single colours, which aimed to diminish the mass of the object so that it possessed greater unity with the surrounding environment.

IN THE 1920S the ideas of Rodchenko and the Constructivists, and Strzemiński and Kobro, merged with a wider tendency known as 'constructive' or 'concrete' art. The De Stijl, Bauhaus and concrete art movements in Europe all promoted the unity of painting, sculpture, architecture and life. The 'Manifesto of Concrete Art' (1930) envisaged a modern art driven by a utopian faith in geometric abstraction as a universal language, one through which the artist could explore the basic formal principles of line, shape, colour and texture. The manifesto emphasized, for example, the idea that a work of art is a material object: 'The picture must be entirely constructed from purely plastic elements, that is, planes and colours. A pictorial element has no other meaning than "itself" and thus the picture has no other meaning than "itself".'[11] The Swiss artist Max Bill, an important exponent of concrete art in the post-Second World War period, argued that this new art applied a rigorously scientific, mathematical and intellectual approach: 'Concrete Art, when it is true to itself, is the pure expression of harmonious measure and law. It organizes and gives life to these arrangements, through the means of art. It is real and intellectual, anaturalist while being close to nature.'[12]

Rational procedures, including seriality, modularity and repetition, dominated 'concrete art', with colour remaining subordinate to line as it was considered too inherently ambiguous and emotional. But the monochrome's rejection of internal compositional division and its reduction to just one colour seemed much too reductive.

Indeed, the wider movements that in the post-war period began to challenge geometric abstraction's claim of a monopoly on the true spirit of the modern were also largely hostile to the perceived austerity of the monochrome. The unleashing of dynamic expressive possibilities within Art Informel, Tachisme and Abstract Expressionism dramatically reflected a loss of faith in utopian rationalism and seemed to better reflect the sense of social crisis that characterized the period. As a result, the potential of the monochrome as a new form of realism went into abeyance.

An important exception to the general lack of interest in the monochrome during this period was the work of the American artist Ellsworth Kelly (1923–2015), who brought concrete art into alignment with the art-for-art's-sake aesthetic and thereby revealed for the first time the potential of the monochrome as a sensual, colour-centric art. From 1948 Kelly was based in Paris, where he encountered concrete art, and in 1954 he moved to New York, where he continued to develop a style of painting dedicated to shape and colour. Kelly aimed to equate the format of his painting precisely with its colour. As he emphasized: 'In my painting, the painting is the subject rather than the subject, the painting.'[13] In this way, Kelly strove to ensure the total identification of shape with colour. 'I am less interested in the marks on the panel than the "presence" of the panels themselves . . . My work is about structure,' he said.[14]

In *Red, Yellow, Blue II* (1965), for example, Kelly confronted head-on the legacy of Rodchenko, presenting in a triptych format the three primary colours in all their purest splendour. But Kelly's intentions in making such a work were very different to Rodchenko's. This was not the end of painting but rather the means through which to sustain it. Indeed, Kelly's colourist commitment inevitably led him to treat the monochrome as a specific option within a wider practice rather than as an ideological choice. Some of his works include single-colour panels but are often part of larger, multi-panelled works, and Kelly also often juxtaposed two or three colours on the same support, thereby returning to relational colour painting.

But in the late 1950s, another American, Frank Stella (b. 1936), began pursuing a far more austere and pragmatic version of the new abstract realism or literalism. Stella made paintings comprising parallel black stripes the width of the flat-ended house-painter brush he used. In *Jill* (1959), for example, he set the stripes at 45 degrees from the four right-angled corners of the support, converging them towards the centre. While the painting looks a little like an overhead view of a pyramid, it seems explicitly to be the result of a desire to expunge any possibility that what is seen is construed as anything more than a pattern that is the result of a methodical working plan. For, as Stella stressed, the striped pattern served only as a regulating system intended to minimize any tendency to read into the surface a sense of illusionistic depth. In terms that could not be further from the metaphysical rhetoric of the 'illuminating' monochrome, and which instead seem closer to those of a technician committed to the smooth running of a machine, Stella said in a lecture:

> There were two problems which had to be faced. One was spatial and the other was methodological. In the first case I had to do something about relational painting, i.e. the balancing of the various parts with and against each other. The obvious answer was symmetry – make it the same all over. The question still remained, though, of how to do this in depth. A symmetrical image or configuration placed on an open ground is not balanced out in the illusionistic space. The solution I arrived at – and there are probably quite a few, although I know of only one other, color density – forces illusionistic space out of the painting at a constant rate by using a regulated pattern. The remaining problem was simply to find a method of paint

> application which followed and complemented the design solution. This was done by using the house painter's technique and tools.[15]

In fact, reproductions of Stella's paintings of this period look more mechanically pristine than they are in real life, and it is worth seeking a real one out. The wobbles in the lines and the drips of paint are clearly visible, and these works have a handmade, even slightly cack-handed, quality that imbues them with more pathos than they convey in photographs, and certainly more pathos than the artist himself intended. But soon, Stella had mastered a much more straight-edged, glossy, hands-off kind of art. He lamented that viewers 'always end up asserting that there is something there besides the paint on the canvas'.[16] But he also believed that the artist was capable of quarantining his or her paintings from this 'something' by educating the viewer to concentrate only on what was visible. 'My painting is based on the fact that only what can be seen there *is* there. What you see is what you get,' Stella declared.[17] As his friend the soon-to-be Minimalist sculptor Carl Andre wrote in 1959, in the catalogue preface to an exhibition including Stella's black stripe paintings:

> Art excludes the unnecessary. Frank Stella has found it necessary to paint stripes. There is nothing else in his paintings. Frank Stella is not interested in expression or sensitivity. He is interested in the necessities of painting. Symbols are counters passed among people. Frank Stella's painting is not symbolic. His stripes are the paths of a brush on canvas. These paths lead only into painting.[18]

Stella's work locates the idea of the monochrome squarely within the tradition begun by Rodchenko, in which circumscribed, repetitious, predetermined procedures signal commitment to the 'real' as something synonymous with materiality. But Stella divests it of the political goals that motivated the Russian, and in their places advocates an art that is purely aesthetic in intention. Overtly severed from all external references, and from an expressive or conceptual agenda, Stella's paintings are not 'abstractions' of anything, and nor are they 'about' anything. This is therefore a form of realism that is much more rigorous than even Strzemiński's. 'Stella's black paintings had gotten down to business,' writes Rosalind Krauss,

> And their business had everything to do with surface, a surface within which nothing would be ambiguous. Everything that 'happened' in the picture would be the result of real manipulation of that surface. Meaning would no longer be a function of illusion, of an imagined 'inside' or 'behind' the surface. Meaning, since it could come from nowhere but in the surface itself, would be an effect of that surface: a meaning-effect.[19]

But it was to be Stella's contemporary Robert Ryman (1930–2019) who would perhaps explore the empirically based notion of monochromatic realism with the most single-mindedness. The technical aspects of the craft of painting that normally lie latent become in Ryman's work directly manifest – the various constituents of painting as a practice, such as brushstrokes, textures, the size and shape of the support, the affixing elements and so on, become the subject of the work.

Ryman arrived in New York in 1953 intending to be a jazz musician, but he switched to painting. He more or less began his practice with the monochrome, and until his death in 2019 continued to work in this way. Rather than an academic institution, Ryman's 'art school' was effectively the Museum of Modern Art in New York, where he served as a guard for several years; one consequence of this apprenticeship, undertaken in the shadows of masterpieces by Van Gogh, Matisse, Picasso, Mondrian and Malevich (*White on White* had been in the collection since 1935), among others, was to nurture in Ryman the idea that art inhabits a cloistered and pristine world.

Like Strzemiński, Ryman recognized that most so-called 'abstract' art still made a reference to something lying outside itself. Ryman argued that his form of 'realism' – a term he himself used in referring to his own work – began with the premise that there is no further point in making a work of art that claims to be about something that isn't actually there. Henceforth, Ryman proposed, the purpose of the artist was to help the viewer to see more acutely what *is* there – to see that which is not an illusion. 'With Realism the aesthetic is an outward aesthetic instead of an inward aesthetic,' he wrote. 'Since there is no picture, there's no story. And there's no myth. And there's no illusion, above all. The lines are real, the space is real, the surface is real, and there's interaction between the painting and the wall plane, unlike in abstraction and representation.'[20]

By limiting himself to the colour white, and to conventional and unconventional materials, Ryman teased out from what might seem an overly minimal repertoire a remarkably rich series of variations. In his painting *Mayco* (1966), for example, six broad bands follow the horizontal axis of the square format, not quite remaining distinct one from the other and in several places almost merging. But the desire to achieve the formalist's coincidence between the delimited two-dimensional support and the painted surface was less important to Ryman than the exploration of textures, brushstrokes, affixing elements and stretcher bars.[21] By being so centrally involved with the material processes involved in constructing a work, Ryman exposed the hidden or latent dimensions of picture-making. His attention to surface texture and reflectance, to the nature of the material support and to how a support attaches to the wall meant that the normally hidden dimensions of picture-making come to light. In Ryman's case, a description of intention is also a description of how the work has been made. He explained *Mayco*, for example, which is related to two other works of the period, *Twin* and *Allied* (1966), as follows:

> They were all on canvas, some linen and some cotton, and done with broad brushes. You see, when you're working with oil paint particularly, and you use it with a certain heavy consistency, it leaves brush marks. And those marks reflect the light. And how the paint is brushed on will determine how the light works on the surface.[22]

A similar pragmatism informs the work of another American, Brice Marden (b. 1938). 'I paint paintings in panels,' he stated in 1971. 'They are not colour panels. Colour and surface must work together. They are painted panels. Colour against a colour makes a colour situation . . . I work with no specific theories or ideas.'[23] In practice, however, Marden avoided the bright hues of Kelly, the serial processes of Stella and the extreme reductiveness of Ryman. Instead, he preferred muted pastel tonalities and used beeswax mixed with oil paint and turpentine – a technique learned from the artist Jasper Johns and which gives the paint a matt, unctuous consistency that enhances its status as a surface in its own right rather than as a surface covering.[24] In reproduction, Marden's monochrome paintings appear to be flat, coloured planes that are absolutely uniform, like Reinhardt's or Kelly's, but in fact they are quite nuanced, with the visible residues of the gestures Marden made when applying the paint with a spatula and palette knife. The bottom edge of the canvas in *Nebraska* (1966), for example, which was shown in Marden's first solo exhibition in the same year as he painted it, is partially exposed, as Marden stopped the application of the paint short of the lower edge, a device he sometimes used in other works. The raw canvas and drips of paint are visible, an effect that adds welcome lightness to the otherwise intense planarity of the composition. The act of condensation for Marden is also one of concentration.

Marden's contemporary Robert Mangold (b. 1937) also adopted the monochrome, considering it the only viable way to continue painting, and he concurred with his friend Marden that it was necessary to go by way of the elemental: in order to reinvent painting, one must start from the beginning. As Mangold said in 1986: 'It seemed to me when I began that the only way to make a painting was to start at zero and add one thing at a time.'[25] He also adopted neutral colours: 'I was attracted to generic or "industrial" colours; paper bag brown, file cabinet gray, industrial green, that kind of thing.'[26]

But Stella, Ryman, Marden and Mangold's work cannot be defined simply in terms of literal flatness. In this sense they all challenge Clement Greenberg's theory of formalist modernism – or 'Modernism' as Greenberg confidently called it – which, as we saw, was especially important in the United States in the 1960s, and served to create a theoretical framework within which the monochrome could be interpreted and critiqued.[27] Mangold, for his part, substituted the notion of 'frontality' for 'flatness', and this permitted him to explore a more nuanced conception of his work. He saw painting as offering the only means through which the image could be experienced as a totality, all at once, thereby delivering the unique experience of frontal unity. Ryman did not limit his paintings to the Greenbergian 'flatness' that was supposed to ensure the status of the artwork as a self-contained, pure object. By exploring variations in surface Ryman invites the viewer to interact optically not only with the painting's surface but with its tactile properties and the space that surrounds the work, thereby diluting the purity of the aesthetic experience as Greenberg conceived it.

THE 'REALIST' MONOCHROME had an especially strong presence in South America in the 1950s and '60s. But here, too, it cannot be assimilated into the narrowly Greenbergian formalist interpretation. But when compared to the monochromes produced by the North Americans, with the exception of Kelly, those of the South Americans were much more emphatically directed towards the sensory – towards colour as an overt stimulant.

Until the 1960s, art made by those who are considered from a Western point of view to be at the 'margins' was often considered limited because it was directed at a particular market lying outside the mainstream, uninteresting because it was not exemplary, ill-informed because it was the result of limited communication with the 'centre', and belated because it occurred after a lag of time, caused by the slow dissemination of information from this centre.[28]

But in addressing instances of monochrome and monochromatic art by artists outside the European and North American arena during the 1950s and '60s we should adopt a much more nuanced model of cultural interaction.

A new phase of globalization had begun in the late 1950s, characterized politically by Western decolonization and Cold War ideological and military confrontations, economically by the increasing globalization of markets, and culturally by greater interaction between countries. As we have already seen in relation to Gutai in Japan, this situation encouraged a new generation of non-Western artists to explore ways both to assimilate and contest the impact of Western culture on their own terms, and while the modern non-Western monochrome is inconceivable without these Western precedents, they were nevertheless rerouted and transformed in significant ways.

In seeking to understand the nature of the complex dialogue between cultures, the art historian and curator Ming Tiampo suggests that the model of transnational 'cultural mercantilism' is a more accurate metaphor than the old one of 'centre/periphery'. By 'cultural mercantilism' Tiampo means that there was a 'two-way exchange' between cultures, one that functioned according to processes of creative 'misreading', by successions and divergences occurring through emulation and the anxiety provoked by the influence of Western precursors.[29]

Tiampo is specifically referring to Japan, the first East Asian nation to embrace Western modernization. As we saw, it was there that the earliest examples of East Asian monochrome art emerged that were indebted to Western models but could not simply be cast as peripheral responses to the cultural centre. Gutai was also well known to European artists by the early 1960s through the wide dissemination of its self-titled journal, and the group's artists participated in exhibitions abroad organized by the foremost critical advocate of Art Informel in Europe, Michel Tapié (who visited Japan in 1957), and showed alongside Western artists associated with the Zero and Nul groups, including Yves Klein, Piero Manzoni and the New York-based Yayoi Kusama. Influences flowed in both directions. For example, the performances of Kazuo Shiraga (1924–2008) involving huge red monochromatic backdrops had an acknowledged influence on the black monochrome series *Goudrons*, made of tar on paper, produced by the French artist Bernar Venet in the early 1960s.[30]

By comparison, South American artists were working much more closely with the same formal vocabulary as their European and North American peers, but like the Gutai group they were motivated by expectations and intentions closely linked to the specific social and political contexts of their home nations. Many South American countries were experiencing a new prosperity and forging a confident cultural identity, and within this situation the geometric and the concept of artistic 'construction' were read as material signs of optimism concerning the new emerging social and political order based on clear, rational principles. Furthermore, through being a practical demonstration of first principles, the monochrome was cast not so much as a negation as a liberating *tabula rasa*. The Spanish Uruguayan artist Joaquín Torres-García (1874–1949) was instrumental in forming the 'constructive art' (arte constructivo) group in Spain in the 1930s, and after the Second World War he moved to Uruguay, where he published a manifesto that announced the birth in a new culture of 'a virgin and powerful art' that could exist away from the 'Babel of Europe'.[31] In Argentina, the Argentinian Italian artist Lucio Fontana organized a group of like-minded artists and in 1946 penned the 'White Manifesto', declaring: 'The new art requires that all of man's energies be used productively in creation and interpretation. Existence is shown in an integrated manner, with all its vitality. *Colour Sound Movement.*'[32]

In Brazil in the 1950s and early 1960s the Neoconcretismo (Neo-Concrete) movement became especially important in extending the possibilities of one-colour painting in a more lyrical, sensual, playful and participatory direction.[33] The artist Hélio Oiticica (1937–1980), for example, united an admiration for the austere and detached neutrality of European concrete art with a Matisse-like voluptuousness. Colour was something that painting possessed in a specific way, Oiticica argued, working in a dialectical relationship with its other elements, such as space, line and texture. 'In painting,' he wrote, 'colour is synthetic and undiluted, and possesses its own meaning.'[34] Colour functions as an expressive medium independent from colour in life. Oiticica's interest was above all informed by the potential of colour to act as a source of sensory experience. 'To me,' he wrote, 'colour is an imaginary, artificial medium that, along with other elements that make up the work, constructs a world detached from nature, one that speaks only to man, and that is characteristic of the world of art.'[35]

Oiticica aimed to free colour so that it could fully occupy the material support and overcome the limits of painting in order to convey feeling eloquently on its own terms. The optimum way to achieve this chromatic intensification was through using a single hue, as only then did 'colour [take] on a "body"'.[36] In practice, this meant that Oiticica promoted colour at the expense of compositional divisions, reducing his works to simple coloured configurations. He explored the subtle nuances within colours that are revealed slowly within the incremental variations of what initially seem to be fully monochromatic surfaces. In his *White Series* (1958–9) and the *Red and Yellow Series* (1959), for example, Oiticica worked with layers of paint in one or two tones that were so close in hue that they at first sight seem to be a single colour, only gradually breaking down into subtle, deep, interwoven veils.

But there was also a strong impulse to go beyond the painting rectangle itself. In a statement from 1960 the Brazilian artist Lygia Clark (1920–1988) described what she saw as the inevitable limitations of the normal rectangular format of painting:

> Before the artist situated himself in front of the rectangle, he projected himself onto it and in that projection he filled the surface with transcendent meaning. To demolish the plane as the support for expression is to become aware of unity as an alive and organic whole.[37]

The goal Clark therefore set herself was to reduce the gap between art and life, and to introduce into the former more properties of the latter by engaging the viewer more actively in the appraisal of her work, making the experience more participatory, with the result that the boundaries between the work of art and the world around it became less clearly defined.[38] In the *Bicho* (Creature) series, for example, such as *Creature-Maquette (320)* (1964), Clark fashioned small, monochromatic, origami-like metal constructions with hinged joints so they could be reorganized into different configurations. The viewer is invited to fold, turn, close and open the works.

In the *Bilateral* series, Oiticica also set about opening his work on to its surroundings, cutting the support into irregular shapes. *Bilateral* (1959), for example, consists of two overlapping white fibreboard planes that together produce a sense of shallow relief. The principle of the fold also implied that a painting could leave the support of the wall altogether. By suggesting that the space of a painting continues beyond the frame, Oiticica invites the viewer to interact not only with the object itself but with the space around it. In his *Spatial Relief (red)* REL 036 (1959), for example, two obliquely angled slightly differently red coloured box-like forms intersect and fold into each other. Oiticica was aiming to emphasize the object's relationship with the surrounding space, blurring the boundaries between object and non-object.[39] His *Grand Nucleus* (1960–66) comprises multiple panels, painted on both sides in tones of violet at the centre of the work and moving outwards into radiant yellows, which hang at 90-degree angles so as to form a maze-like space within which the viewer can move about.[40]

Oiticica spoke of this work as creating a new sense of time in art – a 'sense of colour-time' or 'time-structure', in which duration is extended through engagement with the multiple facets of the work distributed in space.[41] The aim, so Oiticica wrote, was to transpose the work 'from the contemplative attitude that motivates [painting] to a perception of the colour-structures in space and time, [one that is] much more active and complete in its sense of involvement'.[42]

11

FORMAT

The main thing wrong with painting is that it is a rectangular plane faced flat against the wall.[1]
Donald Judd (1965)

Donald Judd (1928–1994), the artist perhaps most indelibly associated with the Minimalist art movement that emerged in New York in the 1960s, argued that the main problem with painting – even monochrome painting – was that it could never avoid the play of illusion. He pointed out that despite the fact that fixed-point perspective and the idea of figurative representation had been abandoned in abstract art, there still remained the fact that colours painted on a surface will seem to lie at different depths. Further, even a single-coloured rectangular plane hung on a wall carries with it a range of associations, such as suggesting an opening – a window or a door – and as a result, however assiduously an artist may strive to attend to the surface, they will never be able to banish the lingering and debilitating surplus of illusion. 'The main thing wrong with painting is that it is a rectangular plane faced flat against the wall,' Judd wrote in his seminal essay 'Specific Objects' (1965). 'The rectangle is a shape itself; it is obviously the whole shape; it determines and limits the arrangement of whatever is on or inside of it.'[2] But three dimensions, by contrast, were for Judd 'real space', and by working with real space an artist is able to '[get] rid of the problem of illusionism and of literal space, space in and around marks and colours – which is riddance of one of the salient and most objectionable relics of European art.'[3] Once the rectangle hung on the wall has been abandoned, Judd argued,

> a work can be as powerful as it can be thought to be. Actual space is intrinsically more powerful and specific than paint on a flat surface. Obviously, anything in three dimensions can be any shape, regular or irregular, and can have any relations to the wall, floor, ceiling, room, rooms or exterior or none at all. Any material can be used, as is or painted.[4]

The first step in getting away from the window-like aperture, as the Brazilians Lygia Clark and Hélio Oiticica had shown, was to break free of the inherited convention of the rectangular format. Despite their closeness to the 'objectionable relics of European art', several European artists had also been coming to a similar conclusion to Judd: the painted rectangle was a limiting condition.

The monochrome relief – the wall-based square or rectangle that possesses overtly three-dimensional properties – had been an early solution. An early pioneer was the British artist Ben Nicholson, who between 1934 and 1939 produced several white monochrome reliefs. Nicholson was unaware of the innovations of Malevich and Strzemiński, and was most strongly influenced by Piet Mondrian. The relief format allowed Nicholson to explore the properties of real rather than illusionistic light. The three-dimensional relief generated real shadows rather than depicting them.[5]

In the 1950s the monochromatic relief was also especially exploited by a number of European artists associated with Zero and the closely allied Nul group of Dutch artists. Zero artist Heinz Mack (b. 1931), for example, embossed sheets of aluminium by hand, creating corrugated surfaces whose metallic shine produces a complex reflective field. Another Zero artist, Günther Uecker (b. 1930), hammered nails into canvas or wood supports. In his *Informal Structure* (1957), Uecker drove large numbers of nails into the surface of his canvas and then poured plaster over them. The Dutch artist Jan Schoonhoven (1914–1994) limited himself to all-over white surfaces so as to capitalize on the fugitive effects of shadows, and produced wall- and floor-based relief constructions out of materials such as papier-mâché, chipboard and corrugated cardboard.

Like Judd, Otto Piene (1928–2014), co-founder with Mack of the Zero group, also identified the traditional format of painting as an oppressive legacy. From the late 1950s he began to explore monochrome surfaces, using not only paint but soot, and perforating canvases and other materials with holes. But he felt that it was necessary to go further: 'The pictures of the old world were equipped with heavy frames,' Piene wrote. 'The viewer was forced into the picture, pressed as though through a tube, he had to make himself small to see this channel; he was brought low to experience the realm of art.'[6] The solution was to distance the art object from not only the frame on the wall, but the limitations imposed by paint. 'My greatest dream is the projection of light into the vast night sky, the probing of the universe as it meets the light, untouched, without obstacles.'[7]

In fact, Piene soon began to work with electric light, producing installations such as *Light Ballet* (1961), in which a motorized metal globe projects variable light through perforations onto the floor, ceiling and walls of a darkened space.

In the United States, Ellsworth Kelly also explored the shaped monochrome canvas. In *Yellow Piece* (1966) he rounded off the top-right and bottom-left corners of the canvas's typical rectangular form, while in *Green Angle* (1970) he created a gentle, horizontally stressed form. 'Unenclosed by the usual rectangle, Kelly's monochromes do not establish an impermeable barrier between pictorial space and the space of the gallery,' writes the critic Carter Ratcliff.[8] Kelly paintings seem to exist within the viewer's own space, rather than simply functioning as wall-based objects or pictures.

In Frank Stella's *Avicenna* (1960), angled stripes of aluminium paint sit obdurately on the canvas, reflecting the light, with the aim of making it appear two-dimensional. But the sharp corners of the traditional canvas have also been replaced by right-angled incisions, and a rectangular hole has been cut into the middle of it – the site where we would expect to see something significant in a representational work. As a result, the inclination to seek content in a work or to explore possible associations is resoundingly countered. In a shaped canvas the absence of internal relations and the smoothness of the painted surface, achieved through the more methodical and non-expressive application of paint Stella adopted by this point, mean the eye is able to freely graze across the plane, an experience arrested only by the physical edge of the canvas, or where the canvas ends and the wall begins, or at the place where one shaped coloured panel abuts another. Similarly, in the mid-1960s Robert Mangold began to airbrush paint onto Masonite supports to create geometric, but irregular, formats. In works such as *1/3 Gray-Green Curved Area* (1966), Mangold's support is curved at the bottom and reaches an apex at the top centre, from where it is bisected by a straight, vertical black line.

Donald Judd was increasingly convinced that painting was naturally evolving into an object: 'Frank Stella says that he is doing paintings, and his work could be considered as paintings,' Judd wrote in a review. 'Most of his works, though, suggest slabs, since they project more than usual, and since some are notched and some are shaped like letters.'[9] Judd himself moved on from experimenting with the monochrome canvas towards three-dimensional works that communicate a robust sense of their status as an object. He sought a means to overcome what he saw as the relational, divisive and arbitrary nature of the pictorial, and dedicated himself to seriality and repetition. The aim was to create works that would be experienced all at once, with nothing concealed.

In 1963 Judd exhibited a series of plywood objects all uniformly painted in bright Cadmium Red Light. In the simple, coloured, eccentrically geometric forms, such as in *Untitled (DSS 41)* (1963), the single hue of Cadmium Red Light was not used with an aesthetic function in mind but instead with the aim of effecting a unified experience of the object, with the object itself having no function. Judd called this new kind of work 'specific objects' and from 1964 began commissioning a factory to manufacture his pieces, using materials with no traditional connection to art, such as Plexiglas, concrete and steel. Judd's work took on an overtly impersonal and industrial look as he continued to explore the literalist monochrome. From the heights from which he surveyed the art of his time, it seemed that the only way forward was via the 'specific object'. 'The thing as a whole, its quality as whole is what is interesting,' he declared.[10]

Typical of this period in the United States was the artist Dan Flavin's resistance to any attribution of metaphysical, narrative or symbolic significance. Like Otto Piene, Flavin added electricity to the repertoire of the monochrome artwork, choosing to use fluorescent lighting as a medium. In *'Monument' 1 for V. Tatlin* (1964), for example, Flavin rigged together seven commercially produced fluorescent tubes in a format that alludes to the unbuilt utopian 'Monument to the Third International' designed in 1919–20 by the Soviet Constructivist artist Vladimir Tatlin, installing the piece on the floor against a wall. Fluorescent lighting had been commercialized in the 1930s; its incandescent glow is produced when an electric current in mercury vapour produces short-wave ultraviolet light, which causes the phosphor coating on the inside of the bulb to become luminous. Flavin was soon generating coloured light in works such as *greens crossing greens (to Piet Mondrian who lacked green)* (1966), in which bottle-green light suffuses the room; such works greatly developed the possibility of dematerializing colour by radiating it into the environment. At the same time, the fluorescent lamp casings are obdurate material presences within the actual space of the work. For Flavin, the choice of fluorescent lighting rigs was done largely in order to create distance from the familiar forms of art. In 1966, for example, he declared:

> I believe art is shedding its vaunted mystery for a common sense of keenly realized decoration. Symbolizing is dwindling – becoming slight. We are pressing downwards toward no art – a mutual sense of psychologically indifferent decoration – a neutral pleasure of seeing known to everyone . . . [The fluorescent tubes] lack the look of a history.[11]

For Flavin, like Judd, notions of purity, origin or the essential were replaced by the more empirical terms 'clarity' and 'specificity'. Indeed, in this period, as the art historian Briony Fer notes, the term 'infinity' became a 'literalist watchword' that effectively supplanted terminology derived from the 'aesthetic of revelation'.[12] The preoccupation with unity, modular sequencing and repetition distanced the new 'minimalist' art from any lingering expressive or spiritual contexts. By the mid-1960s the tide seemed to have decisively turned towards such readings of the monochrome, as artists extended the idea of the monochrome from its dependence on the picture, and instead turned it into an object.

12

SIGN

> tabletops, studio floors, chart, bulletin boards – any receptor surface on which objects are scattered, on which data is entered, on which information may be received, printed, impressed – whether coherently or in confusion.[1]
>
> Leo Steinberg (1972)

In insisting on colour *as* colour, and by avoiding internal divisions within their compositions, monochrome artists hoped to restrict the tendency of the art-viewing audience to default to learned responses, the already consciously familiar. They did this by limiting the possible fields of external reference that could be explored, wanting their audience to perceive their work without the distractions of allusions or pre-existing associations. In this sense, the monochrome was intended to strip painting of the props through which these responses inevitably occur. These artists did not want their audience to use what Barnett Newman called the 'nostalgic glasses of history', which always potentially act as a shield that blocks access to direct experience.

But they soon learned that even a canvas covered in just one colour will potentially bring with it a range of learned associations or symbolic meanings. Discussing his black paintings of 1951–3, Robert Rauschenberg recalled being surprised to find that viewers identified expressive intentions even in the simple black surfaces he presented: 'They moved immediately into association with "burned-out," "tearing," "nihilism" and "destruction".' Rauschenberg, however, was only interested in 'black as pigment', explaining: 'I don't mess around with my subconscious. If I see any superficial subconscious relationships that I'm familiar with – clichés of association – I change the picture.'[2] He believed that, like him, viewers would also inevitably jettison the 'clichés of association'.

Ad Reinhardt explained that he had abandoned the use of all colours other than black because 'colour is always trapped in some kind of physical activity or assertiveness of its own; and colour has to do with life.'[3] Nevertheless he was keenly aware of the deep-rooted symbolism of the black he used, noting its role in mainstream Christianity, where it is associated with the Devil, and in Christian mysticism, where black takes on more positive connotations. Looking beyond Western culture, Reinhardt noted that in Islam black is celebrated as an evocation of the transcendent God in the Kaaba cube in Mecca, and that in the *Tao Te Ching* the Tao is described as 'dim and dark'.[4] But what counted for Reinhardt, and what should also count for his audience, he declared, was 'the idea of black as intellectuality and conventionality', and not black as a symbol or emotion.[5]

The colour white was also a popular choice for monochromists, for similar reasons: its apparently non-associative and non-expressive potential. The Italian Piero Manzoni, for example, claimed that his all-white monochromes, or *Achromes*, as he called them, begun in the late 1950s, were 'simply a white surface and nothing else (a colourless surface that is just a colourless surface)'.[6] What was important, Manzoni insisted, was that the viewer attend to the surface – what they perceived before them.

For Yves Klein, by contrast, colour's extra-visual associations were actively invited. As we saw, ultramarine blue was central to his art because of its traditional association with the sky and infinity. But he also believed that blue is the least tangible of hues, and so in Klein's opinion it was the colour least dependent for its emotional impact on conventional, codified, psychological and symbolic associations. 'Blue has no dimensions, it is beyond dimensions, whereas the other colours are not,' he explained. 'They are prepsychological expanses, red, for example, presupposing a site radiating heat. All colours arouse specific associative ideas, psychologically material or tangible, while blue suggests at most the sea and sky, and they, after all, are in actual, visible nature what is most abstract.'[7] In other words, for Klein, the semiotic value of blue was not dependent on some external symbolic reference but derived directly from the experience.

But the struggle to isolate the work from its wider relationship to memory was bound to fail. Even a painting in one-colour-all-over involves the reception of a dual and inseparable message that is both optical and discursive. An audience draws on both 'bottom-up' information, coming from the external stimulus of a work, and on 'top-down' information derived from the storehouse of memories and imagination. To be 'visible' – that is, meaningful – a painting must also be 'legible'. In other words, any work of art, including a monochrome, will bring with it a potential explanation of itself that is consciously discursive, as well as stimulating levels that are preconscious and felt. Even a monochrome cannot ever be fully quarantined from extra-visual associations. It will always also be a *sign*.

However, a work of art will potentially *show* what it refers to, rather than just speaking of it, as is the case with verbal language or a symbol. While verbal language is limited to articulating meaning in an abstract linear sequence, the two-dimensional and poly-dimensional use of space within visual art can supply directly structural equivalents or isomorphisms for objects, events and relations. This means a work of art has some significant advantages over verbal language. It can represent through sameness of form the abstract dimensions necessary for theoretical thought.[8] Feelings also have visual equivalents, associations acquired over time, and as a result, in a work of art feelings and thoughts are closely related to formal properties, so that much of its content is to an extent inherent rather than added. The problem is distinguishing what kind of relationship a work's form has to its content. Is this content 'motivated', that is, an *intrinsic* aspect of formal properties, or is it 'unmotivated', and then a supplement added from outside via the artist's or audience's interpretative frameworks?[9]

In the late nineteenth century the philosopher C. S. Peirce proposed a taxonomy of three types of visual sign. The 'symbol' was a sign that is conventional or learned, and so it is the one most dependent on learning. To understand what a symbol refers to one must know the code within which it functions, because there is no directly visual relationship between form and meaning, and once a code is learned, a 'symbol' will deliver a precise and unchanging message. An 'icon', by contrast, directly resembles or imitates its referent and therefore is significantly different from a set of verbal signs like the alphabet – which are arbitrary tokens – or from visual symbols such as iconography. Peirce suggested that an icon functions according to three modalities – as an 'image', a 'metaphor' and a 'diagram'. An image has a direct resemblance to something; a metaphor produces a parallelism in something else; and a diagram shows the relations of the parts of an object or a concept through an analogy or isomorphism with the work's own spatially extended parts.[10] Peirce's third sign is the 'indexical', which is connected to its referent by dint of some existential link, as when smoke signifies fire, or in painting, when a mark on a canvas refers back to the body of the artist who made the gesture and deposited the paint. An indexical sign casts painting as closely connected to the imprint or trace, such as with a footprint or a photograph. It depends on sensory features and is more fundamental and 'natural' than both the symbol and the icon, which rely to a much greater extent on acquired knowledge and interpretation and involve cognitive skills acquired later in an individual's mental development. Indeed, the interpretation of an indexical sign is often fast and pre-conscious. It is also a sign that requires only minimal cues. In terms of semantics, an indexical sign often functions as a synecdoche, that is, through substituting a part for the whole.

As the earlier discussion of the 'spiritual', 'transcendent' and 'ineffable' dimensions of the monochrome, epitomized by Malevich, Klein, Rothko, Newman and (to some extent) Reinhardt, suggested, the potential indexicality of the monochrome meant that its minimal form could directly correlate with complex feelings or ideas that are pre-conscious, wordless or difficult to put into words – 'indefinable', as Yves Klein liked to put it. In the previous two chapters we saw how the monochrome could be indexical of the physical properties of painting itself, and thereby constitute a new kind of realism based on the logic of the trace, and substitution of the part for the whole.[11] By reducing painting to its essential properties, artists hoped to render it as purely indexical as possible.

A monochrome can make a directly iconic or indexical reference to the human body. Through the equivalence of seemingly similar qualities, reference to body height, upright proportion and skin colour, for example, can be cued. In fact, painting in general can also function metaphorically in relation to the body, a part of the body or something assimilated to the body.[12] Even when it does not represent a body as such, a painting can mimic the proportions, bilateral symmetry and vertical positioning of a human form, or the internal functions and sensations of being embodied. Axial symmetry, the use of a single or few colours of a closely valued hue, a lack of compositional hierarchy, vertical orientation and an overall sense of unity make manifest a structural relationship between the monochrome painting and the basic bodily schema. Its format and surface then function as substitutes for similar corporeal qualities, such as body height, upright posture and proportion, while the use of a single colour can suggest skin tone and texture. Such corporeal associations can be triggered directly via perception rather than through discursive reference, and in this sense are indexical. They are affective and are aroused by one's response to the picture as a whole, or to large areas of it, rather than given in a piecemeal fashion.

An especially obvious example of the monochrome referencing human corporality is the work produced by the Italian artist Alberto Burri (1915–1995). Burri served as a military doctor during the Second World War and while imprisoned in a camp in the United States began his *Sacchi* (Sackcloth) series, which involved the sewing and patching of fragments of burlap into monochromatic textiles. These works clearly conjure associations with tattered garments covering a body.[13] Unsurprisingly, allusions to the human body *in extremis* were especially prevalent in the art produced in a devastated Europe recovering from war. Associations with the body also seem suggestive in relation to the *Spatial Concepts* of Lucio Fontana. His canvases suggest human skin and the slashes open wounds, or even, perhaps, a sexual assault on the 'virginal' monochrome surface.[14]

Then again, a monochrome may also produce a more or less obvious, more or less intended, correspondence with similar and familiar flat, vertical, two-dimensional objects and surfaces. In the early 1950s the Catalan artist Antoni Tàpies (1923–2012) began producing monochromatic paintings with rough, gouged surfaces that seem directly to evoke the old walls of his native Barcelona. In *Great Painting* (1958), for example, Tàpies used oil paint mixed with sand to create a heavy, rough paste which he laid on the canvas, also gouging into its surface with the blunt end of a paintbrush.[15] He thereby made an explicit connection between the flat surface of his painting and the flat surface of the architecture that surrounded him.

The kind of surface with which a monochrome can be iconically associated may also be one customarily used to carry some kind of two-dimensional code – a text, for example. As we saw earlier, the term *tabula rasa* was often used to convey the idea of the monochrome as an 'origin'. In fact, a *tabula* was a surface used in the Roman period for inscription that could be erased or blanked by heating wax and then smoothing it over. In this sense, even as artists declared that they were starting with a blank slate or making a new beginning, they were also latently acknowledging that a monochrome is analogous to a surface that is directly implicated in semiosis. It is a carrier of signs, a site awaiting inscription.

A monochrome can, for example, have a 'motivated' semiotic relationship with a stone tablet, blackboard or noticeboard, or other rectangular surfaces that are not necessarily intended to be hung vertically, such as a book, scroll or newspaper. In his black monochrome works of the early 1950s, Rauschenberg painted onto newspaper, making a direct connection between the monochrome as both a text-covered surface and as an erased surface. The American painter Cy Twombly (1928–2011), meanwhile, made several monochromatic works that suggest surfaces covered with illegible or semi-legible writing.

In the early 1960s the art historian Leo Steinberg referred to the 'receptor surface' and the 'flatbed picture plane', which he saw replacing the conventions of perspectival picturing in the works of many contemporary artists. He wrote that paintings now often alluded directly to hard surfaces, such as 'tabletops, studio floors, chart, bulletin boards – any receptor surface on which objects are scattered, on which data is entered, on which information may be received, printed, impressed – whether coherently or in confusion'.[16] Steinberg interpreted the new emphasis on the 'flatbed picture plane' not as signalling painterly autonomy but rather as demonstrating a more general reorientation marking a shift away from the vertical, in which spatial depth is implicit and a painting functions as a window-like aperture on to a space of illusion, towards the horizontal orientation central to inscribing code. Rauschenberg, who was Steinberg's special focus, was prone to conceive of his work as 'receptors', even – as in the case of his white monochrome series – if just as a 'receptor' for the vagaries of ambient light. (We might recall here how the composer John Cage described his friend's white monochromes as 'airports for light'.)

But the 'receptor surface' with which the monochrome will perhaps come to have the closest structural affinity is another kind of receptor of light: the vast, vertically hung white rectangular planes that in the early twentieth century began to appear in theatres across the Western world – the cinema screen. It is surely no coincidence that the monochrome's birth more or less coincided with the beginning of the screen-based technology of the cinema, the dominant new visual information medium of the twentieth century. The cinema screen introduced a new kind of substrate or support, one that offered a novel interface between the concrete and the immaterial. Unlike a painting, a movie screen sustains two separate and seemingly incompatible functions. It is an empty object and also virtual space for the display of images, keeping them distinct through temporal and spatial displacement. Unlike a painting, whose surface must be imprinted with an image, a screen only loses its pristine, virginal status for as long as it is used to focus and frame the imagery of the projected film. When not in use, a movie screen becomes, in effect, a vast white monochrome.

In this sense, the invention of cinema definitively transformed the meaning that can be attributed to a blank rectangle. It was no longer something that simply signified a beginning, an end, an essence or an absence. Instead, the cinema screen inaugurated the era of the blank rectangle as a receptor surface available for countless projections. As the philosopher Gilles Deleuze noted, the cinema screen is 'the frame of frames'. It is a two-dimensional surface but plays host to a virtual world within which, according to Deleuze, the image has lost its moorings in embodied experience; the screen gives 'a common standard of measurement to things which do not have one – long shots of countryside and close-ups of the face, an astronomical system and a single drop of water – parts which do not have the same denominator of distance, relief or light. In all these senses the frame ensures a deterritorialisation of the image.'[17]

The screen analogy is also suggestive from a psychological point of view. Indeed, in Freudian theory the metaphor of the screen was directly applied in relation to the interpretation of dreams. In Freudianism, the 'dream-screen' is 'totally blank, it's blankness reproducing the infantile experience of that against which our first dreams were dreamt, the mother's breast', writes the art historian Richard Wollheim.[18] In this context, the emptiness of the monochrome cannot possibly be voided of content. Its very blankness in fact makes it available for the projected exploration of unconscious fantasies. It serves to mobilize 'memories of what nightly goes on in our heads'.[19]

The potential of the monochrome to function as a surrogate screen for image projection is overtly explored in a different way in some of Andy Warhol's paintings from the 1960s. In several of the *Death and Disaster* series, begun in 1962, Warhol used a diptych format, juxtaposing a single, flatly coloured canvas with another that is imprinted with a silk-screened image. *Blue Electric Chair* (1963), for example, features two canvases painted in a flat monochrome field of blue, one of which is overprinted with repeated images of an electric chair. Through placing a pure, one-coloured field next to one that could be described as 'stained' or 'polluted' with a photojournalistic image, Warhol effectively engineered a meeting that the modernist artwork was meant to ensure never happened. He therefore implies that the monochrome's much vaunted autonomy makes it all the more incapable of resisting incursions from mass culture. Furthermore, by using a monochrome as the colourful screen upon which to project the unsavoury facts of modern American life transmitted via the mass media, Warhol exposed the vanity and impotence of the empty canvas when placed in the context of wider social issues.[20]

13

IDEA

Ut pictura theoria[1]

W.J.T. Mitchell (1994)

In 1897 the French journalist and humorist Alphonse Allais published what he called an *Album primo-avrilesque* (April-foolish Album), which featured several one-colour rectangular blanks surrounded by ornately drawn frames labelled with grandiose titles. An all-white blank, for example, was entitled 'First Communion of chlorotic young girls during snowy weather', while a red one was labelled 'Apoplectic cardinals harvesting tomatoes on the shore of the Red Sea'. Another, in yellow, was called 'Dazed young recruits on seeing for the first time your azure, oh Mediterranean'.[2]

A few years earlier, Allais had exhibited a dark piece of fabric which he entitled *Total Eclipse of the Sun in Darkest Africa*, and in the preface notes to the *April-foolish Album* noted that he had been directly inspired by a certain 'celebrated painting in black, called *Combat of Negroes in a Cave at Night*'. This work, although Allais didn't say so in his album, was by Paul Bilhaud, another member of the group to which Allais belonged, Les Arts Incohérents (The

Incoherents), and Allais also included in his album a black blank with the same title, but with the addition of the label '(a reproduction of a famous picture)'.[3] So his album was another iteration of an already established idea among a certain sector of the avant-garde, one for whom the monochrome rectangle was a useful tool in an intellectual game: as a joke or kind of serious nonsense that aimed to debunk art at the basic level of semantics.

Allais' album signals another interesting point of origin for the monochrome, one that has nothing to do with spiritual transcendence, existential nothingness or formal purity. Rather, Allais places the monochrome within a lineage that we would now term 'conceptual'. He foregrounds the complex relationship between words and pictures, the visual and extra-visual, exemplified by the power of a work's title.

A title is, in effect, something like an 'invisible colour', in that it can potentially imbue a work with an associational range that extends well beyond the purely visual or formal.[4] For his most uncompromisingly monochromatic works, Kazimir Malevich opted for descriptive titles – *Black Square*, *White on White*. But for several of his more elaborate, though still wholly 'objectless', Suprematist works, he sometimes invented highly suggestive titles reminiscent of those of Allais. His titles often offer a possible, if ludicrous, correlation with something visible in the real world, such as, for example, in a work entitled *House under Construction* (1915–16), where the arrangement of coloured geometric shapes within the painting are plausibly like those of a building site. But Malevich's titles could also be far more suggestive and elusive, as in one called *Self-portrait in Two Dimensions* (1915), where there is no obvious connection between what we see and what we read about what we see.

Yves Klein, as we saw, called his first publicly presented monochrome *Expression of the World of the Colour Lead-orange*, a title that is almost as overblown as those of Allais. Subsequently, however, Klein opted for far more prosaic nomenclature, such as the generic *Blue Monochrome*, followed by a date. The difference is telling. While the former leads us into a mental space external to the work itself, the latter directs us only to the visual facts (the colour) and archival data (the date). The title of Brice Marden's monochrome painting *Nebraska*, mentioned in Chapter Ten, refers to a specific American state, while the actual greenish-grey colour of the work relates to that location in only the most generalized way. The title is not meant to suggest that Marden's painting is a specific duplication or representation of a place – although in fact it does draw on the artist's memories of driving through that state the previous summer. But we would never make such an association if unaided by the title. The title nevertheless serves to guide us towards a certain contextual space of possible inference. It is a cuing or priming device, used by Marden to direct our thoughts and imagination beyond the purely formal. Several of the titles of paintings by Agnes Martin also allude to landscape or nature – *Spring Field* (1962), *Starlight* (1963), *Drift of Summer* (1964) and *The Rose* (1965), for example – but here too the artist's goal seems to have been to cue the viewer to a specific associational space rather than provide descriptive labels. But Martin, for her part, quickly recognized that her strategy could easily backfire – that viewers would mistake her tiles as directly denoting rather than connoting meaning, and therefore as functioning as a 'motivated' reference to nature. These titles were being taken too literally, thereby reducing her paintings to little more than attenuated landscapes. As a consequence, she increasingly opted for the neutral *Untitled*, just like many other abstract artists. Like Marden, what Martin sought was to prompt a viewer to be open to an experience encouraged by the inner resources of her works themselves, which might also be familiar from the experience of nature. Frank Stella, by contrast, chose another strategy. His paintings have very evocative titles. *Avicenna*, *Getty Tomb* and *The Marriage of Reason and Squalor, II* are the names of some of his black paintings. But there is no obvious logical connection or causal relationship between the titles and the works, and Stella seems to have actively sought to dissociate the caption from the content.

BY THE 1960S there was the sense that all painting, whatever its genre, was in a certain sense involved in putting something on top of a monochrome.[5] In other words, the monochrome was now the starting-point, not the ending-point. A flat field of colour was construed as a neutral and receptive ground for some content. Whatever the intentions of the individual artist, there was the increasing sense that after the monochrome became art 'worthy of the name', all paintings could be classed as 'failed monochromes', as the artist and art historian Jeff Wall has pointed out. That is, 'all genres now continue through the act of putting something on top of a monochrome – by effacing, supplementing, or disfiguring a monochrome.'[6] In other words, the monochrome made manifest the 'ground' of painting as a medium, in the sense of revealing its foundation, or its self-recognition as painting.

While Warhol explored the implications of this through staining a coloured ground with a printed image, several artists in the 1960s chose instead to inscribe texts on their single-coloured surfaces.

This became particularly compelling because it was increasingly recognized that the monochrome's much vaunted autonomy, which was supposed to be guaranteed by the purification of the compositional paraphernalia of painting, does not produce an empty space within which the invasion of language is resisted, but on the contrary prepares a space within which discourse can be copiously incubated. As Allais had already perceived, words circulate around the apparently autonomous space of abstract art, and *especially* around the blankness of the monochrome. The lack of visual content obliges the viewer to seek elsewhere for meaning. In fact, as W.J.T. Mitchell observes, 'the fewer verbal promptings provided by a painting in the form of title, narrative clues, or subject matter, the more demand for the spectator to fill the void with language.'[7] As a result, abstract art as a whole is really an 'elaborate language game', a 'visual machine for the generation of language'.[8] Indeed, as Mitchell argues, while abstract art 'kept out a certain kind of visual contamination . . . it absolutely depended, at the same time, on the collaboration with another kind of discourse, which we may call, for the lack of a better term, the discourse of theory'. When art becomes objectless or non-representational, what takes the place vacated by traditional literary or narrative content and iconographic reference is not necessarily nothingness or the infinite, or even a heightened experience of material surface and colour, but, all too often, words. 'If we summarize the traditional collaboration of painting and literature under the classic Horatian maxim, *ut pictura poesis*, as in painting, so in poetry,' writes Mitchell, 'then the maxim of abstract art is not hard to predict: *ut pictura theoria*.'[9] In the exemplary place poetry once sat, theory was installed. Mitchell's maxim seems especially appropriate in relation to the developments in art in the late 1960s and early 1970s, a period during which monochrome surfaces literally started to fill up with the words that had been invisibly circulating around them. This was the era of the 'text-assisted' monochrome.[10]

Emblematic of this new conceptual and avowedly self-reflexive attitude are a series that self-consciously addressed the aspirations of monochrome art made by the American artist Sol LeWitt (1928–2007) between 1961 and 1962, which he called *Structures*. They carry lettered inscriptions that describe the hue and shape of the monochrome surfaces – for instance, 'RED SQUARE' – and also descriptions of the inscriptions themselves, such as 'WHITE LETTERS'. The goal was to supplement a style of work that had become primarily construed as a formal, visual entity by linguistic definitions. As Benjamin Buchloh writes:

> Since these inscriptions named either the support or the inscription . . . they created a continuous conflict in the viewer/reader. This conflict was not just over which of the two roles should be performed in relation to the painting. To a larger extent it concerned the reliability of the given information and the sequence of that information: was the inscription to be given primacy over the visual qualities identified by the linguistic entity, or was the perceptual experience of the visual, formal, and chromatic element anterior to its mere denomination by language?[11]

A few years later, another American, John Baldessari (b. 1931), began taking found texts and having a professional sign-painter inscribe them in black on otherwise blank white canvases. One of them carries the following laconic sentences:

> WHAT IS PAINTING
>
> do you sense how all the parts of a good picture are involved with each other? not just placed side by side. art is a creation for the eye and can only be hinted at with words.[12]

Baldessari borrowed his text from a book intended for 'Sunday painters' – it was 'readymade' – and in this new avant-garde setting the seemingly innocuous phrase became a wry parody of formalism and an exemplary instance of Mitchell's *ut pictura theoria*. Furthermore, by not painting the work himself, Baldessari also fulfilled the promise of the idea of the authorless monochrome, while simultaneously deconstructing the idea that the result was an autonomous form of empirical realism.

In 1965 the New York-based Japanese artist On Kawara (1932–2014) painted a triptych of three deep pinkish-red monochromes that he called *Title*. The left canvas carries the text 'ONE THING', the central one (which is slightly larger) reads '1965', and the right side canvas, 'VIETNAM'. Here, evidence of the world that purist modernist art had hoped to hold at bay seems to be infiltrating the space of its greatest icon – which, far from being modernism's firmest foundation stone, turns out to be its most vulnerable point. Kawara's reference to the ongoing war in Vietnam through the simple expediency of a written name collides with the declaration of modernist-style specificity signalled by the words 'ONE THING', while the date sets Kawara's work squarely in a particular moment in time. While Warhol had silkscreened onto the surface of a monochrome images from the mass media, Kawara's texts signified an event through the use of a name and a date, putting into play the kinds of socio-temporal frameworks that become publicly attached to them, and which the modernist ideal of the monochrome was intended to keep at bay. A year later, Kawara began his epic *Today* series, in which in meticulously hand-painted sans-serif letters, in white acrylic paint on usually red-brown, grey or black (but sometimes green, blue or orange) monochrome grounds, he recorded the day, month and year on which he produced the modestly sized painting, also accompanying each painting with a cardboard box containing a newspaper printed the same day.[13] The events signalled by Kawara in words, like Warhol with his silkscreened images, reflect a period of prosperity in the West but also one in which the Cold War threatened to erupt into nuclear conflagration, the United States was increasingly embroiled in Vietnam and protests, especially among students, were widespread. In France in 1968 the crisis erupted into what briefly seemed open revolution when the 'Events' of May brought the country to a temporary standstill. As the French philosopher and historian Michel Foucault wrote of that time, there was

> a sort of general feeling that the ground was crumbling beneath our feet, especially in places where it seemed most familiar, most solid, and closest to us, to our bodies, to our everyday gestures. But alongside this crumbling and the astonishing efficacy of discontinuous, particular, and local critiques, the facts were also revealing something . . . beneath this whole thematic, through it and even within it, we have seen what might be called the insurrection of subjugated knowledges.[14]

In this situation, radicalism in art often went hand in hand with political radicalism. But first it was necessary to expose the shaky premises on which modernist art was founded. It was necessary to expose the spuriousness of faith in 'inner necessity' and spiritual vision. At the bottom of an off-white canvas whose top right-hand corner is bisected by a black triangle, the German artist Sigmar Polke (1941–2010) painted the following words, so that they look as though they were typed on a typewriter: *Höhere Wesen befahlen: Rechte obere Ecke schwarz malen!* (Higher powers command: Paint the upper right-hand corner black!) (1969). Even more explicit in its desire to launch an assault on the idea of the 'spiritual', in the sense used by Kandinsky and the other pioneers of abstraction, is *Secret Painting* (1967–8) by the British artist Mel Ramsden (b. 1944). The work consists of a medium-size black monochrome square in oil, on canvas, hung next to a smaller work in a black frame containing a photostatted text on white paper that reads: 'The content of this painting is invisible; the character and dimension of the content are to be kept permanently secret, known only to the artist.'

In the United States, Greenberg's formalist modernism became an increasingly assailed target. The critic and art historian Rosalind Krauss, who began her career as a Greenbergian formalist, increasingly saw the art of the late 1960s and early 1970s as challenging the basic Modernist assumption of an 'indivisible instant of seeing', in which 'to absolutize this "now," to insist that Painting exists within the indivisible present of the extremest possible perceptual intensity: the rush of pure colour; the shock of light-on-dark as ground pulls level with figure; the reduction of the world to pattern.'[15] But Greenberg's Modernism was actually based on a fantasy, one that the art historian and critic Hal Foster, writing from the vantage point of the early 1980s, called a spurious 'will-to-purity' that by the 1960s was no longer capable – perhaps never had been capable – of delivering a critical challenge. Foster wrote:

> Once, this will-to-purity was subversive: in its negations, conventions – social ones encoded in the aesthetic – were delimited if not transgressed, and the artist, immersed in artistic practice, his or her true history, was rendered autonomous, transcendentally critical. However, seen dialectically in retrospect, such a strategy seems decorous and politically retrograde. 'Purity' abets a division of labour within culture which, as result, comes to partake of both the special professionalism of the academy and the commercial commodity-production of industry. It also affirms the idea of art as its own issue, engendered from a special history: and this is indeed how art history is institutionally presented: as a line of works, a lineage of artists, in the historicist terms (*post hoc, ergo propter hoc*) of influence or continuity.[16]

The art collective Art & Language, which began in Britain around 1967 and of which Ramsden was part, adopted the resolutely anti-formalist premise that an artwork achieves its status as art through an assertion of its metalinguistic status. As another member of the group, the art historian Charles Harrison (1942–2009), observed, the goal must now be 'the ruination of those mechanisms of validation which were identified with the beholder', that is, the basic assumption of modernism concerning the role in the encounter with art of disinterested, detached contemplation.[17] The focus was on critical readings of art, rather than on looking, or on 'interpretative reading', as Harrison put it.[18]

The question of the frame moved to centre stage. The process through which it could become more porous and contested had begun with the confusion around its limiting condition in relation to the work of abstract art, and the monochrome in particular.

It seemed increasingly clear that the 'framing' condition existed not only in relation to an object defined by its material limits but on wider conceptual and institutional levels, or what the American artist Joseph Kosuth (b. 1945), another member of Art & Language, called the 'first frame' of the mediums of painting and sculpture, and the 'second frame' of institutional mechanisms.[19] A critique of the framing conditions established by both the 'first' and, more especially, the 'second' frame – the institutions of the art world itself – was inaugurated.

Kosuth noted that 'In the philosophical *tabula rasa* of art, "if someone calls it art," as Don Judd has said, "it's art."'[20] This recognition in its turn led Kosuth to argue that what was important was not the material object but rather the definition or proposition that guaranteed the status of that object as 'art'. For him, the lesson of Ad Reinhardt's black monochromatic paintings, for example, had little to do with art's opening on to a 'beyond' or with ontological negation. Kosuth took Reinhardt at his word when he declared that 'The object of fifty years of abstract art is to present art-as-art and as nothing else, to make it into the one thing it is only, separating it and defining it more and more, making it purer and emptier, more absolute and more exclusive – non-objective, non-representational, non-figurative, non-imagist, non-expressionist, non-subjective.'[21] What was important for Kosuth was that Reinhardt's paintings had made manifest 'that self-reflexive spiral which was also painting's self-erasure in its very act of completion'.[22] As such, Kosuth concluded, 'it was necessary to shift from material vehicle to conceptual content.'[23]

The fact that many of the works mentioned in this chapter can be described in words without losing much of the intended meaning or aesthetic value of the original, suggests that their content is indeed almost entirely discursive. But this, as already noted, has always been an implicit part of the story of the monochrome. As a consequence of its anti-visual status and conceptual motivations, a monochrome will easily invite the adoption of a critical stance that assumes that any distinction between the original and a copy, or an original and a description of it, may no longer be of much significance. While, as we have seen, no monochrome is amenable to photographic reproduction, nevertheless, from the beginning there was always the possibility that it remains essentially a 'monochrome' whatever the technique used to make one. In other words, that the monochrome is a concept not a specific material work.

Malevich's *Black Square* began a tendency that the conceptual turn of the late 1960s subsequently made central to avant-garde practice. The monochrome was cast as a finished object supporting an intention in the mind of an agent – the artist. It was an embodied idea. The implications for the future were made clear in a statement from 1969 by the American artist Lawrence Weiner (b. 1942):

> The artist may construct the piece;
> the piece may be fabricated;
> the piece need not be built.
>
> Each being equal and consistent
> with the intent of the artist
> the decision as to condition
> rests with the receiver upon the
> occasion of receivership.[24]

Once the idea or concept was what was important, an object was no longer the necessary outcome of the creative process. As the critic Lucy Lippard wrote in an influential article from 1968, many artists were committed to 'the dematerialization of art'.[25]

This was something that Yves Klein had already explored in 1958 with his exhibition 'The Void'. Eleven years later, the American artist Robert Barry staged exhibitions in Amsterdam, Turin and New York that consisted only of sending out an invitation card that stated 'During the exhibition the gallery will be closed', and two pieces of paper attached to the locked door of the galleries. One announced the dates of the exhibition, the other repeated the same information as the invitation card. Like Klein, Barry produced an empty gallery – but in his case, the monochrome had facilitated entry not to a space replete with the possibility of mystical transcendence, but to one where a concept could be explored unencumbered by the obdurate finitude of an object.

DURING THE LATE 1960s and the 1970s monochrome painting did not entirely disappear, of course. But it seemed that grey was the most appropriate hue. The British artist Alan Charlton (b. 1948), for example, began making paintings uniquely in grey tones, covering rectangular canvases of different sizes and proportions that he meticulously constructed himself. Grey was chosen for its ability to diminish the sensual possibilities of colour and its symbolic resonances, even rendering a painting banal.

The German painter Gerhard Richter (b. 1932) also resorted to the grey monochrome, albeit much more briefly. By painting in all-over grey, Richter wrote in 1975, he believed he would expose the essential meaninglessness of his actions: 'To me, grey is the welcome and only possible equivalent for indifference, noncommitment, absence of opinion, absence of shape.'[26] As he explained in an interview: 'When I first painted a number of canvases grey all over, I did so because I did not know what to paint, or what there might be to paint: so wretched a start could lead to nothing meaningful.' But Richter also discovered something surprising, something that signalled the potential of painting to exceed the rational intentions imposed upon it: he found that there were unexpected nuances within the greys he painted so 'meaninglessly', and that each painting had its own constitutive values. 'I observed differences of quality among the grey surfaces – and also that these betrayed nothing of the destructive motivation that lay behind them. The pictures began to teach me. By generalizing a personal dilemma they resolved it.'[27]

However, in the United States, two artists would nevertheless seek to keep the two principal forms of the monochrome – the metaphysical and the literal – alive. Joseph Marioni (b. 1943) made monochromes using paint rollers, layering different colours one on top of the other so that the surfaces seem to be like veils. The resulting paintings communicate a deep and indeterminate chromatic space. There is something intangible and ineffable about his works, and they self-consciously continue a tradition that goes back to Newman and Rothko in conceiving of the monochrome as a vehicle for evoking the spirituality and immateriality of light-colour. Like their work too, Marioni's is neither wholly transcendental nor fully literal, but seems rather to work in-between such polarities. Marioni himself describes them as 'portraits of colour'.[28]

Marcia Hafif's (1929–2018) work, meanwhile, was more closely allied with developments in art since minimalism, although like Marioni she also imbued it with a more subjective mood. Of her work, Hafif noted: 'I do not make painting so much as I make installations. Each series has its inherent way of hanging, though it is difficult to make firm rules. In each case – with one work or many – I look for how the painting(s) will join with the wall to unite space. Every location is different.'[29] In practice, these series involved Hafif exploring different pigments, binders and supports, often with a conscious awareness of the history of the materials she employed, combined with investigations of the locations where the works were exhibited and personal responses to their associations. Hafif's intention in adopting the monochrome form was to focus attention on the procedures involved in the use of colour, and to avoid the kinds of formal and expressive concerns associated with abstraction in general. As she explained: 'I am using paint in a kind of experiment to find out what happens with paint.'[30] But she also sought to bring these reductive methods into alignment with broader issues. Of her *Roman Paintings* from the mid-1980s, for example, Hafif said: 'I recalled the colours of architecture in that city where I once lived. This series began with four vertical canvases that became *Roman Painting I* using colours traditionally those for representing flesh. Other works in the series were single or with multiple parts, the canvases vertical, the strokes as well, and again I was working all over the entire canvas several times.'[31]

In 1978 Hafif wrote an essay for the influential American art magazine *Artforum* entitled 'Beginning Again', where she laid out her commitment to the literalist, or realist, narrative of the monochrome, giving it especially clear articulation:

> Paintings were once seen as surfaces on which were created illusions representing real life; or they were seen as the 'flat-bed plane' on which to place objects. Now they exist (perhaps since

> Suprematism) to be related to other objects in the world. The experience of seeing such works is very different from the earlier way of looking. The eye stops on the surface, where once it expected to go within. Where we used to read a surface, ignoring the material it was made of, we now look at that surface's very materiality. This work accepts the objectness of the painting. No illusion is created in terms of three dimensions, and associations outside the object are almost nonexistent. Although it is an object, the painting is painted like the particular kind of object it is – a painting. The paint is applied by an artist and the brushstrokes are visible. The surface is painted, but not the edges.[32]

In the 1980s Hafif collaborated with the French artist Olivier Mosset (b. 1944), who was based in the United States. In France in the late 1960s Mosset had been part of team of four painters calling themselves BMPT, after their surname initials – Daniel Buren, Olivier Mosset, Michel Parmentier and Niele Toroni. BMPT staged a series of performances and exhibitions that set out to blur the nature of authorship, uniqueness and economic value, and to undermine the connection between the painterly mark and meaning. The artists argued that painting could no longer claim to stand apart from the wider context of social, political and economic reality, and it was necessary to reveal how a work functioned within a complex network that not only comprised artists, audiences, critics, curators, institutions and collectors but which extended further into the world of economics and political power. BMPT declared that in one way or another it was necessary to acknowledge this wider context or setting, rather than claim or attempt to bracket it out. Their first public 'performance', at the 18th Salon de la Jeune Peinture in 1967, featured the four artists publicly producing their works and then signing one another's.

The paintings of Michel Parmentier (1938–2000) subverted the monochrome from within. In 1966 he began to use rolls of unstretched canvas, folding them into even pleats before spray-painting the exposed areas in gloss blue, in part-homage to Yves Klein. At this stage he seemed to have made a monochrome, but this was only a temporary state, because when the canvas was unfurled the reserves of primed white canvas were exposed, creating a striped pattern. Parmentier used automobile lacquer and a serial process that deliberately excluded any metaphysical goals. Blue had no intrinsic meaning, he stated, and Parmentier declared that the colour he used would change annually. The result was very different in both appearance and intention to Klein's works. By the 1967 performance, for example, they were matt grey.[33]

In Hafif's collaboration with Mosset, they described what they aspired to as 'Radical Painting'. Radical was meant in both the formal and political senses, and the goal was to 'begin again' from first principles. Since his work with BMPT, Mosset had developed into a painter of large, single-colour paintings hung closely together to create installations that evoke a powerful sense of material literalness and spatial organization. For Mosset, the anonymity offered by seriality and the non-expressive mark signalled engagement in systems of distribution and modes of production, rather than in painting as a mode of individual expression. In this sense, Mosset's work recalls the principles expounded by Rodchenko in the early 1920s.[34]

14

ALLEGORICAL

False pictures, pseudo-artifacts which beckon me into the desire to look at a picture.[1]
Craig Owens (1983)

By the late 1970s, it seemed to many 'insiders' that the 'monochrome adventure', as Yves Klein called it, was finished. Writing as a new postmodernist wave of figurative expressionism, known as Neo-Expressionism, Transavantgarde, Bad Painting or Neue Wilden, arrived on the art scene, the art historian and critic Yve-Alain Bois cast Robert Ryman as belonging to an earlier era. Ryman could only be involved in a melancholy task of mourning, and was patiently working through the death of painting by exploring basic manual procedures, Bois asserted.[2] Thinking specifically of the metaphysical aspirations associated with the monochrome, in the early 1990s the critic Thomas McEvilley wrote that it was time to acknowledge that 'as a major conquest, like the discovery of a continent or a galaxy, in the adventure of art [the monochrome] lies in the past, exhausted and wrung dry of meaning. It is the banner on the grave of the mad ambition of Modernist abstraction.'[3] Around the same time, with

Malevich in mind, Arthur Danto opined that 'my sense is that the faith in art as a primary means and agency of spiritual transformation has almost totally vanished, and that this explains the vanishing of art movements as such. Art today is pretty much just art.'[4]

The potential banality and inherent elitism of monochrome paintings of all kinds was becoming increasingly obvious to a younger generation. The exposure of the repressed or occluded dimensions of earlier phases of the avant-garde intensified. If much abstract art had been advocated by artists and critics who believed that the primary goal was to seek out an unassailable origin, a sensibility rooted in a broadly Platonist conception, this was now judged to be a 'profoundly conservative' position, so argued the art historian Mark Cheetham, 'in the sense that it remembers an ultimate, past authority very like the complete unity of Plato's Forms, and because it strictly curtails any further change'.[5] Authoritarian tendencies were lurking within the seemingly empty spaces of the monochrome. The critic Donald Kuspit made a telling comparison between Mondrian and Malevich, arguing that while 'Mondrian's dialectical geometry suggests a differentiated wholeness', 'Malevich's authoritarian geometry is in effect an undifferentiated totality.'[6] While 'wholeness', as Kuspit explained, implies mutuality and inclusion, 'totality', by contrast, 'evokes a Gestalt in which an absolute boundary is emphasized'.[7] In this light, the monochrome seemed dangerously close to functioning as the pictorial equivalent of rigid intolerance. Benjamin Buchloh examined Yves Klein's career, and concluded that Klein's paintings had always lacked the authenticity of the earlier radical 'moment' of the pre-war avant-garde as epitomized by Malevich and Rodchenko. By the time Klein was at work the monochrome was already domesticated and trivialized:

> Even a strategy like the systematic withdrawal of perceptual information could be altered in the postwar moment. If the notion of an autonomy of the visual had once been constitutive of a new spectatorial self-awareness, one that would gradually lead away from the empirical certainty of the visual to one of epistemological doubt, in Klein's hands the withdrawal of perceptual data – rather than wean his audience from the dependence upon an ontologically and phenomenologically grounded visuality – functioned as a well calibrated *choc* for the initiated, a call to partake in a silent consensus that the neo-avantgarde and its increasingly professionalized apparatus were complicit in the initiation into the spectacularization of experience.[8]

With a utopian faith in the future, the early twentieth century avant-garde had focused on the critical practice of relentlessly purifying painting, but Klein, Buchloh argued, merely adopted the monochrome as a ready-made style. He shifted the focus to the monochrome's reception, using it as a well-planned strategy that played to a specific audience for art. Not only had the monochrome's moment passed, it was also necessary to subject its legacy to rigorous critique. The modernist preference for essentialism – for the immediate, the pure and the Real – required comprehensive deconstruction. The new postmodernism sought to establish art on the basis of a fundamentally anti-modernist assumption: cultural productions are wholly coded, and so there can never be access to the 'pure', 'essential' or 'real' values that modernism so vaunted.

For feminist critics especially, the monochrome was one of the dubious foundation stones of patriarchal modernism. Its blankness had been exploited in the service of sexual inequality. As the critic

Ann Eden Gibson wrote, there was an implicit chauvinist assumption behind modernist painting in general: *it must be male*.[9] But, as she was at pains to emphasize, 'the point isn't that there is anything intrinsically "male" about monochrome paint surfaces; the point is that as the epitome of a modernism that has been a male preserve, monochrome painting has appeared at its apex.'[10] The task, as Gibson saw it, was therefore either to expose the monochrome's complicity, or somehow to extricate it from the prison of the outdated ideology into which it had been born and forced to develop. It was necessary to read the monochrome against the grain by placing it within another story, one that 'attempts to escape the phallocentrism of language, the violence of representation, and the control of bodies as different'.[11]

In the event, the reductiveness of modernism's 'visualist' stance was to be most effectively countered through a critical discourse informed by semiotics, Marxism, psychoanalysis and feminism. 'Modernism's optical field is like a protective shield,' writes the art historian Briony Fer, 'whose function is to cover over the repressed "gaps" within the ideology.'[12] What was required was 'a break in the logical circuitry of the modernist imagination'.[13] In her influential book *The Optical Unconscious* (1993), Rosalind Krauss argued that while modernist art was ostensibly concerned with the omniscient, panoramic eye, and dedicated to the detached, aesthetic contemplation of art, this was far from the case in practice. The flat, non-representational surfaces of the modernist painting may have seemingly signified purification, specificity and transcendence, assuming the presence of a disengaged and contemplative viewer, but when submitted to Krauss's critical analysis, the conscious motivations of the modernists were shown to conceal unconscious drives that embodied the very impurities they claimed to banish.

Krauss heralded the 'return of the repressed'. When brushed against the grain, modernism was revealed to be replete with motivations relating to decomposition, erasure, obliteration, cancellation, pulverization and emasculation. The apparently detached viewer was in fact far from the ideal assumed by modernism and was instead a deeply motivated subject who, like the artists themselves, was unconsciously exploring their desires.

In this light, none of the manifest intentions associated with the modernist monochrome were any longer sustainable or credible. They merely concealed the true motivations that Krauss now claimed to expose. Instead, she celebrated the Duchampian antiretinal impulse, exposing the monochrome to a counter-history in which art is suffused with what Krauss termed the 'optical unconscious', which, as in the work of Marcel Duchamp, involved the uncontrollable forces of embodied desires, which uncouple perception from any logical system. The 'optical unconscious' deals not in oppositions but in differences, and is constantly involved in flux, mutation, metamorphosis, undermining, complementarity and the seemingly random blocking together of different incompatible elements.[14] In the fluid spaces of the unconscious, the 'good form' of the figure/ground gestalt, and of demarcated zones of line and colour, are disdained. The unconscious, Krauss wrote, allows 'two, or three, or five things to be in the same place at the same time. And these things are themselves utterly heteroclite, not variations on one another but things in total opposition.'[15]

Within the new critical climate characterized by Krauss, the monochrome was largely irrelevant, and any contemporary examples were stranded out of time. The monochrome spoke of a historical moment within the avant-garde's development, one in which defiant autonomy and negation were briefly the basis for a critical assault on the status quo. In short, the monochrome was inextricably tied to issues that had ceased to be pertinent in anything but a critical, archival, museological or sociological sense. It was hopelessly elitist and, insofar as it was an object, too easily manipulated as a commodity. In a key text from 1979, Krauss wrote: 'Within the situation of postmodernism, practice is not defined in relation to a given medium . . . but rather in relation to the logical operations on a set of cultural terms, for which any medium – photography, books, lines on walls, or sculpture itself – might be used.'[16] In postmodernism, Hal Foster wrote, 'the artist manipulates old signs in a new logic: he or she is a rhetorician who transforms rhetoric.'[17]

As Krauss and Foster saw, a new generation of neo-avant-garde artists in the late 1970s and 1980s self-consciously signalled that they were making a fundamental break with the modernist system. Rather than ontology or form, they put interpretability at the centre of their practice. In this context, as Buchloh suggested, the most important legacy of the monochrome had nothing to do with transcendence or autonomy, but rather with how it drew attention to the institutional framework within which all art functions. In retrospect, Klein's primary importance had nothing to do with any Zen or mystical agenda, Buchloh wrote; rather, Klein was involved in 'dissecting abstraction's historical corpse', and he 'uncovered its mechanical and institutional organs, the technical aspects of its formal conventions, and its fictions of signification'.[18]

Writing in the early 1980s, the critic Craig Owens saw that two tendencies had emerged in the 1970s, both of which 'shift attention away from the work and its producer and onto the *frame*'. In the first, this was done 'by focusing on the *location* in which the work of art is encountered', and in the second 'by insisting on the *social* nature of artistic production and reception'.[19] Above all, as Owens noted, this 'frame' was taken in a very different sense to the modernists, who had limited it to the formal structure of the work itself. Now, by contrast, for the neo-avant-garde, 'the "frame" is treated as that network of institutional practices . . . that define, circumscribe and contain both artistic production and reception.'[20] This shift from the work to the frame – from attention to the formal, expressive, iconographical or spiritual status of the artwork to the complex ways in which it is located within a social nexus – was geared above all towards a critique of the commodification of art, and aimed to undermine the assimilation of modernist art into the marketplace through exposing the mechanisms of power that lurked behind its pure surfaces. The dominant form of the neo-avant-garde work was the palimpsest. Artists indulged in a general confusion of traditional categories, using fragmentary and appropriated imagery and preferring strategies of impermanence, repetition, accumulation, the sequential and the discursive.[21] The most challenging new work, suggested Owens, was informed by an 'allegorical impulse'.

In relation to the monochromes of the American artist Allan McCollum (b. 1944), Owens emphasized how they reflected a key strategy of the neo-avant-garde: to 'expose the contradictions of cultural production in a market economy: the inescapable fact that, in exchange, all works of art are reduced to equivalents'.[22] McCollum's 'Surrogates', as the artist termed them, such as *Collection of One Hundred Plaster Surrogates* (1982), consist of variously sized casts of black and framed works that look like small monochromes clustered together in profusion across the wall. As Owens noted, these Surrogates are 'false pictures, pseudo-artifacts which beckon me into the desire to look at a picture, but which are complete in doing that, and that alone'.[23] As such, McCollum had cast the monochrome as 'utter conventionality, banality', in Owens's words.

It was an icon of the 'repetitive culture' of late capitalism in which virtually identical objects masquerade as difference, thereby hiding the deeper fact that the economy functions according to the rule of technologically facilitated mass duplication or production.[24]

The allegorical monochrome therefore shifts attention from the autonomy of the work of art to its status as a signifier of wider social questions. In *Synecdoche* (1991–present), a work by the Korean American artist Byron Kim (b. 1961), the relationship between the 'skin' of paint and the human skin that had been alluded to in Marcia Hafif's painting becomes overwhelmingly explicit, a sign that the focus has decisively shifted from optical and formal issues to conceptual and social concerns. The work's title refers to the literary trope of using a part to refer to a whole, and Kim thereby signals his interest in recasting painting as belonging within an expanded semantic field. As of the time of writing, Kim has made four hundred small wooden panels as part of this piece, displayed in a grid, each panel painted in a different skin tone. The sources for Kim's paint colours have been strangers, friends, family, neighbours and fellow artists, and the work is accompanied by a text that records the names of the sitters, arranged alphabetically by first name. Kim implies that the body that was suppressed within modernism's optical field has been lurking there all the time within the seemingly pure colours of monochrome paintings.

But it is another American, Stephen Prina (b. 1954), who represents the allegorical monochrome in perhaps its clearest form. In 1988 Prina began a project titled *Exquisite Corpse: The Complete Paintings of Manet*, in which offset lithographs representing a visual index of Édouard Manet's entire body of work are arranged to scale as 'blanks' based on the contour and dimensions of each painting or drawing in relation to size, creating a kind of index of Manet's oeuvre.

Prina's works are shown beside monochromatic sepia ink drawings made by hand to the exact size and format of the corresponding works by Manet. Concerning the ink drawings, Prina explains:

> They may be the lowest common denominator of expressivity. The surfaces are sponged with a diluted sepia ink wash. Some people see them as being vacant or empty images. They are subtle, but they aren't empty. In some ways they're as full as they could be. There's pigment edge to edge. Every square inch has been mapped out, plotted and occupied. They are quite clearly hand-made . . .[25]

In a related project from 1988–9 entitled *Monochrome Painting*, Prina 're-enacted' or duplicated in uniform grey-green the formats of monochromes from various twentieth-century artists.[26] The strikingly different dimensions of each monochrome, each painted by a different artist in a different place and time and for different reasons, becomes the dominant feature, and through the levelling of each work to the same treatment and colour of surface, these variations become the manifest content of the work.

The allegorical monochrome cast as the fallen icon of modernism is also a central aspect of the work of the American artist Sherrie Levine (b. 1947). Like Prina, Levine was concerned with investigating modernism's utopian legacy, using it as the raw material for her own gently deconstructive work. In 1991 Levine made a series entitled *Melt Down (After Yves Klein)*, which investigated and parodied the identification Klein had made with International Klein Blue by displaying eight differently coloured monochromes. Levine suggests a kind of schizophrenic identification or 'meltdown' in which several colours vie for identification with the artist, a strategy that willingly adopts the posterior position in relation to modernist art, working 'after' by re-quoting in subtly disorienting ways. In another project, *Salubra* (2007), also on mahogany panels, Levine made three sets of fourteen monochrome paintings based on the colour charts for wallpapers made in 1931 for the Swiss company Salubra by the modernist architect Le Corbusier.[27] Levine's works after Le Corbusier, like those she made after Klein, are not exact copies. She didn't make the work related to Klein using Klein's signature style, but rather, as with the Le Corbusier project, had a conservator paint mahogany panels according to her specifications. Mahogany as a painterly support is one very far from the modernist universe, but it was also chosen by Levine for technical and aesthetic reasons: mahogany is one of the few trees that can produce wood panels wide enough for her needs, and she was also interested in the way the grain revealed itself through the painted surface.

What Levine's project harnesses is not so much the act of repetition but one of concentration and extreme compression.[28] Levine's attitude to her sources was also far from purely cannibalistic or parodic; as she noted: 'I love monochrome paintings. I think monochrome paintings are the apex of modernist painting. For years I've been trying to figure out how to make a monochrome painting that made sense in the context of my work and I was very pleased when I came up with a solution.'[29] For Levine, as for Prina, it was necessary to first take a long detour via cultural and social formations so as to eventually reach the point at which they could feel capable of getting the monochrome to function in a way that made it relevant once again. But such relevance still seems mostly emblematic, for the monochrome was now the privileged sign of the lost utopian spirit of modernism. It was a historical fact to be addressed critically and analytically.

15

NEW MEDIA

The spirit of the time is surely not that of the merely pleasant: its mission remains . . . that of alluding to the nondemonstrable.
Jean-François Lyotard (1982)

The monochrome had been living a parallel life within photography since the early twentieth century. In the first three decades of the twentieth century, Alfred Stieglitz (1864–1946) and his circle had sometimes photographed what can be described as found 'monochromes' within the natural and urban environments of New York and its environs. Stieglitz produced, for example, a series called *Equivalents* in the 1920s and early 1930s that comprised photographs of the empty sky, thereby creating what were in effect black-and-white photographs of 'natural' monochromes.[1] The photographers Edward Steichen (1879–1973) and Paul Strand (1890–1976) also occasionally veered towards the monochrome. Steichen's *Between the Walls, New York* (c. 1922), for example, shows the decidedly monochrome-like expanse of a tenement building's blank brick wall.[2] In effect, photography, which is a chemical process for registering light, has the effect of binding the monochrome directly to the everyday world.

In the 1970s, within the climate generated by the 'conceptual turn', photography became a more overtly avant-garde medium which was intended to overturn the aesthetic connotations of painting. The Japanese American artist Hiroshi Sugimoto (b. 1948) brought the possibilities of the pure-light monochrome photograph to fruition in a series entitled *Theaters*. He initially photographed Art Deco-style movie palaces, then progressed to the halls and drive-in cinemas of the 1950s and '60s.[3] In *Sam Eric, Pennsylvania* (1978), for example, we seem to be looking at a blank white screen surrounded by the Art Deco architecture of the movie theatre. But in fact, the dazzlingly luminous white was created by Sugimoto fixing the shutter at a wide aperture for the duration of an entire film. The long elapse of time has the effect of suppressing the image, or dematerializing it into light. 'Both existence and absence coexist within the photograph,' writes the art historian Kwak June Young. 'The passage of time, the layers of the image fill the screen yet are absent, and while experiential value is created from the narrative and running time of the film, yet there is nothing.'[4] As Kwak also notes, Sugimoto was consciously drawing on his interest in Zen, in which awareness of nothingness brings a deeper connection to existence.

Another consequence of Sugimoto's series was to make clearly manifest the previously more or less unconscious relationship between the history of the monochrome and the cinema screen. This relationship was to be made even more explicit when in 1993 a film written and directed by the British film director Derek Jarman, entitled *Blue*, was premiered. In conscious homage to Yves Klein, a radiant field of ultramarine blue is projected onto the screen for 75 minutes, accompanied by a soundtrack of music, ticking clocks, chimes, gongs, and a narration of poetry and prose.[5] In 1994 Jarman published *Chroma*, a book that gathers together a bewildering variety of quotations and personal reflections as he discusses different colours chapter by chapter, ending with 'Iridescence' and 'Translucence'. Early on, Jarman, remembering his childhood, writes: 'I learnt colour but did not understand it.'[6] The sheer scale, numinous atmosphere, multisensory presentation and complexity of the narrative content of Jarman's *Blue* draws attention to another important dimension of the art of the 1980s and '90s, one that painting was proving less and less capable of exploring: the sublime.

FOR ALL ITS radicalism, the avant-garde of the first half of the twentieth century had held on to the form provided by the traditional media. As we have seen, the limits of these media were increasingly challenged, but it would fall to the postmodern avant-garde to throw itself more wholeheartedly into the indeterminacy made possible by breaking free of these limits. The influential philosopher Jean-François Lyotard linked developments in art to socioeconomic transformations in postmodern society, and declared that art was now wedded to the 'nondemonstrable':

> The governing principle of the post-industrial techno-scientific world is not the need to represent the representable, but rather the opposite principle. To turn away from this principle – that infinity is inherent in the very dialectic of search – is absurd, impractical, and reactionary. It is not up to the artist to reinstate a make-believe 'reality' which the drive toward knowledge, technology, and wealth will continually destroy

> in order to replace it with a version considered more viable – and which itself will eventually be replaced. The spirit of the time is surely not that of the merely pleasant: its mission remains that of the immanent sublime, that of alluding to the nondemonstrable.[7]

For Lyotard, the goal henceforth for progressive art was 'presenting the unpresentable', and he claimed to identify a new kind of art that built on the innovations of the modernist avant-garde but pushed it much further, towards a 'postmodern sublime'.

Actively seeking to shift the viewer's perceptions between literal and virtual readings of a monochromatic space, and to engender a powerful sense of the 'nondemonstrable' or 'unpresentable' on a phenomenological level, certainly became a central goal of the British Indian artist Anish Kapoor (b. 1954). In *Adam* (1988–9) and *It Is Man* (1989–90), for example, Kapoor worked with blue pigment of an intensity exceeding even that of Yves Klein, incorporating a rectangular 'monochrome' in the smooth surface plane of an otherwise roughly hewn sandstone rock that is approximately the size and shape of a imposingly large human being. Ambiguity is generated through becoming aware that what seems to be a flat black rectangle is in fact a deep blue incision into the stone. Because of the lack of sufficient spatial readings, this cavity seems without perceptual limits. As Kapoor noted: 'I have a curious overlap with painting, in that the space of painting is the space of illusion. I seem to be making sculpture about the space beyond, illusory space.'[8] In this sense, Kapoor consciously undermines the binary distinctions between the literal and the virtual through exposing their interaction in the very activity of perceiving. In *Angel* (1989), for example, a large irregular slab of slate has been completely coated in deep blue pigment, and the colour seems to imbue the heavy rock with gravity-defying potential, as if transforming earth into sky.

But it is above all in ambient light installations that the potential of the 'postmodern sublime' monochrome was to be most clearly developed. The work of the California light artists such as Robert Irwin (b. 1928) and James Turrell (b. 1943) finally freed the monochrome from the material substrate, thereby bringing new phenomenological possibilities characterized by a sense of physical immersion and liminality beyond the reach of painting.

The goal Irwin and Turrell set themselves in the 1960s was to move beyond imitated space and into actual space. They shifted the monochrome away from a preoccupation with surface and towards the intangible transparency of light. As Rosalind Krauss writes, they explore the 'effect that if I am in the presence of mystery, it is one that is unmediated; it is in the same room with me'.[9]

In Irwin's *Untitled* (1966–7), for example, a circular aluminium form painted in cream-coloured acrylic is suspended far from the wall, casting ambiguous overlapping shadows. The boundaries Irwin creates are deliberately intended to be penetrable, but also limited by the play of light. Irwin made several monochrome paintings to test real spatial boundaries, but then started to engage with ambient light as part of his work. It is as if light itself has become the medium.[10] Irwin was interested above all in empirical experience, in how we perceive or fail to perceive within real contexts, and how this impacts on consciousness. 'The intention of a phenomenal art is simply the gift of seeing a little more today than you did yesterday,' he explained.[11] In his text 'Notes Toward a Model' (1977), Irwin defined the new experiential monochrome he was pioneering as 'Conditional Art', which, he wrote, 'simply means it should never be held wholly apart from, or independent of, those grounds from which it is drawn'.[12]

In 1969 Irwin collaborated with Turrell on a joint statement outlining their new goals. 'Art is not object – it is experience – in each case a particular experience defined by the artist', they declared. 'Although much art depends on an object to convey or mediate the experience, this is a condition we have sought to alter by choosing the realm of perception as our art form.'[13] In Turrell's own work, light comes to play an even more central role; while Irwin dissolved materials into light, Turrell treated light as the medium itself. Using electric light and light generated by nature in increasingly ambitious installations involving monochromatic fields of colour, Turrell transports the experience of art far beyond the confines of the canvas – outwards into the immateriality of real space – and thereby opening up new possibilities for an intensely experiential monochrome. As Turrell said: 'I want to create an atmosphere.'[14]

In Turrell's *Gard, Pale Blue* (1968), an early projection piece that spans the corner of a room, a triangle of pale blue light is projected within a space suffused with deep blue light. In *Milk Run II* (1997), one of his *Wedgeworks*, a powerfully diffuse red light projection produces variously opaque, translucent and transparent light within the space, creating highly ambiguous locational readings. Turrell also often intentionally generates in his viewers a Ganzfeld effect, and is interested in how the loss of perceptual coordinates can have a direct impact on mental states. Turrell describes the experience of light as 'not so much something that reveals as . . . itself a revelation'.[15]

He used the medium of light to explore in a far less mediated fashion the experiential potential of a field of colour. In this sense, like that of Irwin, his work can be seen within the broader context of the artists discussed earlier, who set out to create and test ontological and cognitive boundaries. But once the medium of the monochrome had abandoned the limitations imposed by placing paint pigment on a material surface, the possibilities of evoking an expanded awareness of boundary-free subjectivity through colour as pure light became more fully obtainable. In Irwin and Turrell's work these boundaries are more decisively created and breached.

These effects and affects can also be contextualized in relation to the spiritual and religious goals discussed earlier. Turrell has drawn attention to the influence of his Quaker upbringing on his work. A Protestant Christian denomination, the Quakers believe that in seeking to commune with God as directly as possible, it is necessary to reject the mediation of images, dogma and doctrine, and instead to rely on the power of 'inner light'. But Turrell's work also connects with the Eastern ideas related especially with Zen discussed earlier. 'My work is about how we constitute reality. The real illusion is that we aren't aware of how we give reality to things,' Turrell emphasizes, in terms that reflect his interest in the spirit of Zen. 'We have awarded them concreteness or reality and we are unaware of how we did it.'[16] Turrell refers to his works as 'visual koans',[17] and when he declares, 'In working with light, what is really important to me is to create an experience of wordless thought, to make the quality seemingly intangible, yet it is physically felt,'[18] he is also close to Zen.

16

DANSAEKHWA

When [I encounter] a canvas with brushes and painting, a work of art comes into existence. Therefore, strictly speaking, it is wrong to say that [I have] painted a canvas with paint and brushes. This would be a Western-European mistranslation.[1]
Lee Ufan, n.d.

Just when monochrome painting in the West was being displaced from its iconic position, in the Republic of Korea it emerged as a significant dimension of avant-garde practice, as part of the stylistic tendency that became known as Dansaekhwa (or 'Tansaekhwa', meaning 'one-colour', 'monochrome' or 'monotone' painting).[2] As with the works of Japanese artists in the 1950s and '60s, discussed earlier, paintings made by South Korean artists in the 1970s and '80s not only arose as a consequence of a growing awareness of modern Western art among non-Euro-American artists, but derived from indigenous artistic techniques and situated philosophical traditions that lent themselves to the 'monochrome effect'. These exogenous sources also in their turn fed back into Western practices and, as we saw in Chapter Nine, influenced the works of Western artists like Yves Klein.

In Japan, from the late 1960s to the mid-1970s, Mono-ha ('School of Things') played an important role in pushing forward the avant-garde. Mono-ha artists went further than Gutai towards bridging the gap between the natural and the man-made, aiming to minimize the level of human intervention in their work and to assert the primacy of productive nothingness through celebrating the 'untouched'. Mono-ha artists thus often worked with unaltered organic materials, juxtaposing them with ready-made industrial forms to create (usually temporary) earthworks and installations.

One of the founders of Mono-ha was the Korean Lee Ufan (b. 1936), who had moved to Tokyo to study philosophy. Lee assimilated many influences from traditional Japanese culture, in particular from Zen Buddhism, but he also studied Western philosophy and Japanese contemporary philosophers of the Kyoto School, who actively linked East Asian traditions to modern Western thinkers such as Friedrich Nietzsche, Martin Heidegger and Jean-Paul Sartre. During the 1970s, however, Lee was to be central to the development of a much more pervasively monochromatic painting in his native South Korea: Dansaekhwa.

Unlike the Japanese avant-garde – which in the 1960s largely abandoned painting to pursue more immersive, experiential and fugitive practices, epitomized by Mono-ha – in Korea a more cautious embracing of modernism was undertaken because of an oppressive political situation and a poor economy. The Republic of Korea was poised between the closure of a tragic period of civil war and confrontation with a belligerent communist North, and the dawning of a new prosperous, and eventually democratic, state. The specific traits and temporalities of modernization in South Korea therefore meant that Korean-style monochrome painting effectively marked a moment when the society that gave birth to it appeared almost as a cultural *tabula rasa*.[3]

Artists associated with Dansaekhwa had a preference for earth-toned or white and off-white colours, and applied paint in emphatically repetitive, process-based ways. Park Seo-bo (b. 1931) scratched rhythmically into a dull off-white oil paste with a pencil (see illus. 7), while Ha Chong-hyun (b. 1935) squeezed earth-toned oil paint from the reverse side of a canvas through the surface to the front. Chung Sanghwa (b. 1932) pleated canvases into monochromatic grids and then cut and painted into the cracks he produced. Yun Hyong-keun (b. 1928) treated oil paint as a fluid medium, staining large pieces of unprimed canvas that he worked while they were laid on the floor. Lee Ufan used a brush loaded with a paint composed of stone-based pigment and glue, and progressively depleted the amount of paint deposited by repeating a sequence of horizontal, vertical or random brushmarks according to a predetermined system. Furthermore, several Dansaekhwa artists used *hanji*, a traditional Korean paper made from the mulberry bush, instead of or in addition to canvas. For example, Chung Chang-Sup (1921–2011) laid *hanji* in a collage-like fashion onto canvas and then worked it into a rough terrain using oil paint.

As we have seen, by the time Korean monochrome painting emerged in the 1970s, the once seemingly inexorable progress towards the 'ultimate' monochrome painting had already faltered in the West. As a result, linking Korean monochrome painting to the Euro-American chronology may suggest a case of belatedness, of the 'periphery' lagging behind the 'centre'. In this sense, Korean monochrome painting can be read as a cultural placeholder, signalling South Korea's alignment with the United States through the 'obedient' adoption of Western-style modernism. The uncompromising 'abstractness' of Dansaekhwa works would, in this view, then correlate with the dominant Western politico-cultural narrative in which the repudiation of figuration becomes the visual equivalent for the individualism and freedom of expression made possible under American protection.

In the Korean situation, such defiantly abstract paintings were also readily presented as the politically charged antithesis to the Socialist Realist art propagated north of the border in the People's Democratic Republic of Korea. Artists began eschewing figurative imagery, whether derived from the conventions of their traditional culture or from earlier periods and styles of Western art, in favour of simple, flat, all-over and repeated motifs made with reductive gestures and single colours. As such, their works appear to be interpretable in line with the kinds of meanings we have encountered so far. These artists treated painting as anti-illusionistic and grounded in two-dimensionality, and like Western monochromists they sought to remove from the painted rectangle the lingering illusionism created by the organization of forms into figures and grounds. Dansaekhwa therefore does share several formal characteristics with the 'cool', all-over or 'colour field' painting that characterized the end of the Abstract Expressionist period. For example, the paintings of Park Seo-bo bear a passing resemblance to the work of the American Cy Twombly, and those of Yun Hyong-keun to Mark Rothko.

However, an analysis based on cross-cultural influence fails to adequately take into account the variable pace and character of the modernizing project within different cultures. Within the temporality of unfolding modernity, some South Korean artists turned to their indigenous cultural traditions just as much as absorbing the new Western art. While the works of Dansaekhwa artists markedly display qualities that set them apart both from the kinds of painting styles that had dominated Korean art for centuries, and also from those very recently adopted under the 'modernizing' agendas of Chinese and North Korean communism, they also signal important underlying continuities with pre-modern Korean culture. Monochrome painting in Korea, like Gutai in Japan, must therefore be assessed in relation to a local history and social context that embeds it within endogenous forms of modernity.

To some extent, these local narratives are constructions produced in the service of forging a workable identity, and as such they are inextricably tied to a political agenda, which can be described as seeking a way to accommodate Korea within a Western, and pre-eminently American, sphere of influence. But while there is no timeless, essential quality of 'Japanese-ness', 'Korean-ness' or 'East Asian-ness' (just as to speak of 'Britishness' or 'Americanness' inevitably implies an ideological agenda), these countries nevertheless possess resilient and linked worldviews. These traditions are also highly contingent and open to questioning and renegotiation, however, and this is especially the case in relation to the South Korea of the 1970s, which was struggling to forge a new modern identity that could somehow bridge the widening chasm between the pre-modern Korea of only one generation before, the model of modern Communist Korea being mandated in the North, and the demands imposed by a pro-capitalist Republic under a repressive military government.

In viewing Dansaekhwa paintings 'in the flesh' rather than in photographs, it soon becomes evident how different from Westerners the Korean painters' use of materials is, informed as it is by the melding of the spontaneous and the ascetic. A strong sense of rhythmic but controlled repetitive process is conveyed in the work of Lee Ufan, as for example in his *From Point* (1976). While for Westerners these qualities may seem to have certain affinities with the notion of painting as performance or the 'informalism' and action painting espoused especially during the 1950s, in Dansaekhwa they should more properly be located within an indigenous tradition that values the artwork as existing in an intimately indexical relationship with its maker, who seeks to link the work with the world through channelling *qi* energy.

The typically repetitive, process-based approach of Dansaekhwa artists like Lee Ufan and Park Seo-bo is grounded in physicality – the use of the hand – but also in controlled action. As a result, this is a kind of painting that 'conveys something quite different from the cold and rigorous formal aspect of minimalism'.[4] As the art historian Joan Kee notes, Dansaekhwa 'demanded of the viewer a deeper level of somatic involvement than could otherwise be achieved through essentializing views of medium'.[5] The haptic vision that Dansaekhwa artists explore takes little account of colour; it considers the holistic 'field', rather than analysing specifics, and is more inclined to deliver an ambiguous and empathetic grasping of the total field than is the focused eye.

The specific context within which Korean artists self-consciously emerged seemed to compel these artists to engage with traditions that were endangered by modernization. These traditions established the basis for a complex weaving of ideas and beliefs coming from indigenous Korean shamanism, Taoism, Buddhism and Confucianism that both intersects with and differs from that employed in relation to the Western monochrome. For example, *shan shui* – literally 'mountain' and 'water' painting – was the pre-eminent subject of literati or scholar-painter art in China, especially during the

Song and Yuan periods (960–1368 CE), and subsequently became important in regions under Chinese cultural influence such as Korea and Japan. On the level of the representational motif, imagined rather than specific or real landscapes were depicted, and these were intended to serve as phenomenal analogues for a state of mind. As the artist and writer Wucius Wong puts it:

> From his mind-heart [the artist] selects mountains, which he can then rotate and reshape; directs water to wind as springs, jump as waterfalls, or flow as rivers along folds; plants trees and shrubs at choice locations; and combines these elements in a harmonious orchestration displaying vital breath. What results is the creative equivalent of nature.[6]

Unlike in Western landscape painting, in which the location of the viewer in relation to a depicted panorama is usually firmly identified as being on the ground and in a specific position, in much East Asian landscape painting the goal was to provide multiple viewpoints, including the aerial, and to set the landscape at a distance. The result was a lack of single focus and a distribution of visual attention more evenly across the whole surface. As the philosopher and sinologist François Jullien writes, this effect 'not only makes it possible to take in a vaster landscape but also renders it more accessible to contemplation, for distance, as it were, rids the landscape of all the weight of inessentials and restores it to the simple movement that gives it form and existence.'[7]

By gathering the forces of *yin* and *yang* into a synergy conveyed through brush and ink, a painting would communicate a condition 'when plenitude has not yet broken up and dispersed', as Jullien writes.[8] As we discussed earlier regarding the influence of Zen on the monochrome and Western art, one result is that what to Western eyes might register as emptiness, sketchiness or incompletion was deemed within East Asian art to be of the utmost importance. *Qi* ('breath', 'energy' or 'life force') is associated with the void, 'emptiness' or 'nothingness', and with the performative traits of effortlessness and spontaneity. Analogues of the void in nature, which are common in East Asian landscape painting, include water, clouds, mists, moonlight and smoke, which manifest traits of indistinctness and structureless impermanence. The representation of such formlessness was not intended to imply the limit beyond which forms vanish at the horizon, as it would be within the conventions of Western landscape painting; rather, such vagueness, as Jullien writes, 'also permeates the interiority of forms, opens then, aerates them, liberates them, and makes them evasive'.[9] As the curator Lee Joon writes:

> From the perspective of Western art, which explicates everything based on forms, the void of Asian painting may appear, to certain extents, to suggest a lack of forms or a space of incompletion. As a matter of fact, it is difficult to find a term corresponding to the concept in the Western artistic lexicon. 'Empty space', a negative element, implies absence of physical representation or is synonymous with 'blank space'. In the theory of East Asian painting, however, void exists as a complete, legitimate part of a work, and, in a more active sense, is an 'unpainted painting'. In that sense, void does not mean the renunciation of the use of space but rather the encouragement of space and is absence-cum-presence.[10]

The 'emptiness' of Dansaekhwa paintings can therefore be considered from within a tradition in which the undifferentiated carries very different connotations in the West, where, as we have seen, emptiness or nothingness usually signifies non-being, the negation of being or the absence of something. 'Even when negativity is actively or even ardently grasped, in the end it is grasped as a self-negation of being that serves to elevate being itself,' writes the contemporary Japanese philosopher Ueda Shizuteru of the Western position. In the East Asian model, by contrast, Ueda continues, 'nothingness is not only non-being . . . as the negation of being . . . but also contains a sense that goes beyond this, and this "additional sense" is brought to life when the originariness of nothingness is existentially realized and thoughtfully cultivated.'[11]

The prevalence of white or off-white tones in many Dansaekhwa works can be related not only to the evocation of void but to uniquely Korean responses to Confucian concepts as revealed in the ascetic moral code installed by the Joseon dynasty that ruled Korea between 1392 and 1897. In this Neo-Confucian ideology, ostentatious display was frowned upon and the studious life of the scholar highly esteemed. The promotion of an austere and self-abnegating philosophy is clearly evident in the architecture and interior furnishings of the nobility of this period and in the preferred styles of pottery, which are distinguished from Chinese and Japanese examples by their pronounced austerity. Furthermore, the dominant form of Buddhism in Korea, Seon (developed from Chinese Chan Buddhism, as with Japanese Zen), advocates physical self-control through strict regimes of contemplation and meditation in order to achieve a level of inner peace. The ability to combine self-discipline and naturalness was especially admired, and the achievement of the latter was understood to come through rigorous training. Thus in Taoism, Confucianism and Buddhism we see the exemplary figure of the peaceful sage who lives in perfect harmony with nature through complete control over the body and mind.

In a panel discussion, the artist Lee Ufan declared that 'Dansaekhwa is rooted in ascetic tradition,' and he went on to argue that such asceticism was grounded in Confucianism 'or a uniquely Korean somatology' in which 'we use our bodies consciously without violence or force.'[12] As such, Lee concluded, 'It is difficult to talk about Dansaekhwa without talking about how it is created by the actions of mindful bodies.' But as one of the other panel participants noted, while 'the ascetic nature of the works [of Dansaekhwa] seems clearly to relate to this tradition . . . foreigners are unfamiliar with and may be unable to discern [it].'[13]

But the choice of white was also grounded in a more prosaic, everyday symbolism. As the critic and curator Yoon Jin-sup writes:

> The colour white was present in many corners of Korea's life: It was the colour of our ancestor's garments, the famous moon jar as well as other various white porcelains, *baeksulki* (traditional rice cakes) . . . the different hues of *hanji* (traditional paper) and so on. It existed as a cultural base to form part of a collective identity, which was revealed through Dansaekhwa.[14]

The quality of incompletion and the seeming crudeness of execution evident in Korean monochrome paintings are often cited as particularly important attributes of the Korean aesthetic in general, which, by comparison to Chinese or Japanese aesthetics, was more concerned with conveying an air of nonchalance or unconcern with technical perfection. An ethos of spontaneity, seemingly paradoxically fused with an ascetic sense of restraint, is usually associated with traditional Korean art and artefacts, as well as music and dance. This emphasis on spontaneity can be traced in part to another uniquely Korean cultural heritage: the trance state central to its shamanism, which is fundamentally ecstatic and led to a pervasive admiration among Koreans for the encouragement of a temporary absence of order. Fused with the desire for naturalness, the ethos of spontaneity resonated especially strongly, and rawness, nonchalance and individuality, as well as humour and expressiveness, are usually identified as components of a particularly Korean aesthetic.[15]

As mentioned above, the emphasis on controlled, concrete and repetitive processes is one of the most striking characteristics of the works of Dansaekhwa artists. It is not so much optical properties that are emphasized as the more intimately tactile, haptic and bodily or somatic. A sense of tactility is 'the outstanding feature' of the works of these artists, writes Yoon Jin-sup.[16] 'Tansaekhwa artists shared an interest in getting to know the object through its most basic material properties,' notes Joan Kee. 'That so many Tansaekhwa artists insisted on showing what paper, paint, or canvas could do, even to the point of stressing the obvious, was a means of establishing concreteness, albeit temporarily.'[17] In other words, these artists were exploring various permutations in the interaction between specific bodily action and specific materials.

The painters associated with Dansaekhwa also pursued a practice that emphasized self-negation. 'As one sheds one's exterior shell, like the surface of granite exposed to time,' Chung Chang-sup noted, 'I will open myself to embrace time, ego, and nature in all traces, stains, and chance happenings.'[18] Park Seo-bo declared, in a similar vein: 'I want to reduce and reduce – to create pure emptiness. That is an Asian idea, an approach to nature. Nature and humans can connect in this way.'[19] Park's works from the 1970s and early 1980s, such as *Écriture, No. 14–79* (1979) (illus. 7), display a far more controlled, rhythmic relationship to the marks he makes across the surface of his monochromatic oil-painted panels than those of, say, Cy Twombly, appearing overtly to signal a desire to relate to the calligraphic traditions of his culture. At the same time, however, the *Écriture* series title, the French word for 'writing', indicates a relationship, or intention to establish an affiliation, with Western art.

'My kind of minimalism is a method that requires the space around the work to be energized more than the work itself,' writes Lee Ufan of his practice. 'The work is not a text made up of signs. I want it to be an energetic living body possessing variability and contradictions.'[20] In one text, Lee discusses what he see as the fundamental difference between his goals and those of some of the key artists I have discussed:

> Contemporary painting has developed by focusing on the means by which a painting becomes a painting rather than what the artist paints. Lucio Fontana demonstrated how a painting could be brought into being by cutting into canvas, Yves Klein by painting over the canvas and objects with a single colour, Barnett Newman by dividing the pictorial surface into separate areas of color and Robert Rauschenberg by combining four white canvases.
>
> The work of these painters was quite innovative, but they were restricted by the idea that it is enough for a painting simply to be a painting, giving painting a more self-contained

> character than in the past. This excessive concentration on the autonomy of painting closed off connections and passages to the outside world.
>
> I want to pay renewed attention to how the conditions of painting are established (how it is given an intermediary role) by means of the body.[21]

Both completion and its antithesis, the Korean monochrome suggests an interesting parallel life for our subject. It is a reminder that the monochrome is concerned with meetings and overlaps, but also about where such meetings and overlaps cease. While the Korean artists were cognizant of Western developments, and drew on them, they were also able to reinterpret and redirect these foreign tendencies through blending them with their own indigenous and unfolding concerns. As a result, interpretation of their works requires a different conceptual framework to those applied previously to the Western monochrome. Furthermore, in looking beyond the West we can also problematize what we thought we already knew about the Western monochrome.

IN THE LATE 1970S the French theorist Roland Barthes discussed what he called a 'third space', an interstitial space that eludes the dichotomies and binary oppositions that characterize language.[22] He also calls it the 'neutral,' and in the course of his examination of the concept refers to a kind of painting that 'substitutes for the idea of opposition that of the slight difference, of the onset, of the effort toward difference, in other words, of nuance', and which as a result goes on to produce a 'shimmering' space 'whose aspect, perhaps whose meaning, is subtly modified according to the angle of the subject's gaze'.[23] This seems a useful way to describe a monochrome – or some of them, at least.

In framing his concept of the neutral Barthes was influenced by East Asian philosophical traditions, a connection deepened by François Jullien in his discussion of traditional Chinese aesthetics. Jullien also draws attention to a pervasive concept that celebrates the 'neutral', one that in China deploys a metaphor drawn from the sense of taste, for an especially valued quality was *dan*, which Jullien translates into French as *fadeur* and into English as 'blandness'.[24] *Dan* refers to a mental state that does not seek to make distinctions. While strong flavour 'provokes attachment . . . overwhelms us, clouds our minds, reduces us to a state of dependence', blandness, by contrast, 'provokes detachment . . . liberates us from the pressure of the external world, from the excitement of sensations, from all false and short-lived intensities. It frees us from fleeting infatuations and silences the wearying din and clamour.'[25] As such, *dan* can be compared to emptiness, tranquillity, indifference, insentience or non-action, and corresponds to the human capacity for inner detachment. It assumes that reality 'projects no meaning beyond itself, and nothing else lends it variety or attraction'.[26] Ultimately, writes Jullien, *dan* is the 'experience of transcendence reconciled with nature – and divested of faith':

> By taking us to the limits of the perceptible, that place where perceptions assimilate and nullify each other, the bland brings us to experience a world beyond. But this movement does not open onto another, metaphysical world, cut off from the senses. It simply unfurls and expands this world (the only one): drained of its opacity, returned to its original, virtual state, and opened up – forever – to joy.[27]

In the art of China, Korea and Japan the aspiration towards achieving a state of *dan* gave birth to 'pale paintings, composed of the rare brush stroke opening onto vast, empty spaces (of sky and of water), where nothing forces itself on the gaze and everything is equal and seems on the verge of disappearing'.[28] Indeed Jullien's description sounds very much like a painting by Lee Ufan, or one by other Dansaekhwa artists, but it also evokes many Western monochromes – works whose 'blandness' or 'neutrality', especially when encountered amid great complexity, encourage a distinct kind of attention that has to do with nuanced vision, inner-directed thought, contemplation, slowing down, silence, simplicity – and letting go.

17

CONTEMPORARY

The dumbest kind of painting that it is possible to make.[1]
David Batchelor (2009)

Writing in 2006 in his book on the monochrome, Denys Riout lists an impressive number of major international exhibitions held since the early 1970s that focused, in one way or another, on the monochrome.[2] Such institutional attention is clear evidence that the monochrome's capacity as a disruptive force has been severely eroded. An online search made while I was writing this chapter brought to my attention a number of websites concerned both with the contemporary monochrome and the historical monochrome. One announces an exhibition at the Richard Taittinger Gallery in New York called 'Untitled (Monochrome), 1957–2017', which was held in 2018 to celebrate the gallery's third anniversary. The exhibition charted its subject over sixty years and included paintings and sculptures by Americans such as Ellsworth Kelly, Marcia Hafif, Joseph Marioni, Allan McCollum and Stephen Prina, and Europeans such as Alan Charlton, Yves Klein, Piero Manzoni and Olivier Mosset. There was also a generous sampling of younger monochromists working in a variety of media: Henry Codax, Claudia Comte, Edith Dekyndt, Will Kerr, the LAb[au] group, Teresa Margolles, Navid Nuur, Fabrice Samyn, Peter Scott, Turi Simeti, Morgane Tschiember and Kees Visser.[3] Today, all developed nations seem to have their own small quota of male and female 'pure' or pure-ish monochrome painters. In 2018, as I write this book, in Britain there are, among others, Jason Martin, Zebedee Jones and Robert Holyhead. South Korea has a thriving culture of 'post-Dansaekhwa' artists, such as Kim Taek-sang, Kim Tschoonsu and Jang Seung-taik.[4] China has caught up, and now has its own monochrome painters, such as Su Xiaobai and Wang Guangle.

But what critical role do such monochrome paintings play within our technologically advanced society and post-medium art world – an art world in which such paintings have been outflanked by 'radical' practices, and can be located comfortably within the familiar history of modern art? One thing is for sure; as the semantic tide has gone out, monochrome painting is increasingly distanced from the critical shoreline where decisions about what does and does not constitute 'art' are made.

The art historian Terry Smith takes a sceptical stance in relation to the possibilities of painting in general, arguing that the term 'contemporary' describes a pot-pourri of 'remodernist', 'retro-sensationalist' and 'spectacularist' strategies, fleshed out by a globalism that permits artists working at the margins to now participate in a unified art world.[5] In Smith's reading, examples of new monochrome paintings are probably to be found primarily in the first category: remodernist. What is clear is that the 'ideal' monochrome and monochromatic painting have been comfortably absorbed into the contemporary stylistic category of small 'm' minimalism. The Minimalism with a capital 'M' of the 1960s was characterized by procedures that through serial repetition and extreme formal reduction, simplification, condensation and concentration aimed to convey a pronounced sense of the impersonal, objective and emotionally neutral, often expressed in objects rather than paintings. Contemporary monochrome and monochromatic paintings, while visually close to the language of 1960s Minimalism, are much less 'pure' to the extent that they are often intended to have an expressive content. In this sense, the visual language first pioneered by Malevich and Rodchenko, and brought to fruition by Donald Judd, say, has been accommodated within a more conservative vision of art that remains wedded to the ideal of the artist as originator, as an author of a unique work of art who is intent on communicating their emotional, spiritual or intellectual reality. Indeed many monochrome paintings have been referred to disparagingly as part of what in some quarters is dubbed a retrogressive 'zombie' formalism.[6]

Whatever the case, *all* forms of painting today must vie with a plethora of globalized practices that take impurity and hybridity as givens. This is a post-media context in which art has extended far beyond the painted canvas to include photography, film, video, electronic lighting technologies, performance, multimedia installations and collaborative, 'open' works with no fixed form, such as conceptual art, Land Art, installation and performance art. Artists no longer adhere to binding programmes, movements or groups. The ideological definitions, manifestos and entrenched theoretical positions that once gave indispensable motivation and structure to the avant-garde, and were inextricably bound to a linear conception of progress in art, are a thing of the past.

Contemporary art unfolds within a fluid situation, one that encourages an open relationship in which the viewer collaborates in a work in progress; indeed the whole idea of art itself has been transformed. An artist is defined no longer by a signature style manifested in a specific medium but by an 'attitude' – by their mode of engaging with the network.

The influential French critic and curator Nicolas Bourriaud argued in 2002 that because we have moved beyond the confines of a 'postmodern' teleology, a central quality of the contemporary art – which, it should be noted, he himself has done much to promote – is that it does not 'position itself as the termination point of the "creative process" (a "finished product" to be contemplated) but as a site of navigation, a portal, a generator of activities'. As a result, 'we tinker with production, we surf on a network of signs, we insert our forms on existing lines.'[7] Within this 'relational' art, Bourriaud declares, 'meaning is born of collaboration and negotiation between the artist and the one who comes to view the work', and the normal relationship between production and consumption is thoroughly disrupted.[8] Art today is concerned with translation, displacement, transposition, erring. It is nomadic. Bourriaud likens contemporary art to a gas that fills the most diverse cultural forms solidifying once again into something that constitutes the visible.[9] For another influential writer and curator, Boris Groys, writing in 2016, the art of today is no longer even bound to aesthetics, and as a result of the possibilities opened up by the hugely enhanced levels of creative engagement facilitated by the Internet, 'contemporary art has become definitively a mass cultural practice . . . Today's artist lives and operates primarily among art producers rather than among art consumers.'[10]

Not surprisingly, the kind of art Bourriaud, Groys and many other intellectually minded contemporary critics and curators favour tends not to include painting, and definitely not the monochrome variety. Painting as a whole is judged to be old-fashioned and inherently unable to provide the kinds of collaborations and negotiations necessary for it to be contemporary art worthy of the name; it is of interest only to the market. Monochrome painting in particular seems inextricably tied to critical issues that long ago ceased to be of any relevance, and within the new anti-aesthetic climate it speaks of an earlier moment within the avant-garde in which the priority was on pure vision, defiant autonomy and negation.

There is no doubt that today the potential of the medium of the monochrome to challenge boundaries and limits, to evoke the intangible and ineffable, absence or the void, is more likely to be exercised successfully beyond painting. In his study *Monochrome: Darkness and Light in Contemporary Art*, Craig Staff explores examples of 'sublimity' with contemporary monochromatic art, but spends little time discussing contemporary painting as such. He draws attention to how any appraisal of his subject must begin with the inherently ambivalent relationship of much contemporary art to modernism as a whole, and specifically to the narrow reading of modernism in terms of the 'optical' that dominated modernist formalism. Staff also emphasizes the fact that a central characteristic of the monochrome is its complex relationship to various forms of binary opposition, such as figure/ground, literal/spiritual, space/time – oppositions that now seem increasingly irrelevant.[11] But as Staff acknowledges, any discussion of the contemporary monochrome nevertheless has to include the complexities of its hundred-year-long history.

Meanwhile, the critic David Joselit makes a spirited argument in favour of a kind of minimal painting that has successfully abandoned modernist fantasies of aesthetic autonomy and which now exists consciously within an expanded network. This he calls 'transitive painting', referring to works that in one way or another include within their frame of intention an awareness of their location within 'networks of distribution and exhibition'.[12] Joselit argues that 'the rhetoric of modern painting (the allover field, the monochrome and Op) served to suture spectators to extra-perceptual social networks rather than merely situating them in a phenomenological relationship of individual perception, as orthodox modernist criticism would have it.'[13] He identifies the medium of monochrome and monochromatic painting as a prime example of this transitive painting, which now 'invents forms and structures whose purpose is to demonstrate that once an object enters a network, it can never be fully stilled, but only subjected to different material states and speeds of circulation ranging from the geologically slow (cold storage) to the infinitely fast.'[14]

The critic Isabelle Graw, in her book-length defence of painting as a 'formation' – a term borrowed from the historian Michel Foucault – aims to situate painting as a 'historical structure that changes over time while also obeying certain "rules of formation"' and that thereby 'allows us to conceive of changes, boundary shifts, alongside aspects that persist over time'.[15] Graw notes that a salient characteristic of painting as a 'formation' is that is has 'routinely assimilated the lessons of other media', from poetry to dance and from theatre to photography. She continues: 'However, although painting's absorptive capacity has made it an extremely heterogeneous medium, it has also "obstinately maintained itself," as Foucault put it.'[16] Like Joselit, in Graw's view, when understood as a 'formation', painting must be seen to incorporate the wider context in which it arises, beyond the simple boundaries of the medium itself – a context 'defined by a variety of actors, theories, and institutions . . . these include the painters themselves and also apologists, patrons, collectors, gallery owners, critics, agents, and museums, as well as the creation of legends and discourses surrounding painting'.[17] In this definition, painting is not only a set of artistic practices but 'a historically situated set of rules that can resurface and remain effective under new historical conditions'.[18]

For both Joselit and Graw there is still a place for monochrome painting within the 'formation' of painting today. One of the artists mentioned by both writers is the American Wade Guyton (b. 1972). In 2007 Guyton exhibited for the first time a series of black monochromes derived from standard computer-generated rectangular formats, drawn and filled in using Photoshop and then printed on canvas using an inkjet. Seemingly anachronistically, these wall-based works were juxtaposed with a scuffed and dirty black floor covering, bringing the mechanical and virtual into indirect and awkward confrontation with the material. As Guyton said in an interview:

> These objects were made with a computer and my printer. They are dragged across the floor and often are piled up on the floor for weeks or months before being attached to stretchers. So the floor was always an integral part of their making – the scratches on the surface of the works, the dirt the ink would soak up from the floor – all of this. So it made sense for me to bring this floor into the gallery – to give the paintings a context and to connect all of them to each other. It was also the only

> painted surface in the room, so you would feel the painting through your feet.[19]

In another interview, Guyton was asked if his work was about the idea of man versus machine. He replied:

> I don't think it is so oppositional. I think [the computer] is just another tool . . . But you also always develop a relationship with computers these days – something my parents never had. And now, the generation younger than me, has an incredibly different relationship to computers than we have. To me it seems there's always a kind of negotiation, sometimes you are in tune with it and other times you are fighting with it.[20]

Guyton's influential practice enlists the monochrome in exploring one of the most pressing issues in art today. He demonstrates that monochrome painting possesses the capacity to investigate and encourage subtle characteristics of thought and gesture that are in danger of being lost as a result of technological innovation. In this sense, painting as a whole – as a collection of exemplary practice exploring the nature of the relationship between thought and gesture – can be seen as having an enhanced relevance. But perhaps monochrome painting in particular can play a unique part in this task by delineating the possibilities of this relationship at its most refined and nuanced levels.

The monochrome is still potentially provocative from another perspective – one that engages with questions of authenticity and authorship. Graw discusses the British artist Merlin Carpenter (b. 1967), who begins from a position that acknowledges the 'impure' status of painting, its relationship to redundancy and repetition, and its inevitable susceptibility to commodification. In 2009 Carpenter proposed to the well-known British abstract artist John Hoyland (1934–2011) to repaint some of his pathbreaking works from the 1960s.[21] Perhaps not surprisingly, Hoyland refused to grant permission, but Carpenter painted them anyway, and to avoid complications of copyright infringement he had the copies boxed in cardboard carrying cases, complete with packing tape and transport labels, which he then hung on the wall for exhibition. Potential purchasers of the works were contractually bound to keep their work wrapped until 2081, when the copyright would expire, and at which time they can enjoy the Hoyland copies.[22] In the meantime, the actual outcome of Carpenter's project is a collection of paintings packed in cardboard that take on the appearance of monochromes. The narrative in which the monochrome functions as both the negation, erasure or veiling of painting and also as a readymade is brought into intimate relationship. Carpenter's strategy is certainly witty and thought-provoking, but like so much contemporary painting, it prioritizes intellectual rewards over any others. Carpenter trades on the fact that within contemporary art the monochrome has become a familiar and debased sign.

Within a culture stripped of the faith in essentialism central to modernism, the monochrome's relationship to more quotidian and banal forms, like cardboard boxes, now becomes explicit and interesting, as does its relationship to more overtly conceptual approaches to art. In *Monochrome Till Receipt (White)* (1999), the British artist Ceal Floyer (b. 1968), turns a humble printed receipt from the UK supermarket chain Morrisons into a 'monochrome' by attaching it to the gallery wall without a frame. The receipt shows that the items purchased by Floyer were all white or have the word 'white' in their name. She thereby focuses on a possibility that has always been inherent: the monochrome is something of such little visual interest that it is often ignored, and is intrinsically banal and uninteresting. But as Duchamp already showed in the early twentieth century, through the artist's nomination and presentation of any object – a men's urinal, for example – as art worthy of the name, it can be so. Floyer notes that her interest in the uninteresting has its roots in her time as a gallery invigilator while she was an art student: 'I watched a lot of art being seen. And a lot of art being not seen. That was a training in itself. I discovered that presumption is a medium in its own right.'[23] Floyer's response to this period of coexisting with art in a museum setting is therefore similar in many ways to that of Robert Ryman at the Museum of Modern Art in New York thirty years earlier: the focus of both was drawn towards the overlooked.

But it is another British artist, David Batchelor (b. 1955), who has perhaps explored in the most systematic fashion the status of the monochrome as something that exists ready-made and unnoticed within the everyday. In one of his writings, Batchelor also catches the monochrome's paradoxical allure, as well as what is no longer possible – at least for him:

> My original motives for making monochromes – back in the late 1980s – were vaguely malicious. The subject was interesting because it seemed to be pretty much the dumbest kind of painting that it is possible to make. A single uninterrupted plane of flat unmodulated colour spread evenly across a given surface – a monochrome appears to involve no composition, no drawing, no subtlety; and it requires no skill, and certainly no craft skill, to make one. Anyone who can paint a door can paint

> a monochrome . . . This was painting as low comedy, the *reductio ad absurdum* of high abstraction. Having said that, a part of what attracted me to the monochrome was also the awareness that for many artists this form of painting had promised a great deal more – the freeing of colour from the tyranny of line, the liberation of painting from the register of representation and the possibility of a brush with some sublime void or other metaphysical nothingness. It's just that I didn't believe that anyone could still seriously maintain its claims to transcendence, be they formal, spiritual or otherwise.[24]

In an ongoing series of photographs called *Found Monochromes*, begun in 1997 (illus. 8 and 9), Batchelor discovers 'monochromes' on vacant billboards, hoardings, noticeboards and windows – tatty, abjectly empty rectangles that remain visible while a location's function as a venue for advertising is suspended or interrupted – and photographs them.[25] Here the monochrome meets the Duchampian readymade and Warhol's deliberately shallow urban aesthetic. Batchelor writes of these works:

> A plane and a void. But not a mysterious void-in-general, rather a contingent void, a void in a place, here, today, on this particular railing in this particular street; here today, and probably gone tomorrow. A void in a place, but not in every place: these incidents are not, I noticed, distributed evenly throughout the city; they have a tendency to cluster in more overlooked and transitional environments, and are scarce in more refined and elegant districts. For me, and perhaps only for me, these bits of peripheral vision are little heroic moments, small monuments to modernity – if modernity can still, in part,

> be defined in that great phrase of Baudelaire's as 'the ephemeral, the fugitive and the contingent'.[26]

As Batchelor points out, the ubiquity of monochrome coloured surfaces within today's urban environment has rendered them a familiar and unthreatening part of our daily lives. In fact, the status within culture in general of 'blankness' as a whole, and with it of visual 'nothingness', has fundamentally changed. Modern architecture, technology and mass culture routinely provide examples of empty coloured rectangles. We are surrounded by monochromatic surfaces. Blank surfaces were once rare – interior walls were usually covered in patterned wallpaper, for example. But now, after a century of 'less is more' in architecture, and technological innovation, blank surfaces are everywhere. Many of these blanks that surround us are electronic – dormant televisions, computers and smartphone screens, waiting to be activated. In short, the potential of blankness within art to deliver an experience that is a subversive challenge to the habitual, an experience which is a negation, an encounter with nothingness or the 'ground of being', has been much diminished both from within and without.

Can the shocking frisson of the monochrome still be delivered further upstream of the found or readymade monochrome, with examples of the contemporary dematerialized work of art – the ones we cannot see but can sense, consider and read about? Since Yves Klein's intervention at the Galerie Iris Clert in Paris in 1958, which signalled the moment when the monochrome became the final threshold before dematerialization, the ostensible absence of an art object has itself become an increasingly familiar potential content of art. As the critic Anna Dezeuze writes: 'Every time the audience of modern and contemporary art is led to believe that the avant-garde reduction of the artwork to a minimal, barely perceptible form can go no further, along comes another artist who creates another even more minimal, even less perceptible, artwork.'[27]

Another work by Ceal Floyer is interesting in this context. In *Auto Focus* (2002) she uses a Leica Pradovit P-150 projector – the analogue predecessor to today's digital projector, which at that time was beginning to take over – sitting on a stand and emanating an empty beam of light against the nearby wall. As the function of a projector is usually to project images, Floyer's work evokes the absence of the image, but in a way that is deliberately divested of what she now considers to be a dubious and outdated sense of the numinous.

For the Danish-Icelandic contemporary multimedia artist and sometime monochromist Olafur Eliasson, however, this loss of metaphysical justification need not necessarily lead to a purely conceptual or parodic practice. Eliasson notes that 'the monochrome is often seen as having an aura of exclusivity about it – as being hermetic, sealed off, mystical even (think Kazimir Malevich).' But once freed from its debilitating role as modernist icon, so he argues, the medium of the monochrome can finally come into its own and be 'about inclusion':

> It can be open and hospitable once we trust ourselves to step into it. The 'mono' of monochrome does not mean the elimination of complexity; rather the monochromatic space holds plurality in it – it welcomes multidimensionality and offers it to us as viewers. Some art seems to tell you what to think, and may even make you feel inadequate and that you don't fit in. Or else it simply ignores you. Other artworks address you as a subject and urge you to become active in making the

> experience your own. Monochrome is the latter. It allows you to be in charge of defining what you are and of assuming authorship of your experience.[28]

For his *Room for One Colour* (1997) (illus. 10), Eliasson suffuses a space with single-frequency sodium-yellow light, which has the effect of suppressing every other colour in the spectrum. As a result, when we are standing inside the room we appear to ourselves and to others only in shades of black and white. The effect is uncanny; Eliasson describes it as 'a sort of hyper-vision that gives us the feeling of having a particularly sharp ability to perceive the space and people around us'.[29] As he also explains, in terms that neatly summarize the function of the monochrome on the level of the directly phenomenological and unmediated:

> By reducing an artwork to only one colour, you eliminate narrative entirely, even compositional narrative. This makes it possible to pay attention not only to the monochromatic matter in front of you but also to the conditions in which your experience takes place, to the peripheral stimuli and noise that surround it, to the emotional state you are in when you encounter the work, and to the nature of perception itself. It is not the monochrome itself – the abstraction – that is the subject matter, but your perception and experience, at once abstract and very close.[30]

CONCLUSION

To be able to see Nobody! And at that distance, too![1]
Lewis Carroll, *Through the Looking-glass* (1871)

Yves Klein cast his decision to make monochromes in the form of a short fable:

> A flute player one day began to play only a single and unique continuous sound.
>
> Having done so for more than twenty years, his wife finally pointed out to him that other flute players have produced many harmonic and melodic sounds, etc., and that this was perhaps more interesting and varied.
>
> To this the 'monotone' flute player replied that it was not his fault that 'he' had found the note for which the others were still in the process of searching![2]

What 'simple truth' did Klein believe he possessed? What special insight did he have that is apparently denied all the rest of humanity except those who Klein believed possess the special capacity to see beyond the obvious, and for whom his works are an open invitation? Within the metaphysics Klein embraced and that his art was intended to embody, there are two distinct levels of consciousness, an outer one directed towards and engaged with the phenomenal world, and that is available to all and sundry, and another that is much more exclusive – an inner-directed world which ostensibly brings union with the transcendent One, the 'ground of being' – and that only the special few can enter. For Klein, only those capable of 'reading' his blue monochromes 'correctly' in relation to this second world will ever grasp their true meaning.

But seen from a purely sociological perspective, we could interpret the presentation of a coloured rectangle as art as above all an uncompromising emblem of social distinction based on a rare refinement of the judgement of taste. The monochrome offers those who claim to value it what Pierre Bourdieu calls 'cultural nobility'.[3] Indeed, within a society in which the old hierarchies have disappeared, the monochrome is especially useful because it guarantees such 'cultural nobility' based on what seems to be a gratuitous leap of faith, that is, it is based on esoteric factors lying beyond the capacity of the 'uninitiated' or the 'outsider' to comprehend. While 'we' – meaning the 'insiders' – talk eloquently of the 'spiritual', or 'autonomy' or 'allegory', what 'they' – the 'outsiders' – see is just an empty canvas, displaying no evidence of skill in the making, or narrative or aesthetic content. 'They' scratch their heads in confusion or laugh in derision, or just ignore the foolishness; sometimes, as we saw in relation to the hapless Reinhardt painting at Christie's, they resort to more direct action. Occasionally, and for whatever reason, 'they' may take the time to reconsider, and perhaps become one of 'us': those who can see a monochrome as worthy of being called 'art'. 'I see nobody on the road,' says Alice in *Through the Looking-glass.* To which the White

King replies, 'in a fretful tone': 'I only wish I had such eyes . . . To be able to see Nobody! And at that distance, too! Why, it's as much as I can do to see real people, by this light!'[4]

What the evolution of modern art has shown with special clarity is that within a context where the criteria for judgements of value are no longer securely defined or are in metamorphosis, personal understanding and feelings about a work of art often defer to knowledge relayed as verbal information provided by cultural 'gatekeepers'. Such information, coming from a trusted source, not only impacts us at a conscious cognitive level but, as neurological research shows, delivers an unconscious neurochemical reward that is so compelling it will effectively determine a viewer's response.[5] In the case of something as visually parsimonious as a monochrome, we can easily imagine how the inclination is especially strong to default to a 'trusted source' in order to gain this neurochemical, intellectual and social reward.

SO MUCH OF what was shocking and innovative about the monochrome is now commonplace, or even judged to be comprehensible. Its gesture of revolt has become a stylistic option. Once we climb down from the Olympian heights to which artist like Malevich, Klein, Reinhardt and Ryman in their different ways carried it, what remains of the monochrome? From the perspective of today, the monochrome often seems to be a quintessentially urban and urbane art form.[6] In the city, monochrome surfaces are everywhere. The streamlined forms of engineering, industry, technology and urban planning are clearly reflected in the appearance of monochromes, and are often overtly celebrated in those of the realist tradition. But it could be argued that even Malevich's description of the monochrome as a 'desert' that prepares for the emergence of a metaphysical reality is also, on a more grounded level, evoking the desert of bulldozed land that must precede any new phase of urban development. The blue of Yves Klein's infinity, which is supposed to liberate the imagination from its bodily shackles, can seem to uncannily foretell the disembodied states we inhabit within the city in the twenty-first century as we hook up to the technologically produced world of virtual reality.

The constructed environment in which the majority of artists, like most people in the 'developed world', now live is increasingly removed from nature. Urban society effectively shelters humanity from its unpredictable and often destructive forces by producing an artificial buffer zone. The urban is also linked to a specific idea of progress, one that is envisaged as a flight from the original givens of nature.

Modern secular culture is founded on faith in the universal applicability of the idea that 'intellectual inquiry can disclose the structure of things to humankind', as the philosopher John Gray puts it.[7] It fosters a worldview that is above all committed to rationalism, and as such, writes the philosopher Charles Taylor, assumes that

> an agent who is perceiving the world takes in 'bits' of information from his or her surroundings, and then 'processes' them in some fashion, in order to emerge with the 'picture' of the world he or she has; who then acts on the basis of this picture to fulfil his or her goals, through a 'calculus' of means and ends.[8]

This idea pits the human against the non-human, culture against nature. Indeed, the modernization project central to Enlightenment humanism, for which urban culture is indispensable, is also founded on the compulsion to appropriate and exploit the non-human world, and as a result opposes the natural and organic. What was once a specifically Western compulsion has now been exported globally, and this expansion has coincided with the growing recognition that despite the evident benefits of Enlightenment humanism in terms of economic, technological and political progress, it has also bred a pervasive sense of nihilism, and tipped the world towards ecological disaster.

The current physical condition of Malevich's *Black Square* of 1915 can be read as a kind of allegory of the fate of the Enlightenment humanist dream, and also of our current relationship to it. The pristine simplicity of the original conception has been cruelly betrayed by the attrition of time. Malevich painted the *Black Square* over two earlier works, one of which is clearly visible as the surface layer of black and white paint has cracked and fissured to reveal the ghost of a Suprematist composition (see illus. 3). The other, painted in his Cubo-Futurist style of a few years earlier, has only recently been revealed through X-ray analysis. But the problems with the painting's condition began almost immediately, which is one reason why Malevich painted another version of *Black Square* between 1923 and 1924. He then painted a third in 1929, and a fourth in the late 1920s or early 1930s – which was the one carried at his funeral in Leningrad in 1935. Malevich's willingness to repeat the same simple motif underscores the suggestion made earlier that *Black Square*, like many subsequent monochromes, was always intended more as an idea than as a unique plastic reality. In this sense, the deterioration of one physical example does nothing to diminish the potency of the idea that was meant to imbue the object with meaning.

But yet more layers of meaning have recently been uncovered below the surface of *Black Square*. In 2015 the same analysis of the painting that revealed the second buried painting showed that partly legible words, which previously were thought to be the artist's signature, actually say in Russian: 'A battle of negroes . . . [continuation illegible].' No doubt Malevich was intending to allude to the visual puns of Alphonse Allais and others, mentioned in Chapter Thirteen.[9] But this revelation adds yet another level of potential meaning to *Black Square*, one that, however briefly and for whatever reason, was part of Malevich's consciously intended meaning.

The recently discovered text has now become another component in the wider story of Malevich's pioneering work, which also includes its unintended material disintegration. All these potential contexts, and surely many others, are intrinsic to any response to the work itself today. In assessing Malevich's painting today, we cannot ignore the evidence of our eyes, and the additional information supplied by the X-ray analysis, thinking of it as primarily a concept in the mind, without severely limiting our experience of it. The deterioration of the painting is part of what it now means, as is the scribbled text. The chance effects caused by the instability of the materials used by Malevich have contributed additional levels of affect and association which are part of the work's reception, and these suggest a vulnerability, decay and abjectness that were far from the artist's mind when he made it, while the words open the painting up to a decidedly 'impure' context.

But above all, the sorry material state of *Black Square* reminds us that the monochrome is more than a hundred years old. An art hell-bent on erasing the traces of history now definitely has its own, and the values that underpinned it have brought us to the edge of extinction. Thus, any attempt to understand the monochrome from the perspective of the present day will require the inclusion of this history and the various interpretative frameworks that belong to it. The 'contemporary' monochrome needs to be seen as both a summation of that history, and as part of an ongoing process in which new meanings continuously emerge to challenge previous dogmas. As we saw, the existence of non-Western monochromy, such as the Korean Dansaekhwa, for example, is especially significant in this context as it reveals that there are other possibilities for the monochrome.

One important and still incomplete legacy of the monochrome is how it can serve to foreground a deep and ongoing cultural problem determined by the specific Western worldview outlined above. This concerns the relationship between making and thinking, crafting and knowing, and how we understand the way raw materials are transformed into stable, ordered and meaningful forms through mental activity combined with bodily action. In this context, tracing the evolution of the monochrome through modern art has revealed how it serves an important role in consolidating a specific cultural idea: that a work of art is preconceived form imposed on a minimal, inert and in itself meaningless material artefact. It is interpreted as simply an outcome that is the consequence of a sequence of antecedent conditions traceable to an idea in the mind of the artist. A fundamental distinction is made between conceiving and making, and between a concept and the material outcome.[10] As a result, the intellectual aspect of art is elevated to the highest position, and the mental is sundered from the material and physical. The mind is raised over the body.

This tendency is evident in many aspects of modern and contemporary art, where knowledge associated with intellectual analysis is emphasized over the implicit and personal. But while the monochrome often seems inextricably bound to this 'calculus', we have seen how it can also be understood to challenge such assumptions. With special clarity a monochrome can draw attention to the fact that when we seek to make sense of a work of art we are using a combination of the formal and conceptual as well as the preconceptual, non-formal and felt, and that the categories of thought we employ have experiential and perceptual origins, and the way in which our embodied mind experiences art informs the concepts we articulate. The making of meaning is essentially a creative act, and is inextricably bound to sensorimotor, felt, performative and personal levels of experience. In this sense, the monochrome serves to draw attention with special clarity to how perception combines observation with memory, reflection and imagination.

IN THE 1960s the psychologist and art theorist Rudolf Arnheim wrote that where art is concerned, 'simplicity is not enough':

> If simplicity were the overriding goal of art, evenly stained canvases or perfect cubes would be the most desirable art objects. In recent years, artists have in fact provided us with such examples of 'minimal art.' Historically, they were needed to soothe the eyes of a generation that had gotten lost in complexity and disorder, but they also served to prove that once it has fulfilled its therapeutic function, so bland a diet does not satisfy.[11]

Arnheim is surely correct. In most cases, 'so bland a diet' is definitely not enough to sustain critical interest, and as an artistic goal is rarely enough to sustain a whole career. But I think Arnheim is too sweeping in his judgement. When considered within a holistic context, as part of a network, and within the contemporary cultural situation, simplicity in art certainly does have its place.

Perhaps today more than ever we shouldn't be quite so quick to dismiss the importance of the broadly 'therapeutic' potential of an art dedicated to visual simplicity. After all, we are certainly no less 'lost in complexity and disorder' than we were in the 1960s, and many of the ideological agendas that once sustained modern art have lost credibility. In fact, the potential of a work of art to serve a therapeutic function, where 'therapeutic' is defined as 'relating to the treatment of disease or disorders by remedial agents or methods' – seems especially valuable today in what has been called our 'burnout society'.[12]

Humans are voracious gatherers of both physical and mental sustenance, and if information were food we would see that today we are all massively overweight. The new electronic systems have reached unprecedented levels of pervasiveness and targeted specificity, and are cleverly designed to capture our attention and to direct us towards specific, often trivial and commercialized goals. Far from producing greater freedom, the new digital communication technologies seem to be enslaving us. Mega-data and the multitasking capacities offered by digital technology exponentially increase our levels of physical, psychological and moral fatigue. In such a world, one in which high levels of attentional interference, distraction and manipulation are increasingly the norm, the future of personal and societal well-being is far from certain. We may have acquired enormously enhanced technological powers, but this doesn't seem to have brought greater peace of mind. Attention has become a lucrative commodity, and we seem to have voluntarily surrendered this, our most precious resource, permitting our minds to be infiltrated by the 'attention merchants'.[13] This massive expansion in the control of attention is especially worrying, because we have no choice but to pay attention to *something*. In this situation, one characterized by an inflated and devalued economy of attention, the arts can function as specific 'attention capture devices' that exist alongside those derived from natural stimuli, human social interactions and the technical devices that, in one way or another, seek to attract our attention.[14] But rather than trying to counteract this spectacular sensory and cognitive overload, the attentional spaces demarcated by contemporary art often seem to be actively aiming to emulate and compete with it. Or, alternatively, our galleries of contemporary art display predominantly non-aesthetic and discursive content that directs the mind towards intellectual concepts, that is, towards articulated knowledge that often engages with explicitly socio-political issues.

There is, however, another kind of attentional space that art can nurture.[15] Within contemporary society the unknowable or ineffable has largely been removed from the centre of human life, and there is an enormous lack of viable space and time within which to perform contemplative rituals, a fact to which the current boom in the 'wellness' industry attests. In this context, the arts can be understood as extending an invitation to spend attention profitably in ways that are predominantly contemplative rather than active. The *Oxford English Dictionary* defines 'contemplation' first as 'the action of beholding, or looking at with attention and thought', and second as 'the action of contemplating or mentally viewing;

the action of thinking about a thing continuously; attentive consideration, study'. Contemplation counters the scattering of attention that is the dominant feature of our culture through providing space and time for the imagination to be grounded in inner integrity. In this sense, the monochrome's apparent simplicity can be experienced as an especially effective means of accessing a contemplative space that resists the dissipating forces which increasingly surround us and invade our consciousness.

REFERENCES

INTRODUCTIONS

1 John Logan's more recent hit play *Red* (2009), which is about Mark Rothko, also revolves around a single colour, attesting to the continued fascination with the monochrome.

2 Alain Badiou, *The Century*, trans. Alberto Toscano (Cambridge, 2007), p. 56.

3 Heinz Mack, Otto Piene and Günter Uecker, 'Untitled', published on a poster and in a leaflet, 1963, reprinted in *Zero: Countdown to Tomorrow, 1950s–60s*, exh. cat., Solomon R. Guggenheim Museum, New York (New York, 2014), p. 228.

4 An exhibition at the National Gallery, London, adopted the term 'monochrome' in order to explore the black or white characteristic of grisaille. But this use of the term seems to be far removed from how it is understood in relation to modern art, and caused several problems for the curators when they arrived at to the twentieth century. See Leila Packer and Jennifer Sliwka, eds, *Monochrome: Painting in Black and White*, exh. cat., National Gallery, London (London, 2017).

5 In fact, the 'squares' are not geometrically square – they are more like 'impressions' of squares. Since *White on White* entered the New York Museum of Modern Art's collection as long ago as 1935, it was an especially influential example of white monochromatic painting.

6 Heinz Mack writing in *Group Zero* magazine, 1958, quoted in Gladys Fabre, 'Monochromes of Light in Time and Space: Colour as Becoming', in *Monochromes: From Malevich to the Present*, ed. Barbara Rose (Berkeley and Los Angeles, CA, 2006), p. 106.

7 Willem de Kooning quoted in Mary Lynn Kotz, *Rauschenberg: Art and Life* (New York, 1990), p. 108.

8 In 1960 Klein had himself photographed heroically leaping from the second storey of a building and called it *Leap into the Void*. In fact, Klein was rather more cautious than it seems. A mattress was provided to break his fall and then artfully removed from the final image by his photographers Harry Shunk and János Kender.

9 Denys Riout, for example, describes the monochrome as a genre. See Denys Riout, *La Peinture monochrome: histoire et archéologie d'un genre*, revd edn (Paris, 2006). A stylistic reading of the monochrome is obviously redundant – the equivalent to categorizing a variety of objects simply because they share the same colour (which I will do anyway, for rhetorical ends, in Chapter Two).
10 On 'fantasy' in abstract art, approached from a psychoanalytical perspective, see Briony Fer, *On Abstract Art* (New Haven, CT, and London, 1997). For the 'authoritarian' dimensions of abstract art, see Mark A. Cheetham, *The Rhetoric of Purity: Essentialist Theory and the Advent of Abstract Painting* (Cambridge, 1994).
11 Barnett Newman, 'The Sublime Is Now' [1948], in *Barnet Newman: Selected Writings and Interviews*, ed. Paul O'Neill (Berkeley and Los Angeles, CA, 1990), p. 173.
12 Quoted in Brandon Joseph, *Random Order: Robert Rauschenberg and the Neo-Avant-garde* (Cambridge, MA, and London, 2003), p. 86.
13 'Questions to Stella and Judd by Bruce Glaser' [1966], excerpted in *Theories and Documents of Contemporary Art: A Sourcebook of Artists' Writings*, ed. Kristine Stiles and Peter Selz (Berkeley and Los Angeles, CA, 1996), p. 121.
14 Ibid., p. 118.
15 Donald Judd, 'Specific Objects', in *Donald Judd: Complete Writings, 1959–1975* (New York, 1975), p. 184.
16 Ellsworth Kelly, 'Notes of 1969', in *Theories and Documents*, ed. Stiles and Selz, p. 93.
17 Yves Klein, 'The Monochrome Adventure: The Monochrome Epic' [1960], in *Overcoming the Problematics of Art: The Writings of Yves Klein* (Putnam, CT, 2007), pp. 135–71.
18 Wassily Kandinsky, 'Reminiscences' [1913], quoted in Sixten Ringbom, 'Transcending the Visible: The Generation of the Abstract Pioneers', in *The Spiritual in Art: Abstract Painting, 1890–1985*, ed. Maurice Tuchman, exh. cat., Los Angeles County Museum of Art (Los Angeles, CA, 1986), p. 133.
19 Ibid.
20 Klein, 'The Monochrome Adventure', pp. 167–8.
21 Kirk Varnedoe, *Pictures of Nothing: Abstract Art since Pollock* (Princeton, NJ, and Oxford, 2006), p. 244.
22 Ibid.
23 Gilles Deleuze and Félix Guattari, *A Thousand Plateaus: Capitalism and Schizophrenia*, trans. Brian Massumi (Minneapolis, MN, 1987), p. 21.
24 Alva Noë, *Strange Tools: Art and Human Nature* (New York, 2016), p. 97.

25 Ibid., p. 206.
26 Mark Johnson, *The Meaning of the Body: Aesthetics of Human Understanding* (Chicago, IL, and London, 2007), p. 272.
27 See John Onians, *European Art: A Neuroarthistory* (New Haven, CT, and London, 2016), p. 324.
28 See Mark Johnson, *The Meaning of the Body*, and David Freedberg, 'Memory in Art: History and the Neuroscience of Art', in *The Memory Process: Neuroscience and Humanistic Perspectives*, ed. Suzanne Nalbantian, Paul M. Matthews and James L. McClelland (Cambridge, MA, and London, 2011), pp. 337–58.
29 Noë, *Strange Tools*, p. 137.
30 Onians, *European Art*, p. 15.
31 Park Seo-bo, interview with Robert Morgan, *Brooklyn Rail* (10 July 2006), at www.brooklynrail.org.
32 Ming Tiampo, *Gutai: Decentering Modernism* (Chicago, IL, and New York, 2011), p. 5.
33 See Sherry Turkle, *Life on the Screen: Identity in the Age of the Internet* (New York, 1997).
34 For a more recent works by Turkle see *Alone Together: Why We Expect More from Technology and Less from Each Other* (New York, 2012), and *Reclaiming Conversation: The Power of Talk in the Digital Age* (New York, 2016). From the growing number of books seeking to explore this new digital world, see, for example, Nicholas Carr, *The Shallows: What the Internet Is Doing to Our Brains* (New York, 2011); Tim Wu, *The Attention Merchants: The Epic Scramble to Get Inside Our Heads* (New York, 2016); Adam Gazzaley and Larry D. Rosen, *The Distracted Mind* (Boston, MA, and New York, 2016). The authors cite studies that report that, at the time of publication, U.S. adults and teenagers on average checked their phones up to 150 times a day, or every six to seven minutes that they are awake.

1 SETTING

1 Yves Klein, 'Overcoming the Problematics of Art', in *Overcoming the Problematics of Art: The Writings of Yves Klein*, ed. and trans. Klaus Ottmann (Putnam, CT, 2007), p. 58.
2 Robert Hirsch, *Seizing the Light: A Social History of Photography* (New York, 2008).
3 For a discussion of cave painting, see David Lewis-Williams, *The Mind in the Cave: Consciousness and the Origins of Art* (London and New York, 2009). For a discussion of the origins of languages in prehistory, see Steven Mithen, *The Singing Neanderthals: The Origins of Music, Language, Mind and*

Body (London, 2011). For the latest on the current consensus on the date of the earliest cave paintings, see Doyle Rice, 'Earliest Cave Paintings of Animal Discovered in Indonesia, Dating back 40,000 years', www.usatoday.com, 8 November 2018.

4 W.J.T. Mitchell, *Picture Theory* (Chicago, IL, and London, 1994), p. 220. I will be returning to this important point.

5 Benjamin H. D. Buchloh, 'Plenty of Nothing: From Yves Klein's *Le Vide* to Arman's *Le Plein*', in *Neo-Avantgarde and Culture Industry: Essays on European and American Art from 1955 to 1975* (Cambridge, MA, and London, 2000), p. 263.

6 This seems to be one of the conclusions come to by the author of the only book-length study of the history of the monochrome, Denys Riout, in his excellent *La Peinture monochrome: histoire et archéologie d'un genre*, revd edn (Paris, 2006), which has a central section of just 4 small colour images and 21 in black and white, few of which are actually of individual monochromes. Riout's argument is that since a monochrome is about the absence of the image, it is not necessarily necessary to see one. In fact, Riout claims that there is no real difference between what is inevitably lost in reproducing a monochrome as compared to a figurative painting. He notes that people claim that reproducing a coloured monochrome in black and white is nonsensical, but argues against this that they make the mistake of assuming that a monochrome is only interesting because of its colour. Referring to the white monochromes of Robert Ryman, Riout points out that a reproduction in black and white transmits a good deal of important information, and that a colour reproduction is anyway misleading because it can never correspond to the real colour. But Riout then concludes that since a monochrome is a work about the absence of an image, a photographic image of an image of absence will convey the work's important function (pp. 218–22).

2 RECEPTION

1 Ad Reinhardt, '[The Black-Square Paintings]' [1955], in *Art as Art: The Selected Writings of Ad Reinhardt*, ed. Barbara Rose (Berkeley and Los Angeles, CA, 1991), p. 83.

2 '"Black" Painting by Reinhard is Vandalized', *New York Times*, 17 November 1977, www.nytimes.com, accessed 4 April 2019.

3 For a discussion of attacks on the works of another artist featured in this book, Barnett Newman, see Dario Gamboni, *The Destruction of Art: Iconoclasm and Vandalism since the French Revolution* (London, 1997), pp. 206–11.

4 Reinhardt, '[The Black-Square Paintings]', p. 83.

5 Robert Rauschenberg, letter to Betty Parsons, postmarked 18 October 1951, reproduced in Walter Hopps, *Robert Rauschenberg: The Early 1950s* (Houston, TX, 1991), p. 230. Since Rauschenberg painted the first coat, repainters of the white surface have included the artists Brice Marden and Cy Twombly.
6 Susan Sontag, 'The Aesthetics of Silence' [1969], in *A Susan Sontag Reader* (London, 1982), p. 184.
7 Here I draw on and elaborate the discussion of the 'covenant' between art and audience in David Morgan, *The Sacred Gaze: Religious Visual Culture in Theory and Practice* (Berkeley and Los Angeles, CA, 2005), pp. 76–8.
8 Arthur Danto, 'The Historical Museum of Monochrome Art', in *After the End of Art: Contemporary Art and the Pale of History* (Princeton, NJ, 1997), p. 167. Danto stages an imaginary exhibition of red monochromes in his essay to prove the point. But the idea of batching monochromes by a shared colour is rather like batching representational paintings just because they show a nude woman, which as my imaginary exhibition of black monochromes shows is a pointless exercise. The book *Monochromes: From Malevich to the Present*, ed. Barbara Rose (Berkeley and Los Angeles, CA, 2006), tried this form of typology, perhaps not entirely successfully; Rose's essay, which provides an insightful overview, is a useful starting point for anyone interested in the monochrome.
9 Pierre Bourdieu, *Distinction: A Social Critique of the Judgment of Taste*, trans. Richard Nice (Cambridge, MA, 1984), p. 3.
10 Ibid., p. 2.
11 Ibid., p. 3.
12 W.J.T. Mitchell, '*Ut Pictura Theoria*: Abstract Painting and Language', in *Picture Theory: Essays on Verbal and Visual Representation* (Chicago, IL, and London, 1994), p. 226.
13 Kazimir Malevich, 'The World as Objectlessness' [1927], in *Kazimir Malevich: The World as Objectlessness*, ed. Simon Baier et al., exh. cat., Kunstmuseum Basel (Berlin, 2014), p. 188.
14 Quoted in Katherine Hardiman, 'Monochromes and Mandalas', http://shuffle.rauschenbergfoundation.org, accessed 20 September 2017.
15 Yves Klein, 'The Monochrome Adventure: The Monochrome Epic', in *Overcoming the Problematics of Art: The Writings of Yves Klein*, ed. and trans. Klaus Ottman (Putnam, CT, 2007), p. 81.
16 Clement Greenberg, 'Modernist Painting' [1960], in *Twentieth Century Theories of Art*, ed. James M. Thompson (Carleton, ON, 1990), p. 95.
17 Clement Greenberg, 'The Recentness of Sculpture' [1967], in *Minimal Art: A Critical Anthology*, ed. Gregory Battock (Berkeley and Los Angeles, CA, 1968), p. 181.

18 Michael Fried, 'Three Modernist Painters: Noland, Olitski, Stella' [1965], in Fried, *Art and Objecthood* (Chicago, IL, and London, 1996), p. 260.
19 Greenberg, 'The Recentness of Sculpture', p. 181.
20 Thierry de Duve, 'The Monochrome and the Blank Canvas', in *Reconstructing Modernism: Art in New York, Paris, and Montreal, 1945–1964*, ed. Serge Guilbaut (Cambridge, MA, and New York, 1992), p. 280; italics in the original.
21 Ibid., p. 247.
22 Benjamin H. D. Buchloh. 'Plenty or Nothing: From Yves Klein's *Le Vide* to Arman's *Le Plein*', in *Neo-Avantgarde and Culture Industry: Essays on European and American Art from 1955 to 1975* (Cambridge, MA, and London, 2000), p. 267.
23 Jeff Wall, 'Monochrome and Photojournalism: On Kawara's Today Paintings' [1993], in *Jeff Wall: Works and Collected Writings*, ed. Michael Newman and Jeff Wall (Barcelona, 2007), p. 329.
24 See Thomas B. Hess, *The Art Comics and Satires of Ad Reinhardt*, exh. cat., Kunsthalle Düsseldorf and Marlborough Gallery (Rome, 1975).
25 For a discussion of Reinhardt as cartoonist see Michael Corris, *Ad Reinhardt* (London, 2008), Chapter One.

3 COLOUR

1 Yves Klein, 'My Position in the Battle Between Line and Color' [1958], in *Overcoming the Problematics of Art: The Writings of Yves Klein*, ed. and trans. Klaus Ottmann (Putnam, CT, 2007), p. 19.
2 Ibid.
3 Ibid.
4 David Batchelor, *Chromophobia* (London, 2000). For more on the cultural meaning of colour see John Gage, *Colour and Culture* (London and New York, 1995).
5 Leon Batista Alberti, *On Painting* [1435], trans. Cecil Grayson (London, 1991), Book One, pp. 46–7.
6 Giorgio Vasari, *Lives of the Artists* [1550], trans. Julia Conaway Bondanella and Peter Bondanella (Oxford, 1991), Part Three. Vasari, it should be noted, was himself from Florence.
7 'Secreti per colori', fifteenth-century Bolognese manuscript, in *Medieval and Renaissance Treatises on the Arts of Painting* [1849], trans. Mary P. Merrifield (Mineola, NY, 1999), p. 406.
8 Jeremy Gilbert-Rolfe, *Beauty and the Contemporary Sublime* (New York, 1999), p. 31.
9 Yves Klein, 'Selections from *Dimanche*', in *Overcoming the Problematics of Art*, p. 123.

10 Claude Monet quoted in Philip Ball, *Bright Earth: The Invention of Colour* (New York and London, 2001), p. 189.
11 Vincent van Gogh, 'Letter to Theo, late October, 1885', in *The Letters of Vincent van Gogh*, ed. Mark Roskill (London, 1983), pp. 240–41.
12 Paul Signac, 'From Eugène Delacroix to Neo-Impressionism' [1899], in *Art in Theory, 1815–1900: An Anthology of Changing Ideas*, ed. Charles Harrison, Paul Wood and Jason Gaiger (Oxford, 1998), p. 983.
13 Maurice Denis, 'Definition of Neotraditionalism', in *Theories of Modern Art: A Source Book by Artists and Critics*, ed. Herschel B. Chipp (Berkeley and Los Angeles, CA, 1968), p. 94.
14 Henri Matisse, 'Notes of a Painter' [1908], in *Matisse on Art*, ed. Jack Flamm (Berkeley and Los Angeles, CA, 1995), p. 41.
15 Paul Gauguin, 'Notes Synthetiques' [*c*. 1888], in *Theories of Modern Art*, p. 61.
16 Manlio Brusatin, *A History of Colors* (Boston, MA, and New York, 1983), p. 9.
17 Alberti, *On Painting*, p. 45.
18 Ibid., p. 46.
19 One possible explanation for why Matisse painted his studio wall red in *The Red Studio* (1911, Museum of Modern Art, New York) is that he looked out of his window on to the greenery of his garden, and then at the white walls of the studio, and saw the complementary to green. In other words, colours modify each other.
20 Michel Pastoureau, *Blue: The History of a Color*, trans. Mark Cruse (Princeton, NJ, 2001), p. 7.
21 See Gage, *Colour and Culture* (1995). On conceptual paradigms obscuring or biasing the interpretation of empirical evidence in relation to the myth that the Inuit have thirty words for snow, see Piotr Cichocki and Martin Kilarski, 'On "Eskimo Words For Snow": The Life Cycle of a Linguistic Misconception', *Historiographia Linguistica*, XXXVII/3 (2010), pp. 341–77.
22 Pastoureau, *Blue*, pp. 22–3.
23 Ibid., pp. 23–7.
24 On the other hand, it was reported that the tribe had far more words for things described as 'green' than in Western languages, and when the researcher recreated the test by showing a subtle variation in green hue to Westerners, he found that they struggled just as much as the Himba had over blue, while the Himba participants in the test immediately saw the different green. Fiona MacDonald, 'Humans Didn't Even See the Colour Blue Until Modern Times, Research Suggests', www.sciencealert.com, 4 March 2015.
25 Johann Wolfgang von Goethe, *Theory of Colours*, trans. Charles Lock Eastlake (London, 1840), section 759, p. 305, www.gutenberg.org, accessed 1 May 2017.

26 For an interesting short survey of recent research on colour and expression in art see Cynthia A. Freeland, 'A New Question About Color', *Journal of Aesthetics and Art Criticism*, LXXV/3 (Summer 2017), pp. 231–48. For a book-length overview see Pamela Fraser, *How Color Works: Color Theory in the 21st Century* (New York, 2018).

4 GROUND

1 William Hazlitt, *The Collected Works of William Hazlitt*, ed. A. R. Waller and Arnold Glover (Frankfurt, 2018), p. 543.
2 Ibid.
3 Ibid., italics in the original.
4 Robert L. Solso, *Cognition and the Visual Arts* (Cambridge, MA, and London, 1996), p. 23.
5 Maurice Merleau-Ponty, *The Phenomenology of Perception* [1945], trans. Colin Smith (London, 1962), p. 78.
6 V. S. Ramachandran and William Hirstein, 'The Science of Art: A Neurological Theory of Aesthetic Experience', *Journal of Consciousness Studies*, VI/6–7 (1999), p. 23.
7 In the first half of the twentieth century the psychologist Edgar Rubin explored figure/ground assignment: see Edgar Rubin, 'Figure and Ground' [1915], in *Readings in Perception*, ed. David C. Beardslee and Michael Wertheimer (Princeton, NJ, 1958), pp. 194–203. The Gestalt psychologists Max Wertheimer, Wolfgang Köhler and Kurt Koffka built on Rubin's work, investigating what they saw as the organizing principles of perception. Gestalt psychology's insights have been variously confirmed, challenged and modified, but still remain essential to the understanding of the role of cognition in visual perception.
8 Paul Virilio, *Negative Horizon*, trans. Michael Degener (London and New York, 2005), p. 35.
9 Thomas Metzinger, *The Ego Tunnel: The Science of Mind and the Myth of the Self* (New York, 2009), p. 33.
10 For an interesting discussion of the haptic and modern art see Gilles Deleuze, *Francis Bacon: The Logic of Sensation*, trans. Daniel W. Smith (London, 2003), pp. 122ff.
11 'Visit to the Boulevard des Capucines Exhibition by Louis Leroy in Company of M. Joseph Vincent' [1874], in *Art in Theory, 1900–2000: An Anthology of Changing Ideas*, ed. Charles Harrison and Paul Wood (Oxford, 2000), p. 574.
12 Wassily Kandinsky, 'Reminiscences, 1913', in *Kandinsky: Complete Writings on Art*, vol. I: *1901–1921*, ed. Kenneth Lindsay and Peter Vergo (London, 1982), p. 363.

13 James Elkins, *On Pictures and the Words that Fail Them* (Cambridge, 1998), p. 104.
14 Kazimir Malevich, 'Non-Objective Art and Suprematism' [1919], in *Art in Theory*, ed. Harrison and Wood, p. 292.
15 Alexander Rodchenko, 'Working with Mayakovsky' [1921], in *From Painting to Design: Russian Constructivist Art of the 1920s*, exh. cat., Galerie Gmurzynska, Cologne (Cologne, 1981), p. 191, italics in the original.

5 SPIRITUAL

1 Plotinus, *Enneads*, quoted in Sixten Ringbom, 'Transcending the Visible: The Generation of the Abstract Pioneers', in *The Spiritual in Art: Abstract Painting, 1890–1985*, ed. Maurice Tuchman, exh. cat., Los Angeles County Museum of Art (Los Angeles, CA, 1987), p. 132.
2 Robert Rosenblum, *Modern Painting and the Northern Romantic Tradition: Friedrich to Rothko* (New York, 1975).
3 The original German title of Kandinsky's text is *Über das Geistige in der Kunst*; it is worth noting that in German the word *Geist* means 'spirit' but also 'mind', 'intellect' and 'imagination'.
4 Thomas McEvilley, 'Seeking the Primal in Paint: The Monochrome Icon', in Thomas McEvilley and G. Roger Denson, *Capacity: History, the World, and the Self in Contemporary Art and Criticism* (Amsterdam, 1996), p. 82.
5 Aldous Huxley, *The Perennial Philosophy* (London, 1950), p. 29.
6 Francis MacDonald Cornford, trans., *Plato's Cosmology: The 'Timaeus' of Plato Translated with a Running Commentary* (New York, 1937), 48E–51B.
7 Robert Lawlor, *Sacred Geometry: Philosophy and Practice* (London, 1982), pp. 7–8.
8 Plotinus, *Enneads*, quoted in Ringbom, 'Transcending the Visible', p. 132.
9 Richard Temple, *Icons and the Mystical Origins of Christianity* (Shaftsbury, Dorset, 1990), pp. 33–4.
10 St John of the Cross, *Ascent of Mount Carmel* [1578–9], quoted in *Three Mystics: El Greco, St John of the Cross, St Teresa of Avila*, ed. Father Bruno de J. M. (London, 1952), p. 132.
11 Fludd's book is called *Utriusque cosmi, maioris scilicet et minoris, metaphysica, physica, atque technica historia* (The Metaphysical, Physical and Technical History of the Two Worlds, Namely the Greater and the Lesser) and was published in 1617; the etching was by Johann Theodor de Bry. See Riout Denys, *La Peinture monochrome: histoire et archéologie d'un genre*, revd edn (Paris, 2006), p. 413. There is no evidence that Malevich actually knew of this particular print.

12 Quoted in Linda Dalrymple-Henderson, *The Fourth Dimension and Non-Euclidian Geometry in Modern Art*, revd edn (Boston, MA, and New York, 2013), p. 383.
13 See A. Besant and C. W. Leadbeater, *Thought Forms: A Record of Clairvoyant Investigation* (London, 1901). For a discussion of theosophical colour theory and art see Sixten Ringbom, 'Transcending the Visible: The Generation of the Abstract Pioneers,' in *The Spiritual in Art: Abstract Painting, 1890–1985*, ed. Tuchman, pp. 131–53.
14 C. G. Jung, *Mandala Symbolism*, trans. R.F.C. Hull (Princeton, NJ, 1972), and *Psychology and Alchemy*, trans. R.F.C. Hull (Princeton, NJ, 1980).
15 See John Milner, *Kazimir Malevich and the Art of Geometry* (Cambridge, MA, and London, 1996).
16 Maria Taroutina, 'Introduction: Byzantium and Modernism', in *Byzantium/Modernism: The Byzantine as Method in Modernism*, ed. Roland Betancourt and Maria Taroutina (Leiden, 2015), p. 6.
17 Moshe Barasch, *Icon: Studies in the History of an Idea* (New York, 1992), p. 7.
18 Ibid.
19 Taroutina, 'Introduction: Byzantium and Modernism', p. 6.
20 Rainer Crone and David Moos, *Kazimir Malevich: The Climax of Disclosure* (London, 2014), pp. 165–6.
21 Wassily Kandinsky, *Concerning the Spiritual in Art* [1911], trans. M.T.H. Sadler (New York, 1977), p. 49.
22 Ibid., p. 48.
23 Ibid., p. 24; italics in the original.
24 Ibid.
25 Kazimir Malevich, 'The World as Objectlessness' [1927], in *Kazimir Malevich: The World as Objectlessness*, ed. Simon Baier and Britta Dümpelmann, exh. cat., Kunstmuseum Basel (Ostfildern, 2014).
26 Ibid., p. 187.
27 Ibid., p. 188.
28 Ibid., p. 187.
29 Ibid., p. 191.
30 Ibid., p. 188.
31 Ibid., p. 191.
32 Kazimir Malevich quoted in Britta Tanja Dümpelmann, 'The World as Objectless: A Snapshot of an Artistic Universe', in *Kazimir Malevich*, ed. Baier and Dümpelmann, p. 27. See also Myroslava M. Mudrak, 'Kazimir Malevich and the Liturgical Tradition of Eastern Christianity', in *Byzantium/Modernism*, ed. Betancourt and Taroutina, pp. 37–72.
33 Myroslava M. Mudrak, 'Kazimir Malevich, Symbolism, and Ecclesiastic Orthodoxy', in *Modernism and the Spiritual in Russian Art: New Perspectives*,

ed. Louise Hardiman and Nicola Kozicharow (Cambridge, 2017), p. 111.
34 Ibid., p. 96.

6 INDEFINABLE

1 Yves Klein, 'The Monochrome Adventure', in *Overcoming the Problematics of Art: The Writings of Yves Klein*, ed. and trans. Klaus Ottmann (Putnam, CT, 2007), p. 139.
2 Ibid., p. 141.
3 As Thomas McEvilley put it: 'As unmodulated colour = space = Sky = infinity = cosmic sensitivity = omnipresent mind = the absolute = the immeasurable all, so, in a negative and "disquieting" equation, line = obstruction = world = limitation = insensitivity = neurotic personality = the relative = the measurable finite particular.' Thomas McEvilley, 'Seeking the Primal through Paint: The Monochrome Icon', in Thomas McEvilley and G. Roger Denson, *Capacity: History, the World, and the Self in Contemporary Art and Criticism* (Amsterdam, 1996), p. 62.
4 Klein, 'The Monochrome Adventure', p. 138.
5 James Elkins, *On Pictures and the Words that Fail Them* (Cambridge, 1998), p. 43.
6 Ibid., p. 44.
7 Dario Gamboni, *Potential Images: Ambiguity and Indeterminacy in Modern Art* (London, 2002), p. 29.
8 Mieke Bal, *Quoting Caravaggio: Contemporary Art, Preposterous History* (Chicago, IL, and London, 1999), p. 27.
9 John Willats, 'The Rules of Representation', in *A Companion to Art Theory*, ed. Paul Smith and Carolyn Wilde (Oxford, 2002), p. 415.
10 Hubert Damisch, *A Theory of /Cloud/: Toward a History of Painting*, trans. Janet Lloyd (Stanford, CA, 2002), p. 145.
11 François Jullien, *The Great Image Has No Form; or, On the Nonobject through Painting*, trans. Jane Marie Todd (Chicago, IL, and London, 2009), pp. 124–5.
12 Odilon Redon, *À soi-même: journal (1867–1915)* [1922], in *Art in Theory, 1900–2000: An Anthology of Changing Ideas* (Oxford, 2000), ed. Charles Harrison and Paul Wood, p. 1065.
13 Odilon Redon, 'Suggestive Art' [1909], in *Theories of Modern Art: A Source Book by Artists and Critics*, ed. Herschel B. Chipp (Berkeley and Los Angeles, CA, 1968), p. 117.
14 Wassily Kandinsky, *Complete Writing on Art*, vol. I: *1901–1921*, ed. Kenneth C. Lindsay and Peter Vergo (London, 1992), pp. 369–70.

15 Eugène Delacroix, *The Journal of Eugène Delacroix*, trans. Walter Pach (New York, 1937), p. 711.
16 Klein, 'The Monochrome Adventure', p. 139.
17 Gaston Bachelard, *Air and Dreams: An Essay on the Imagination of Movement* [1943], trans. Edith F. Farrell and C. Frederick Farrell (Dallas, TX, 1988), p. 1, italics in the original.
18 Ibid.
19 Quoted ibid., p. 157. The quote is from Bachelard's *Air and Dreams*; in the Farrells' (slightly different) translation of the text (Dallas, TX, 1988), the quotation is on p. 161.
20 Gaston Bachelard, *Air and Dreams: An Essay on the Imagination of Movement* [1943], trans. Edith R. Farrell and C. Frederick Farrell (Dallas, TX, 1988), p. 163, italics in the original.
21 Klein, 'Truth Becomes Reality', in *Overcoming the Problematics of Art*, p. 181.
22 Thomas McEvilley, 'Yves Klein: Conquistador of the Void', in *Yves Klein, 1928–1962: A Retrospective*, ed. Domique Bozo et al., exh. cat., Rice Museum, Houston (Houston, TX, 1982), p. 28.
23 Klein, 'The Monochrome Adventure', p. 143.
24 Klein, 'Overcoming the Problematics of Art', in *Overcoming the Problematics of Art*, p. 58.
25 Klein, 'The Monochrome Adventure', pp. 142, 143.
26 Klein, 'Chelsea Hotel Manifesto, New York, 1961', in *Overcoming the Problematics of Art*, p. 197.
27 Klein, 'Lecture at the Sorbonne', in *Overcoming the Problematics of Art*, p. 75.
28 As Thomas McEvilley explains: 'Of two visually identical paintings, one possessing this substance is art, and the other, lacking it, is not. A sensitive viewer can distinguish it at once.' McEvilley, 'Yves Klein: Conquistador of the Void', in *Yves Klein, 1928–1962*, ed. Bozo et al., p. 46.
29 Klein, 'Truth Becomes Reality', p. 189.
30 Rosicrucianism originated in the early seventeenth century but got a new lease of life when the Rosicrucian Order was founded in the early twentieth century as part of the same general quest for a new religiosity that saw the birth of philosophical systems such as Theosophy and Anthroposophy. Klein was especially influenced by Max Heindel's book *The Rosicrucian Cosmo-conception; or, Mystic Christianity: An Elementary Treatise upon Man's Past Evolution, Present Constitution and Future Development* (1909). See McEvilley, 'Yves Klein: Conquistador of the Void', p. 26.
31 Yves Klein, *The Foundations of Judo* [1954], trans. Ian Whittlesea (London, 2010).
32 Anish Kapoor quoted in Martin Caiger-Smith, *Yves Klein Now: Sixteen Views*, exh. cat., Hayward Gallery, London (London, 1995), n.p.

33 Klein, 'The Monochrome Adventure', p. 162, capitals in the original.
34 McEvilley, 'Seeking the Primal through Paint', p. 65.
35 Quoted in Enrico Crispolti, *Lucio Fontana: Paintings, Sculptures and Drawings*, exh. cat., Skira (Milan, 2005), p. 27.
36 Yve-Alain Bois, 'Klein's Relevance Today', *October*, 119 (Winter 2007), p. 90.
37 Piero Manzoni, 'Free Dimension', *Azimuth*, 2 (January 1960), reprinted in Valerie Hillings et al., *Zero: Countdown to Tomorrow, 1950s–60s*, exh. cat., Guggenheim, New York (New York, 2014), p. 229.
38 Quoted in Germano Celant et al., *Piero Manzoni*, exh. cat., Serpentine Gallery, London (London, 1998), p. 55.
39 Manzoni, 'Free Dimension', p. 229.
40 Klein, 'The Monochrome Adventure', pp. 152–3.
41 For example ibid., p. 141.

7 NOTHINGNESS

1 Arthur Danto, 'Ad Reinhardt', in Danto, *Embodied Meanings: Critical Essays and Aesthetic Meditations* (New York, 1994), p. 206.
2 Rudolf Arnheim, *Visual Thinking* (Berkeley and Los Angeles, CA, 1969), p. 89.
3 The term derives from the work of the influential theologian Rudolf Otto: see *The Idea of the Holy* [1911], trans. John W. Harvey (Oxford, 1958).
4 Dario Gamboni, *The Destruction of Art: Iconoclasm and Vandalism since the French Revolution* (London, 1997), p. 29.
5 Friedrich quoted in Johannes Grave, *Caspar David Friedrich*, trans. Fiona Elliott (New York, 2012), p. 203.
6 Friedrich Nietzsche, 'Towards a Genealogy of Morals' [1887], in *The Portable Nietzsche*, ed. Walter Kaufmann (New York, 1968), p. 454, italics in the original.
7 George Steiner, *George Steiner: A Reader* (Harmondsworth, 1984), p. 11.
8 Theodor Adorno, *Negative Dialectics*, trans. E. B. Ashton (New York, 1973), p. 365.
9 Walter Benjamin, 'The Work of Art in the Age of Mechanical Reproduction' [1935], in *Illuminations*, ed. Hannah Arendt, trans. Harry Zorn (New York, 1969). It should be noted that Benjamin was writing from a Marxist perspective, and his intention was to welcome the severing of art from ritual and its transformation into a form of political praxis.
10 Ad Reinhardt, '[The Black-Square Paintings]' [1955], in 'Autocritique de Reinhardt', newsletter of his Parisian dealer Iris Clert, 1963, reprinted in *Art as Art: The Selected Writings of Ad Reinhardt*, ed. Barbara Rose (Berkeley and Los Angeles, CA, 1991), p. 82, italics in the original.

11 Danto, 'Ad Reinhardt', p. 206.
12 Quoted ibid., p. 208. See Heidegger, 'What is Metaphysics?' [1929], ed. and trans. William McNeil (Cambridge, 1998).
13 Martin Heidegger, 'The Origin of the Work of Art' [1935–6], in *Poetry, Language, Thought*, trans. Albert Hofstadter (New York, 1971), p. 33.
14 Merton quoted in Martin E. Marty, 'Thomas Merton', in *Negotiating Rapture: The Power of Art to Transform Lives*, ed. Richard Francis, exh. cat., Museum of Contemporary Art, Chicago (Chicago, IL, 1996), p. 88. See also Yau John, 'Ad Reinhardt and the Via Negativa', *Brooklyn Rail: Special Edition on Ad Reinhardt*, https://brooklynrail.org (January 2014).
15 Ad Reinhardt, '[Oneness]', unpublished, undated note, in *Art as Art: The Selected Writings of Ad Reinhardt*, ed. Barbara Rose (Berkeley and Los Angeles, CA, 1991), p. 105.
16 Mark Rothko, 'The Romantics Were Prompted' [1947], in *Writings on Art*, ed. Miguel López-Ramiro (New Haven, CT, and London, 2006), p. 59.
17 Mark Rothko, letter of 25 September 1954, cited in David Anfam, *Mark Rothko: The Works on Canvas, Catalogue Raisonné* (New Haven, CT, and Washington, DC, 1998), p. 75.
18 Robert Motherwell, '28 January 1971', in *The Collected Writings of Robert Motherwell*, ed. Stephanie Terenzio (Oxford, 1992), p. 198.
19 Edmund Burke, *A Philosophical Enquiry into the Origin of our Ideas of the Sublime and Beautiful* [1757], ed. Adam Phillips (Oxford and New York, 1990), p. 128.
20 Immanuel Kant, *Critique of Judgement* [1790], trans. James Creed (Oxford and New York, 1973), p. 106.
21 Robert Rosenblum, *Modern Painting and the Northern Romantic Tradition: Friedrich to Rothko* (New York, 1975), p. 202.
22 Robert Rosenblum, 'The Abstract Sublime' [1960], in *Reading Abstract Expressionism: Contexts and Critique*, ed. Ellen G. Landau (New Haven, CT, and London, 2003), pp. 273–8.
23 Rosenblum, *Modern Painting*, pp. 213–14.
24 The *Seagram Murals* were originally intended to fulfil a commission for an exclusive restaurant in New York. Rather disingenuously, Rothko is on record as saying he hoped the paintings would discomfort the rich swells who ate there. But in the end, Rothko refused to complete the commission and returned the money, although not before producing a large number of paintings. A suite of the *Seagram Murals* is permanently installed at Tate Modern, London, while another is in Japan at the Kawamura Memorial Museum of Art.
25 Leo Bersani and Ulysse Dutoit, *Arts of Impoverishment: Beckett, Rothko, Resnais* (Cambridge, MA, 1993), p. 142.
26 Ibid., p. 144.

27 Sigmund Freud, *Civilization and Its Discontents* [1930], in *The Standard Edition of the Complete Psychological Works of Sigmund Freud*, ed. James Strachey (London, 1967), vol. XXI, p. 68.
28 Ibid.
29 Julia Kristeva, *Desire in Language: A Semiotic Approach to Language and Art*, ed. Leon S. Roudiez, trans. Thomas Gora and Alice A. Jardine (New York, 1980), p. 162.
30 Ibid.
31 Ibid., p. 247.
32 Bersani and Dutoit, *Arts of Impoverishment*, p. 144.

8 EXPERIENTIAL

1 Agnes Martin, *Writings*, ed. Dieter Schwarz (Ostfildern, 1998), p. 36.
2 Barnett Newman, 'Ohio, 1949', in *Barnett Newman: Selected Writings and Interviews*, ed. Paul O'Neill (Berkeley and Los Angeles, CA, 1990), p. 174.
3 Ibid.
4 Newman's work, like Reinhardt's, has also suffered at the hands of vandals. As the Stedelijk Museum's website wrote on the occasion of their Newman exhibition in 2014: 'In 1986, allegedly distressed by the work's abstract nature, a confused man slashed with a box cutter *Who's Afraid of Red, Yellow and Blue III*, installed in its gallery of honor at the Stedelijk Museum. It was not the first time a Newman work was vandalized. In 1982, for similar reasons, a student attacked *Who's Afraid of Red, Yellow and Blue IV* in the National Gallery of Berlin. Nine years later, the man who had damaged *Who's Afraid of Red, Yellow and Blue III* returned to inflict five long knife cuts on Newman's *Cathedra*.' www.stedelijk.nl/en/exhibitions/63824, accessed 30 August 2018.
5 See Franz Meyer, *Barnett Newman: The Stations of the Cross: Lema Sabachthani* (Düsseldorf, 2004).
6 'Interview with David Sylvester', in *Barnett Newman*, ed. O'Neill, pp. 257–8.
7 Rosalind Krauss, 'Overcoming the Limits of Matter: On Revising Minimalism', in *American Art of the 1960s*, ed. James Leggio, John Elderfield and Susan Weiley (New York, 1991), p. 123.
8 The neurobiologist Margaret Livingstone suggests that something similar happens when one views the *Mona Lisa*. Leonardo deliberately utilized a peripheral optical effect that simulates less focused vision, in order to render the sitter's expression more elusive. The stochastic quality created by Leonardo means that the *Mona Lisa* appears to be smiling only when the viewer perceives her using their peripheral vision; as soon as they look directly at her mouth the famous smile becomes less pronounced.

In other words, Leonardo did not simply employ *sfumato* to blur his subject's mouth in order to make it ambiguous in all viewing conditions, but rather consciously generated a transitory effect that incorporated the animated, subjective vision of the viewer. Margaret S. Livingstone, 'Is it Warm? Is it Real? Or Just Low Spatial Frequency?', *Science*, CCXC/5495 (November 2000), p. 1299. Livingstone develops her argument in *Vision and Art: The Biology of Seeing* (New York, 2008), pp. 68–73.

9 Robert Motherwell, '28 January 1971', in *The Collected Writings of Robert Motherwell*, ed. Stephanie Terenzio (Oxford, 1992), p. 198.

10 Martin, *Writings*, p. 36.

11 Ibid., p. 96, italics in the original.

9 ZEN

1 Nāgārjuna, *Mūlamadhyamakakārikā*, quoted in Stephen Batchelor, *Verses from the Center: A Buddhist Vision of the Sublime*, trans. Stephen Batchelor (New York, 2000), p. 124. Nāgārjuna was a philosopher and monk from southern India who probably lived around the second century CE. His writings form the basis for the Madhyamaka school, or the school of the Middle Way. Nāgārjuna sought to overcome nihilism through the embrace rather than denial of emptiness.

2 Lao Tsu (Laozi), founder of Taoism and reputed author of the *Tao Te Ching*, *fl.* sixth century BCE; Hui Neng (Nuineng), sixth patriarch of Chan Buddhism, *fl.* seventh century CE; Chuang Tsu (Zhuang Zhou), author of the Taoist text *Zhuangzi*, *fl.* fourth century BCE. Quoted in Jacquelynn Baas, 'Agnes Martin: Readings for Writings', in *Agnes Martin*, ed. Frances Morris and Tiffany Bell, exh. cat., Tate Modern, London (London, 2015), p. 232.

3 Agnes Martin, *Writings*, ed. Dieter Schwarz (Ostfildern, 1998), p. 71.

4 Ibid., p. 39.

5 Thomas Merton quoted in Martin E. Marty, 'Thomas Merton', in *Negotiating Rapture: The Power of Art to Transform Lives*, ed. Richard Francis, exh. cat., Museum of Contemporary Art, Chicago (Chicago, IL, 1996), p. 91.

6 Ad Reinhardt in Barbara Rose, ed., *Art as Art: The Selected Writings of Ad Reinhardt* (Berkeley and Los Angeles, CA, 1991), p. 189. In 1957 Reinhardt drew a cartoon entitled 'A Portend of the Artist as a Yhung Mandala', an affectionate pun and satire on the research of the psychologist Carl Jung into mandalas. See Thomas B. Hess, *The Art Comics and Satires of Ad Reinhardt*, exh. cat., Kunsthalle Düsseldorf and Marlborough Gallery, Rome (Rome, 1975).

7 Reinhardt, 'One', unpublished, undated note in *Art as Art: The Selected Writings of Ad Reinhardt*, ed. Barbara Rose (Berkeley and Los Angeles, CA, 1991), p. 93.

8 See Walter Smith, 'Ad Reinhardt's Oriental Aesthetic', *Smithsonian Studies in American Art*, IV/3–4 (Summer–Autumn 1990), p. 26.
9 See Jacquelynn Baas and Mary Jane Jacob, *Buddha Mind in Contemporary Art* (Berkeley and Los Angeles, CA, 2004); Jacquelynn Baas, *Smile of the Buddha: Eastern Philosophy and Western Art from Monet to Today* (Berkeley and Los Angeles, CA, 2005); Helen Westgeest, *Zen in the Fifties: Interactions in Art between East and West* (Amstelveen, 1996).
10 Keiji Nishitani, *The Self-overcoming of Nihilism* [1949], trans. Graham Parkes with Setsuko Aihara (Albany, NY, 1990), pp. 190–91.
11 D. T. Suzuki, *An Introduction to Zen Buddhism* (New York, 1964), p. 74.
12 Ibid., p. 88.
13 Ibid., p. 75.
14 Arthur Versluis, *American Gurus: From Transcendentalism to New Age Religion* (Oxford, 2014), p. 2.
15 Helmut Brinker, *Zen in the Art of Painting*, trans. George Campbell (London and New York, 1987), p. 21.
16 See Andrew Juniper, *Wabi-Sabi: The Japanese Art of Impermanence* (New York, 2011).
17 For a recent assessment of Tobey see Debra Bricker Balken, ed., *Mark Tobey: Threading Light*, exh. cat., Addison Gallery of American Art, Andover, MA (Andover, MA, 2017).
18 Thomas McEvilley, 'Seeking the Primal in Paint: The Monochrome Icon', in *Capacity: History, the World, and the Self in Contemporary Art and Criticism*, ed. G. Roger Denson (Amsterdam, 1996), p. 84.
19 The Ox-herding pictures were discussed in Suzuki's influential *The Manual of Zen Buddhism* (1934).
20 John Cage, 'Autobiographical Statement' [1990], http://johncage.org, accessed 15 August 2018.
21 John Cage, 'On Robert Rauschenberg, Artist, and his Work' [1962], in *Silence: Lectures and Writing* (Middletown, CT, 1973), p. 102.
22 Quoted in David W. Paterson, 'Cage and Asia, History and Sources', in *The Cambridge Companion to John Cage*, ed. David Nicholls (Cambridge, 2011), p. 97. Paterson notes (pp. 97–8): 'The terminology . . . may seem commonplace at first, yet its similarities to passages found in some of the most commonly read Buddhist literature – while falling short of providing a verifiable textual connection – are rich with innuendo.'
23 Cage, 'On Robert Rauschenberg, Artist, and his Work', p. 105.
24 Yves Klein, 'Lecture at the Sorbonne' [1959], in *Overcoming the Problematics of Art: The Writings of Yves Klein*, ed. and trans. Klaus Ottmann (Putnam, CT, 2007), p. 75.
25 Ibid., p. 83.

26 William C. Seitz, *Mark Tobey*, exh. cat., Museum of Modern Art, New York (New York, 1962), p. 14, www.moma.org, accessed 16 June 2018.
27 Martin, *Writings*, p. 37.
28 See Martha C. Nussbaum, *The Therapy of Desire: Theory and Practice of Hellenistic Ethics* (Princeton, NJ, 1996).
29 Martin, *Writings*, p. 44.
30 I am drawing here on David Wong, 'The Meaning of Detachment in Daoism, Buddhism, and Stoicism', *Dao: A Journal of Comparative Philosophy*, V/2 (June 2006), pp. 207–19. I elaborate on this point in relation to Agnes Martin in Simon Morley, '"Free and Easy Wandering": Agnes Martin and the Limits of Intercultural Dialogue', *World Art*, VI/2 (2016), pp. 247–68.
31 Yves Klein, 'Truth Becomes Reality', in *Overcoming the Problematics of Art*, p. 183.
32 See Shiyan Li, *Le Vide dans l'art du xxe siècle: Occident/Extrême-Orient* (Marseille, 2014), p. 114.
33 See Alexandra Munroe, Ming Tiampo and Yoshihara Jiro, *Gutai: Splendid Playground*, exh. cat., Solomon R. Guggenheim Museum, New York (New York, 2013); Ming Tiampo, *Gutai: Decentering Modernism* (Chicago, IL, and London, 2011).
34 See Paweł Pachciarek, 'Kusama Yayoi in the Context of Eastern and Western Thought', *Journal of Asian Humanities of Kyushu University*, 2 (2017), pp. 1–14.
35 Yayoi Kusama, *Infinity Net: The Autobiography of Yayoi Kusama*, trans. Ralph McCarthy (London, 2011), p. 23. See Akira Tatehata et al., *Yayoi Kusama* (London, 2017). Kusama would return to making *Infinity Net* paintings in the 2010s; see Yayoi Kusama, *White Infinity Nets*, exh. cat., Victoria Miro Gallery, London (London, 2013).

10 MATERIAL

1 Frank Stella and Donald Judd, 'Questions to Stella and Judd by Bruce Glaser' [1966], in *Theories and Documents of Contemporary Art: A Sourcebook of Artists' Writings*, ed. Kristine Stiles and Peter Selz (Berkeley and Los Angeles, CA, 1996), p. 121.
2 Ibid.
3 Alexei Gann, 'Constructivism' [1922], quoted in Boris Groys, *In the Flow* (London, 2016), pp. 68–9.
4 Alexander Rodchenko and Varvara Stepanova, 'Programme of the First Working Group of Constructivists', in *Art in Theory, 1900–1990: An Anthology of Changing Ideas*, ed. Charles Harrison and Paul Wood (Oxford, 1992), p. 317.
5 Rodchenko, '"Slogans" and "Organizational Programme" of the Workshop for the Study of painting in State Art Colleges', in *Art in Theory, 1900–1990*, ed. Harrison and Wood, p. 315.

6 Yve-Alain Bois, 'Strzemiński and Kobro: In Search of Motivation', in Bois, *Painting as Model* (Cambridge, MA, and London, 1990), p. 136. Bois is quoting from Strzemiński's 'Unism in Painting', 1928.
7 Strzemiński, 'What Can Legitimately Be Called New Art' [1924], quoted ibid., p. 136.
8 Strzemiński, 'Statements' [1932 and 1933], in *Art in Theory*, ed. Harrison and Wood, p. 360; the absence of capital letters follows the original.
9 Bois, 'Strzemiński and Kobro', p. 137.
10 See Rosalind Krauss, 'Grids', in *The Originality of the Avant-garde and Other Modernist Myths* (Cambridge, MA, and New York, 1986), pp. 8–22.
11 Published in *Art Concret* (April 1930), reprinted in *The Tradition of Constructivism*, ed. Stephen Bann (London, 1974), p. 193.
12 Max Bill, 'Concrete Art' [1936–49], in *Theories and Documents of Contemporary Art*, ed. Stiles and Selz, p. 74.
13 Ellsworth Kelly, 'Notes of 1969', in *Theories and Documents of Contemporary Art*, ed. Stiles and Selz, p. 93.
14 Ibid., pp. 92–3.
15 Frank Stella, 'Pratt Institute Lecture' [1960], in Robert Rosenblum, *Frank Stella* (New York, 1971), p. 5.
16 Stella and Judd, 'Questions to Stella and Judd by Bruce Glaser', p. 121.
17 Ibid.
18 Carl Andre, 'Preface to Stripe Painting', quoted in Thierry de Duve, 'The Monochrome and the Blank Canvas', in *Reconstructing Modernism: Art in New York, Paris, and Montreal, 1945–1964*, ed. Serge Guilbaut (Cambridge, MA, and London, 1992), p. 244.
19 Rosalind Krauss, 'Overcoming the Limits of Matter: On Revising Minimalism', in *American Art of the 1960s*, ed. James Leggio, John Elderfield and Susan Weiley (New York, 1991), p. 125.
20 Robert Ryman, 'On Painting' [1991], quoted in Robert Storr, 'Simple Gifts', in Storr, *Robert Ryman*, exh. cat., Tate Gallery, London (London, 1993), p. 32.
21 Bois, *Painting as Model*, p. 224.
22 Ryman quoted in Storr, *Robert Ryman*, p. 118.
23 Brice Marden, 'Notes' [1971], in *Theories and Documents of Contemporary Art*, ed. Stiles and Selz, p. 138.
24 Jasper Johns also explored the monochrome in the mid-1950s, making white versions of the American flag, and of rows of numbers. White played a similar role for Johns as it did for Ryman, shifting attention away from the familiarity of the image to the way in which the work was made.
25 Quoted in Richard Schiff, 'Autonomy, Actuality, Mangold', in *Robert Mangold* (London and New York, 2000), p. 31.
26 Ibid., p. 29.

27 See Thierry de Duve, 'The Monochrome and the Blank Canvas', p. 285.

28 I draw here James Elkins's 'Writing about Modernist Painting Outside Western Europe and North America', in *Compression vs. Expression: Containing and Explaining the World's Art*, ed. John Onians (Williamstown, MA, 2006), pp. 188–214.

29 Ming Tiampo, *Gutai: Decentering Modernism* (Chicago, IL, and London, 2011), p. 4. Tiampo here borrows the literary critic and academic Harold Bloom's concept of 'misreading' as expounded in his *The Anxiety of Influence: A Theory of Poetry* (Oxford, 1973) and *A Map of Misreading* (Oxford, 1975).

30 Shoichi Hirai, 'Gutai and its Internationalism', in *Destroy the Picture: Painting the Void, 1949–1962*, ed. Paul Schimmel, exh. cat., Museum of Contemporary Art, Los Angeles (New York, 2012), pp. 204–11; Rosemary O'Neill, *Art and Visual Culture on the French Riviera* (London and New York, 2012), p. 168.

31 See Stephen Bann, ed., *The Tradition of Constructivism* (London and New York, 1974), p. 194.

32 Lucio Fontana, 'The White Manifesto' [1946], in *Art in Theory: 1900–1990*, ed. Harrison and Wood, p. 647.

33 Olivier Berggruen, 'The Realm of Pure Sensations', in *Playing with Form: Neoconcrete Art from Brazil*, ed. Olivier Berggruen, exh. cat., Dickinson, New York (New York, 2011), p. 20.

34 Ibid.

35 Reprinted in Mari Carmen Ramírez, ed., *Hélio Oiticica: The Body of Colour*, exh. cat., Tate Modern, London (London, 2007), p. 247.

36 Mari Carmen Ramírez, 'Hélio's Double-edged Challenge', ibid., p. 18.

37 Lygia Clark, 'The Death of the Plane' [1960], quoted in *Cold American: Geometric Abstraction in Latin America, 1934–1973*, exh. cat., Fundación Juan March, Madrid (Madrid, 2011), p. 444.

38 See Irene V. Small, *Hélio Oiticica: Folding the Frame* (Chicago, IL, and London, 2016), p. 1.

39 Yve-Alain Bois, 'From Arte Concreta to Arte Neoconcreta', in *Playing with Form*, ed. Olivier Berggruen, p. 16.

40 This was the original intention, at least – now its status as a valuable museum piece means we can only admire it from the perimeter.

41 Hélio Oiticica, 'Colour, Time, and Structure' [1960], in *Hélio Oiticica*, ed. Ramírez, p. 206.

42 Hélio Oiticica, 'The Transition of Colour from the Painting into Space and the Meaning of Construction' [1960], in *Hélio Oiticica*, ed. Ramírez, p. 222.

11 FORMAT

1 Donald Judd, 'Specific Objects' [Arts Yearbook 8, 1965], in *Donald Judd: Complete Writings, 1959–1975* (Halifax, NS, and New York, 1975), pp. 181–2.
2 Donald Judd, 'Specific Objects' [1960], in *Donald Judd: Complete Writings, 1959–1975* (Halifax, NS, 1975), pp. 181–2.
3 Ibid., p. 184.
4 Ibid.
5 See Jeremy Lewison, *Ben Nicholson* (London, 1991), pp. 16–17.
6 Otto Piene, 'Paths to Paradise' [1961], in *Zero: Countdown to Tomorrow, 1950s–60s*, exh. cat., Solomon R. Guggenheim Museum, New York (New York, 2014), p. 231.
7 Ibid., p. 232.
8 Carter Ratcliff, 'Ellsworth Kelly's Curves', in *Ellsworth Kelly: A Retrospective*, ed. Diane Waldman, exh. cat., Museum of Modern Art, New York (New York, 1997), p. 59.
9 Donald Judd, 'Local History' [Arts Yearbook 7, 1964], in *Donald Judd: Complete Writings*, pp. 153–6.
10 Judd, 'Specific Objects', p. 184.
11 Dan Flavin, 'Some Remarks . . . Excerpts for a Spleenish Journal' [1966], in *Theories and Documents of Contemporary Art: A Sourcebook of Artists' Writings*, ed. Kristine Stiles and Peter Selz (Berkeley and Los Angeles, CA, 1996), p. 125.
12 Briony Fer, *The Infinite Line: Re-making Art after Modernism* (New Haven, CT, and London, 2004), pp. 47–8.

12 SIGN

1 Leo Steinberg, *Other Criteria: Confrontations with Twentieth-century Art* (Chicago, IL, and New York, 1972), p. 61.
2 Quoted in Brandon Joseph, *Random Order: Robert Rauschenberg and the Neo-Avant-garde* (Cambridge, MA, and London, 2003), p. 86.
3 Ad Reinhardt, 'Black as Symbol and Concept' [1967], in *Art as Art: The Selected Writings of Ad Reinhardt*, ed. Barbara Rose (Berkeley and Los Angeles, CA, 1991), p. 87.
4 Ibid.
5 Ibid.
6 Piero Manzoni, 'Libera Dimensione' [1960], quoted in John C. Welchman, *Invisible Colors: A Visual History of Titles* (New Haven, CT, and London, 1997), p. 37.
7 Yves Klein, 'Lecture at the Sorbonne' [1959], in *Overcoming the Problematics of Art: The Writings of Yves Klein*, ed. and trans. Klaus Ottmann (Putnam, CT, 2007), p. 85.

8 See Rudolf Arnheim, *Visual Thinking* (Berkeley and Los Angeles, CA, 1969), p. 232.

9 See Thomas McEvilley, 'Heads It's Form, Tails It's Not Content', in Thomas McEvilley and G. Roger Denson, *Capacity: History, the World, and the Self in Contemporary Art Criticism* (Amsterdam, 1996), p. 38.

10 C. S. Peirce, 'Logic as Semiotic: The Theory of Signs', in *Philosophical Writings of Peirce*, ed. Justin Buchler (New York, 1955), p. 102.

11 For an important discussion of the role of the index, especially in relation to the influence of photography on avant-garde art of the 1960s and '70s, see Rosalind Krauss, 'Notes on the Index: Seventies Art in America', *October*, 3 (1977), pp. 68–81, and 'Notes on the Index: Seventies Art in America, Part 2', *October*, 4 (1977), pp. 58–67.

12 See Richard Wollheim, *Painting as an Art* (London and New York, 1987), p. 305.

13 Nicholas Cullinan, 'The Empty Canvas', in *Destroy the Picture: Painting the Void, 1949–1962*, ed. Paul Schimmel, exh. cat., Museum of Contemporary Art, Chicago (Chicago, IL, 2012), p. 225. Interestingly, Robert Rauschenberg visited Burri's Rome studio in early 1953, and the encounter evidently proved especially influential. But what struck Rauschenberg in particular was not the works' evocation of the body but the use Burri made of everyday, non-artistic materials, suggesting that a painting could be a collaged repository of the quotidian. Afterwards, Rauschenberg began his black monochrome series, making use of encrusted newspaper. This would soon lead him to abandon the monochrome in order to explore the possibilities of what he called the *Combines*. Cullinan, 'The Empty Canvas', p. 228.

14 See Sarah Whitfield, *Lucio Fontana*, exh. cat., Hayward Gallery, London (London, 2000), p. 19.

15 See Anna Augusti, ed., *Tàpies: Complete Works* (Barcelona, 2002). *Tàpies* actually means 'walls' in Catalan, so in a certain sense the analogy was perhaps predestined, even subconsciously.

16 Steinberg, *Other Criteria*, p. 61.

17 Gilles Deleuze, *Cinema 1: The Movement-image*, trans. Hugh Tomlinson and Barbara Habberjam (Minneapolis, MN, 1986), pp. 14–15.

18 Wollheim, *Painting as an Art*, p. 164.

19 Ibid.

20 It is perhaps pertinent that the printing technique Warhol used is called 'screen-printing'.

13 IDEA

1 'As is painting, so is theory'. W.J.T. Mitchell, '*Ut Pictura Theoria*: Abstract Painting and the Repression of Language', in *Picture Theory* (Chicago, IL, and London, 1994), p. 220.
2 Alphonse Allais, *Album primo-avrilesque* [1897] (Paris, 2000).
3 Allais quoted in Denys Riout, *La Peinture monochrome: histoire et archéologie d'un genre*, revd edn (Paris, 2006), p. 315, my translation; see also p. 516 n. 9.
4 See John C. Welchman, *Invisible Colors: A Visual History of Titles* (New Haven, CT, and London, 1997).
5 This idea is developed by Jeff Wall in 'Monochrome and Photojournalism: On Kawara's *Today* Paintings' [1993], in *Jeff Wall: Works and Collected Writings*, ed. Michael Newman and Jeff Wall (Barcelona, 2007), p. 330.
6 Ibid.
7 Mitchell, '*Ut Pictura Theoria*', p. 219.
8 Ibid., pp. 235, 234.
9 Ibid., p. 220.
10 Welchman, *Invisible Colors*, p. 106.
11 Benjamin H. D. Buchloh, 'Conceptual Art, 1962–1969: From the Aesthetics of Administration to the Critique of Institutions' [1990], in *Conceptual Art: A Critical Anthology*, ed. Alexander Alberro and Blake Stimson (Cambridge, MA, and London, 1999), p. 516.
12 The work is called *What Is Painting* (1968, MOMA, New York).
13 For example, *May 25, 1966, No. 89* in the *Today* series, is juxtaposed with the headline 'A rocket scientist was killed by a foreign-made .25 caliber pistol, Columbus Ohio'.
14 Michel Foucault, *Society Must Be Defended: Lectures at the College de France, 1975–76*, ed. Mauro Bertani and Alessandro Fontana, trans. David Mace (London, 2003), p. 6.
15 Rosalind Krauss, *The Optical Unconscious* (Boston, MA, and New York, 1994), p. 214.
16 Hal Foster, 'Re: Post' [1982], in *Art After Modernism: Rethinking Representation*, ed. Brian Wallis (New York, 1984), p. 190.
17 Charles Harrison, 'Conceptual Art and Critical Judgment' [1990], in *Conceptual Art*, ed. Alberro and Stimson, p. 545.
18 Ibid.
19 Joseph Kosuth, 'Comments on the Second Frame' [1977], in *Joseph Kosuth: Art After Philosophy and After: Collected Writings, 1966–90*, ed. Gabriele Guercio (Boston, MA, and New York, 1991), pp. 169–73.
20 Kosuth, 'Art After Philosophy' [1969], in *Joseph Kosuth*, ed. Guercio, p. 17.
21 Ad Reinhardt, 'Art-As-Art' [1962], in *Art-As-Art: The Selected Writings of Ad Reinhardt* (Berkeley and Los Angeles, CA, 1991), p. 53.

22 Joseph Kosuth, *American Art of the 1960s*, Studies in Art No. 1, ed. John Elderfield (New York, 1991), p. 36 n. 52.
23 Alexander Alberro, 'Reconsidering Conceptual Art, 1966–1977', in *Conceptual Art*, ed. Alberro and Stimson, pp. xviii–xix.
24 Lawrence Weiner, 'Statement' [1968], in *Conceptual Art*, ed. Alberro and Stimson, p. 528.
25 Lucy Lippard and John Chandler, 'The Dematerialization of Art' [1968], in *Conceptual Art*, ed. Alberro and Stimson, pp. 46–50.
26 Gerhard Richter, *Texts, Writings, Interviews and Letters, 1961–2007*, ed. Dietmar Elger and Hans-Ulrich Obrist (London and New York, 2009), p. 91.
27 Ibid.
28 Joseph Marioni, *Joseph Marioni: Paintings, 1970–1998. A Survey*, exh. cat., Rose Art Gallery, Brandeis University, Waltham, MA (Waltham, MA, 1998), p. 51.
29 Quoted in Marcia Hafif et al., *Marcia Hafif: The Inventory: Painting*, exh. cat., Laguna Art Museum (Laguna Beach, CA, 2015), p. 73.
30 'Art and Painting: Marcia Hafif in Conversation with Michael Ned Holte', in Hafif et al., *Marcia Hafif*, p. 237.
31 Marcia Hafif, 'Roman Painting', www.marciahafif.com/inventory/inventory.html, accessed 11 September 2018.
32 Marcia Hafif, 'Beginning Again', *Artforum* (September 1978), available at www.marciahafif.com, accessed 4 September 2018.
33 'Michel Parmentier', in *Color Chart: Reinventing Color, 1950 to Today*, ed. Ann Tempkin, exh. cat., Museum of Modern Art, New York (New York, 2008), pp. 114–15.
34 See *Olivier Mosset (1966–2003)*, exh. cat., Musée Cantonal des Beaux-Arts, Lausanne, and Kunstverein St Gallen, Milan (Lausanne, 2003).

14 ALLEGORICAL

1 Craig Owens, 'Repetition and Difference', in *Allan McCollum: Surrogates*, ed. Owens, exh. cat., Lisson Gallery, London (London, 1985), p. 5.
2 Yve-Alain Bois, 'Ryman's Tact', in Bois, *Painting as Model* (Cambridge, MA, and London, 1990), p. 231.
3 Thomas McEvilley, 'Seeking the Primal in Paint: The Monochrome Icon', in *Capacity: History, the World, and the Self in Contemporary Art and Criticism*, ed. G. Roger Denson (Amsterdam, 1996), p. 87.
4 Arthur Danto, 'Kazimir Malevich', in Danto, *Embodied Meanings: Critical Essays and Aesthetic Meditations* (New York, 1994), p. 172.
5 Mark A. Cheetham, *The Rhetoric of Purity: Essentialist Theory and the Advent of Abstract Painting* (Cambridge, 1991), p. 138. Cheetham is interested specially in Kandinsky and Mondrian, but what he says seems especially valid in relation to the monochromists in the metaphysical line.

6 Donald Kuspit, *The Cult of the Avant-garde Artist* (Cambridge, 1993), p. 50.
7 Ibid., p. 51.
8 Benjamin H. D. Buchloh 'Plenty or Nothing: From Yves Klein's *Le Vide* to Arman's *Le Plein*', in *Neo-Avantgarde and Culture Industry: Essays on European and American Art from 1955 to 1975* (Cambridge, MA, and London, 2000), p. 267.
9 Ann Eden Gibson, 'Colour and Difference in Abstract Painting: The Ultimate Case of Monochrome', in *The Feminism and Visual Culture Reader*, ed. Amelia Jones (London, 2003), p. 192.
10 Ibid., p. 194.
11 Ibid., p. 198.
12 Briony Fer, *On Abstract Art* (New Haven, CT, and London, 1997), p. 5.
13 Ibid.
14 Rosalind Krauss, *The Optical Unconscious* (Cambridge, MA, and London, 1994), p. 220.
15 Ibid., p. 218.
16 Rosalind Krauss, 'Sculpture in the Expanded Field' [1979], quoted in Hal Foster, 'Re: Post', in *Art After Modernism: Rethinking Representation*, ed. Brian Wallis (New York, 1984), p. 194.
17 Foster, 'Re: Post', p. 194.
18 Buchloh, 'Plenty or Nothing', p. 263.
19 Craig Owens, 'From Work to Frame; or, Is There Life after "The Death of the Author"?', in *Beyond Recognition: Representation, Power, and Culture*, ed. Barbara Kruger and Jane Weinstock (Berkeley and Los Angeles, CA, 1994), pp. 122–39: p. 126.
20 Ibid.
21 Craig Owens, 'The Allegorical Impulse: Towards a Theory of Post-modernism', in *Beyond Recognition*, ed. Kruger and Weinstock, pp. 52–3, 54.
22 Owens, 'Repetition and Difference', p. 5.
23 Ibid.
24 Ibid.
25 Quoted in David Joselit, 'Painting Beside Itself', *October*, 130 (Autumn 2009), p. 130.
26 Stephen Prina, *Monochrome Painting*, exh. cat., Renaissance Society, Chicago (Chicago, IL, 1989).
27 Ann Temkin, ed., *Color Chart: Reinventing Color, 1950 to Today*, exh. cat., Museum of Modern Art, New York (New York, 2008), p. 204.
28 Julian Heynen, 'On the Dark Side', in *Sherrie Levine: After All – Works, 1981–2016*, exh. cat., Neues Museum, Nürnberg (Munich, 2016), p. 157.
29 'The Anxiety of Influence – Head On: A Conversation Between Sherrie Levine and Jeanne Siegel', www.aftersherrielevine.com, accessed 22 May 2019.

15 NEW MEDIA

1 Sherrie Levine made a series of inkjet prints after these works in 2006 in which she reduced each panel to monochrome pixels: *Equivalents: After Stieglitz 1–18* (2006).
2 Emmanuelle de l'Ecotais, 'In Search of a New Reality', in *Shape of Light: 100 Years of Photography and Abstract Art*, ed. Simon Baker, Emmanuelle de l'Ecotais and Shoair Movlain, exh. cat., Tate Modern, London (London, 2018), pp. 30–31.
3 See Hiroshi Sugimoto, *Hiroshi Sugimoto: Theaters*, trans. Giles Murray (Bologna, 2016).
4 Kwak June Young, 'Slow and Unfamiliar Images of Thought', in *Hiroshi Sugimoto*, exh. cat., Leeum, Samsung Museum of Art, Seoul (Seoul, 2013), p. 26.
5 In 1974 Jarman saw a Klein work in the Tate Gallery, and at that time made another 'blue film' dedicated to the French artist. The word 'blue', of course, also has very specific connotations in the cinema industry.
6 Derek Jarman, *Chroma: A Book of Colour* (London, 1994), p. 4.
7 Jean-François Lyotard, 'Presenting the Unpresentable: The Sublime', trans. Lisa Libermann, in *The Sublime: Documents of Contemporary Art*, ed. Simon Morley (London and Cambridge, MA, 2010) p. 136. See also Lyotard, 'The Sublime and the Avant-garde', in Lyotard, *The Inhuman: Reflections on Time*, trans. Geoffrey Bennington and Rachel Bowlby (Cambridge, 1991).
8 Anish Kapoor, 'Interview with Marjorie Allthorpe-Guyton' [1990], in *The Sublime: Documents of Contemporary Art*, ed. Morley (London, 2010), p. 92.
9 Rosalind Krauss, 'Overcoming the Limits of Matter: On Revising Minimalism', in *American Art of the 1960s*, ed. James Leggio, John Elderfield and Susan Weiley (New York, 1991), p. 133.
10 Evelyn C. Hankins, 'Experiencing the Ineffable: Robert Irwin in the 1960s', in *Robert Irwin: All the Rules Will Change*, ed. Evelyn C. Hankins, exh. cat., Hirshhorn Museum, Washington, DC (Washington, DC, 2016), p. 33.
11 Quoted in Jan Butterfield, *The Art of Light and Space* (New York, 1993), p. 18.
12 Robert Irwin, 'Notes Toward a Model' [1977], in *Robert Irwin*, ed. Hankins, p. 141.
13 Robert Irwin and James Turrell, 'Statement' [1969], reprinted in Robert Irwin, *Notes Toward a Conditional Art*, ed. Matthew Simms (Los Angeles, CA, 2011), p. 31.
14 Turrell quoted Butterfield, *The Art of Light and Space*, p. 77.
15 Turrell quoted in Michael Govan, 'Inner Light: The Radical Reality of James Turrell', in *James Turrell: A Retrospective*, ed. Michael Govan and Christine K.

Kim, exh. cat., Los Angeles County Museum of Art (Los Angeles, CA, 2013), p. 13.

16 Quoted in Govan, 'Inner Light', p. 51. For Turrell and Zen, see Craig Adcock, *James Turrell: Artist of Light and Space* (Los Angeles, CA, 1990), pp. 212–15.

17 Turrell quoted in Adcock, p. 212.

18 Ibid., p. 2.

16 DANSAEKHWA

1 Lee Ufan, *Selected Writings by Lee Ufan, 1970–96*, ed. Jean Fisher (London, 1996), p. 124.

2 The Korean word is often translated as *Tansaekhwa* because the letter ㄷ is transliterated as 't' in the old McCune–Reischauer romanization system and as 'd' in the new Revised Romanization. Thus Joan Kee's excellent study is titled *Contemporary Korean Art: Tansaekhwa and the Urgency of Method* (Minneapolis, MN, 2013).

3 The early twentieth century saw a brutal period of Japanese colonization (1910–45), followed at the end of the Second World War by the division of the Korean peninsula along the 38th Parallel into a Communist-backed northern and U.S.-backed southern region. Soon, a bloody civil war (1950–53) had begun, a conflict into which the UN and China also entered and which ended with no outright victory. The armistice (which remains in place today) left in existence two rival versions of 'modern' Korea, poised in antagonistic existence. By the 1970s, the Republic of Korea (South Korea) had begun to experience rapid economic growth, driven by an aggressively Westernizing policy supported by the United States and directed under the watchful eyes of military leaders. Democracy was finally established in 1987. Meanwhile, the People's Democratic Republic of Korea (North Korea) lost the support of the Communist bloc after the end of the Cold War and became increasingly isolated, authoritarian and impoverished.

4 Yoon Jin-sup, 'Landscape of the Mind', in *Dansaekhwa: Korean Monochrome Painting*, exh. cat., National Museum of Contemporary Art, Seoul (Seoul, 2012), p. 29.

5 Kee, *Contemporary Korean Art*, p. 93.

6 Wucius Wong, *The Tao of Chinese Landscape Painting: Principles and Methods* (New York, 1991), p. 29.

7 François Jullien, *Detour and Access: Strategies of Meaning in China and Greece*, trans. Sophie Hawkes (New York, 2000), p. 295.

8 François Jullien, *The Great Image Has No Form; or, On the Nonobject through Painting*, trans. Jane Marie Todd (Chicago, IL, 2009), p. 68.

9 Ibid., p. 78.
10 Lee Joon, 'Void: Mapping the Invisible in Korean Art', in *Void in Korean Art*, exh. cat., Leeum, Samsung Museum of Art, Seoul (Seoul, 2008), n.p.
11 Ueda Shizuteru, 'Contributions to Dialogue with the Kyoto School', in *Japanese and Continental Philosophy: Conversations with the Kyoto School*, ed. Brett W. Davis, Brian Schroeder and Jason M. Wirth (Bloomington and Indianapolis, IN, 2011), p. 23.
12 Lee Yong-woo, ed., *Dansaekhwa*, exh. cat., Venice Biennale and Kukje Gallery, Seoul (Seoul, 2015), pp. 281, 287.
13 Ibid., p. 281.
14 Yoon, 'Landscape of the Mind', p. 20.
15 Kwon Young-Pil, 'The Aesthetic in Traditional Korean Art and Its Influence on Modern Life', *Korean Journal* (Autumn 2001), pp 9–34.
16 Yoon, 'Landscape of the Mind', p. 30.
17 Joan Kee, 'Tansaekhwa: Inside and Out', in Joan Kee, *Resonance of Dansaekhwa* (Seoul, 2016), p. 38.
18 Soon Chun Cho and Barbara Bloemink, *The Color of Nature: Monochrome Art in Korea*, exh. cat., Rho Gallery, Seoul, and Wellside Gallery, Shanghai (New York, 2008), p. 27.
19 Ibid., p. 85.
20 Lee Ufan, 'On Infinity' [1993], in Lee Ufan, *The Art of Encounter*, trans. Stanley Anderson (London, 2008), p. 15.
21 Lee Ufan, 'Setting the Conditions of Painting' [1990–94], in *The Art of Encounter*, trans. Anderson (London, 2008), p. 23.
22 Roland Barthes, *The Neutral: Lecture Course at the College de France, 1977–78*, trans. Rosalind Krauss and Denis Hollier (New York, 2005).
23 Ibid., p. 51.
24 François Jullien, *In Praise of Blandness: Proceeding from Chinese Thought and Aesthetics*, trans. Paula M. Varsano (New York, 2008).
25 Ibid., p. 43.
26 Ibid., p. 45.
27 Ibid., pp. 144, 25.
28 Ibid., pp. 133–4.

17 CONTEMPORARY

1 David Batchelor, 'A Bit of Nothing', *Tate Etc.*, 16 (Summer 2009), www.tate.org.uk, accessed 10 September 2018.
2 Denys Riout, *La Peinture monochrome: histoire et archéologie d'un genre*, revd edn (Paris, 2006), pp. 259–60.
3 The exhibition ran from 1 March to 26 April 2018; see www.richardtaittinger.com, accessed 2 September 2018.

4 See for example Yoon Jin-sup, *The Post Dansaekhwa of Korea*, exh. cat., Leeahn Gallery, Seoul (Seoul, 2018).
5 Terry Smith, 'Contemporary Art: World Currents in Transition Beyond Globalization', in *The Global Contemporary and the Rise of New Art Worlds*, ed. Hans Belting, Andrea Buddensieg and Peter Weibel, exh. cat., ZKM Center for Art and Media, Karlsruhe (Cambridge, MA, 2013), pp. 186–92.
6 See, for example, Jerry Saltz, 'Zombie on the Walls: Why Does So Much New Abstraction Look the Same?', *New York Magazine*, 16 June 2014, reprinted online at www.vulture.com, 17 June 2014.
7 Nicolas Bourriaud, *Relational Aesthetics* (Dijon, 2002), p. 19.
8 Ibid., p. 21.
9 Nicolas Bourriaud, *Radicant: pour une esthétique de la globalisation* (Paris, 2009), p. 61, published in English as *The Radicant*, trans. James Gussen and Lili Porten (Berlin and New York, 2009).
10 Boris Groys, *In the Flow* (London, 2016), p. 112.
11 Craig Staff, *Monochrome: Darkness and Light in Contemporary Art* (London and New York, 2015).
12 David Joselit, 'Painting Beside Itself', *October*, 130 (Autumn 2009), p. 125.
13 Ibid., p. 132.
14 Ibid.
15 Isabelle Graw, *The Love of Painting: Genealogy of a Success Medium* (Berlin, 2018), p. 14.
16 Ibid.
17 Ibid., p. 16.
18 Ibid., p. 17.
19 Silvia Simoncelli, 'Interview with Wade Guyton', *OnCurating*, 20 (October 2013), pp. 34–7, www.on-curating.org, accessed 20 September 2018. See also Wade Guyton, *Wade Guyton: Black Paintings* (Zurich, 2010).
20 Christoph Platz, 'Wade Guyton about Efficiency, Inner Logic, and Floors', www.artblogcologne.com, 19 April 2010.
21 Hoyland's work of the period was at the time a highly admired English response to the gestural abstraction associated with American Abstract Expressionism or European Art Informel.
22 Merlin Carpenter, 'Do Not Open Until 2081', Simon Lee Gallery, London (2017). See 'Merlin Carpenter: Do Not Open Until 2018', www.whiteliesmagazine.com, accessed 28 September 2018.
23 Floyer quoted in Anna Dezeuze, 'Nothing Works', *Tate Etc.*, 21 (Spring 2011), www.tate.org.uk, accessed 11 September 2018.
24 Batchelor, 'A Bit of Nothing'.
25 David Batchelor, *Found Monochromes*, vol. I (London, 2010).
26 Batchelor, 'A Bit of Nothing'. The other aspect of modernity for Baudelaire outlined in his *The Painter of Modern Life* (1863) was 'the eternal and

immutable', properties in relation to which Batchelor wisely chooses to remain silent.

27 Dezeuze, 'Nothing Works'. There have been several exhibitions in past years on the theme of nothing and the void, for example 'Vides: une rétrospective' (Voids: A Retrospective) at the Centre Georges Pompidou, Paris (2009), and 'Invisible: Art About the Unseen' at the Hayward Gallery, London (2012).

28 Olafur Eliasson, 'Your Monochromatic Listening', in *Monochrome: Painting in Black and White*, ed. Leila Packer and Jennifer Sliwka, exh. cat., National Gallery (London, 2017), p. 209.

29 Quoted in Jennifer Sliwka, 'Beyond Painting: Monochrome and Installation Art', in *Monochrome*, ed. Packer and Sliwka, p. 208.

30 Eliasson, 'Your Monochromatic Listening', p. 209.

CONCLUSION

1 Lewis Carroll, *Alice's Adventures in Wonderland and Through the Looking-glass* [1865] (Florence, 2002), p. 210.

2 Yves Klein, 'The Monochrome Adventure', in *Overcoming the Problematics of Art: The Writings of Yves Klein*, ed. and trans. Klaus Ottmann (Putnam, CT, 2007), p. 143.

3 Pierre Bourdieu, *Distinction: A Social Critique of the Judgment of Taste*, trans. Richard Nice (Cambridge, MA, and London, 1984), p. 1.

4 Carroll, *Alice's Adventures in Wonderland*, p. 210.

5 John Onians, *European Art: A Neuroarthistory* (New Haven, CT, and London, 2016), p. 15. Onians gives the example of research showing that verbal information provided by a trusted source in relation to the relative quality of expensive and cheap wines can override direct sensory responses, so that participants made choices concerning quality that go against the evidence of the wines themselves.

6 For more on this relationship to the urban see David Batchelor, 'Nothings: David Batchelor in Conversation with Jonathan Rée', in *Found Monochromes*, vol. I: 1–250 (London, 2010), pp. 297–9.

7 John Gray, *Enlightenment's Wake* [1995] (London and New York, 2010), p. 240.

8 Quoted ibid., p. 239.

9 Kelly Grovier, in a BBC article on the discovery, makes a rather swingeing claim that Malevich's words, 'too gutless to show their face in full view, are thought to be an allusion to a racist phrase – used by a French humourist for an 1897 cartoon of a black square. With that disappointing discovery, which succeeded in recontextualizing the work from pioneering masterpiece to appalling misadventure, the inner light of a painting that

had, for decades, been the source of meaningful meditation, suddenly went out.' Kelly Grovier, 'The Racist Message Hidden in a Masterpiece', www.bbc.com, 12 March 2018. Though seemingly obvious to us, the joke was not *consciously* racist for Malevich, who could be no more than a man of his times – that is, someone largely limited by the prejudices of his culture – and primarily had in mind an allusion to Allais and his circle, not an overtly racist joke.

10 I am drawing here on Tim Ingold, *Making: Anthropology, Archaeology, Art and Architecture* (London and New York, 2013).

11 Rudolf Arnheim, *Visual Language* (Berkeley and Los Angeles, CA, 1969), p. 410.

12 Byung-Chul Han, *The Burnout Society*, trans. Erik Butler (Stanford, CA, 2015). Han's bestselling book, first published in 2010 in German, pre-dates the arrival of the smartphone, which has certainly enormously amplified the symptoms he diagnosed. The definition of 'therapeutic' is from the *Merriam-Webster* online dictionary.

13 Tim Wu, *The Attention Merchants: The Epic Scramble to Get Inside Our Heads* (New York, 2016).

14 'Attention capture device' is a phrase used by Wu, ibid.

15 For an especially insightful discussion of this see Sven Birkerts in *Changing the Subject: Art and Attention in the Internet Age* (Minneapolis, MN, 2015).

BIBLIOGRAPHY

Adcock, Craig E., *James Turrell: The Art of Light and Space* (Berkeley, CA, 1990)
Alberro, Alexander, and Blake Stimson, eds, *Conceptual Art: A Critical Anthology* (Cambridge, MA, and London, 1999)
Albers, Josef, *Interaction of Color* [1963] (New Haven, CT, 1971)
Allais, Alphonse, *Album primo-avrilesque* (Paris, 2000)
Anfam, David, *Mark Rothko: The Works on Canvas, Catalogue Raisonné* (New Haven, CT, and Washington, DC, 1998)
Arnheim, Rudolf, *Visual Thinking* (Berkeley and Los Angeles, CA, 1969)
Augusti, Anna, ed., *Tàpies: Complete Works* (Barcelona, 2002)
Baas, Jacquelynn, *Smile of the Buddha: Eastern Philosophy and Western Art from Monet to Today* (Berkeley and Los Angeles, CA, 2005)
Bachelard, Gaston, *Air and Dreams: An Essay on the Imagination of Movement* [1943], trans. Edith R. Farrell and C. Frederick Farrell (Dallas, TX, 1988)
Badiou, Alain, *The Century*, trans. Alberto Toscano (Cambridge, 2007)
Ball, Philip, *Bright Earth: The Invention of Colour* (New York and London, 2001)
——, and Mary Jane Jacob, *Buddha Mind in Contemporary Art* (Berkeley and Los Angeles, CA, 2004)
Banai, Nuit, *Yves Klein* (London, 2014)
Bann, Stephen, ed., *The Tradition of Constructivism* (London, 1974)
Barasch, Moshe, *Icon: Studies in the History of an Idea* (New York, 1992)
Bardaouil, Sam, and Till Fellrath, 'Overcoming the Modern. Dansaekhwa: The Korean Monochrome Movement', *Overcoming the Modern*, exh. cat., Alexander Gray Associates (New York, 2014), pp. 3–14
Barthes, Roland, *The Neutral: Lecture Course at the College de France, 1977–78*, trans. Rosalind Krauss and Denis Hollier (New York, 2005)
Batchelor, David, 'A Bit of Nothing', *Tate Etc.*, 16 (Summer 2009), www.tate.org.uk, accessed 10 September 2018
——, *Chromophobia* (London, 2000)
——, *Found Monochromes*, vol. I: *1–250* (London, 2010)
——, 'In Bed with the Monochrome', in *From an Aesthetic Point of View: Philosophy, Art and the Senses*, ed. Peter Osborne (London, 2000)

——, *The Luminous and the Grey* (London, 2014)
——, ed., *Colour: Documents of Contemporary Art* (Cambridge, MA, and London, 2008)
Battcock, Gregory, ed., *Minimal Art* (Berkeley, CA, 1995)
Belting, Hans, 'Beyond Iconoclasm: Nam June Paik, the Zen Gaze and the Escape from Representation', in *Iconoclash: Beyond the Image Wars in Science, Religion, and Art*, ed. Bruno Latour and Peter Weibel, exh. cat., ZKM Center for Art and Media, Karlsruhe (Karlsruhe and Cambridge, MA, 2002), pp. 390–411
——, Andrea Buddensieg and Peter Weibel, eds, *The Global Contemporary and the Rise of New Art Worlds*, exh. cat., ZKM Center for Art and Media, Karlsruhe (Karlsruhe and Cambridge, MA, 2013)
Berggreun, Olivier, ed., *Playing with Form: Neoconcrete Art from Brazil*, exh. cat., Dickinson, New York (New York, 2011)
Bersani, Leo, and Ulysse Dutoit, *Arts of Impoverishment: Beckett, Rothko, Resnais* (Cambridge, MA, 1993)
Besset, Maurice, ed., *La Couleur seule: l'expérience du monochrome*, exh. cat., Musée Saint-Pierre Art Contemporain, Lyon (Lyon, 1988)
Betancourt, Roland, and Maria Taroutina, eds, *Byzantium/Modernism: The Byzantine as Method in Modernism* (London and New York, 2015)
Birkerts, Sven, *Changing the Subject: Art and Attention in the Internet Age* (Minneapolis, MN, 2015)
Birren, Faber, *Principles of Color: A Review of Past Traditions and Modern Theories of Color Harmony* (Atglen, PA, 1987)
Blazwick, Iwona, ed., *Adventures of the Black Square: Abstract Art and Society, 1915–2015*, exh. cat., Whitechapel Art Gallery, London (London, 2015)
Bois, Yve-Alain, 'Klein's Relevance Today', *October*, 119 (Winter 2007), pp. 73–93
——, *Painting as Model* (Cambridge, MA, and London, 1990)
——, ed., *Ad Reinhardt*, exh. cat., Museum of Modern Art, New York (New York, 1991)
Bourdieu, Pierre, *Distinction: A Social Critique of the Judgment of Taste*, trans. Richard Nice (Cambridge, MA, 1984)
Bourriaud, Nicolas, *The Radicant*, trans. James Gussen and Lili Porten (Berlin and New York, 2009)
——, *Relational Aesthetics* (Dijon, 2002)
Bozo, Domique, et al., *Yves Klein, 1928–1962: A Retrospective*, exh. cat., Institute of Fine Art, Rice University, Houston (Houston, TX, and New York, 1982)
Brinker, Helmut, *Zen in the Art of Painting*, trans. George Campbell (London and New York, 1987)
Brougher, Kerry, Philippe Vergne, Klaus Ottman et al., *Yves Klein: With the Void, Full Powers*, exh. cat., Hirshhorn Museum and Sculpture Garden, Washington, DC, and Walker Art Center, Minneapolis (Washington, DC, 2010)

Brusatin, Manlio, *A History of Colors* (Boston, MA, and New York, 1991)
Bryson, Norman, 'The Gaze in the Expanded Field', in *Vision and Visuality*, ed. Hal Foster (Seattle, WA, 1988), pp. 87–114
Buchloh, Benjamin H. D., 'Plenty of Nothing: From Yves Klein's *Le Vide* to Arman's *Le Plein*', *Neo-Avantgarde and Culture Industry: Essays on European and American Art from 1955 to 1975* (Cambridge, MA, and London, 2000)
Burke, Edmund, *A Philosophical Enquiry into the Origin of our Ideas of the Sublime and Beautiful* [1757], ed. Adam Phillips (Oxford and New York, 1990)
Butterfield, Jan, *The Art of Light and Space* (New York, 1993)
Cage, John, 'On Robert Rauschenberg, Artist, and his Work', in *Silence: Lectures and Writing* (Middletown, CT, 1973), pp. 95–109
Carpenter, Merlin, 'Merlin Carpenter: Do Not Open Until 2018', www.whiteliesmagazine.com, 26 October 2017
Carr, Nicholas, *The Shallows: What the Internet Is Doing to Our Brains* (New York, 2011)
Carroll, Lewis, *Alice's Adventures in Wonderland and Through the Looking-glass* [1896] (Florence, 2002)
Charlton, Alan, *Alan Charlton*, exh. cat., Musée d'art contemporain de Nîmes (Nîmes, 1997)
Cheetham, Mark A., *The Rhetoric of Purity: Essentialist Theory and the Advent of Abstract Painting* (Cambridge, 1991)
Cheng, François, *Empty and Full: the Language of Chinese Painting*, trans. Michael H. Kohn (Boston, MA, 1994)
—, 'Matting the Monochrome: Malevich, Klein, and Now', *Art Journal* (Winter 2005), pp. 95–108
Chévreul, Michel-Eugène, *The Principles of Harmony and Contrast of Colors, and their Application to the Arts*, trans. Charles Martell (Whitefish, MT, 2014)
Chipp, Herschel B., *Theories of Modern Art: A Source Book by Artists and Critics* (Berkeley and Los Angeles, CA, 1968)
Cho, Soon Chun, and Barbara Bloemink, eds, *The Color of Nature: Monochrome Art in Korea*, exh. cat., Rho Gallery, Seoul, and Wellside Gallery, Shanghai (Seoul, 2008)
Clark, T. J., *Farewell to an Idea: Episodes from a History of Modernism* (New Haven, CT, and London, 1999)
Clarke, J. J., *Oriental Enlightenment: The Encounter between Asian and Western Thought* (London, 1997)
Corris, Michael, *Ad Reinhardt* (London, 2008)
Crispolti, Enrico, *Lucio Fontana: Paintings, Sculpture, Drawings*, exh. cat., Ben Brown, New York (New York, 2005)
Crone, Rainer, and David Moos, *Kazimir Malevich: The Climax of Disclosure* (London, 2014)

Crowther, Paul, *How Pictures Complete Us: The Beautiful, the Sublime, and the Divine* (Stanford, CA, 2016)
—, *Phenomenology of the Visual Arts (even the frame)* (Stanford, CA, 2009)
Dalrymple-Henderson, Linda, *The Fourth Dimension and Non-Euclidian Geometry in Modern Art*, revd edn (Boston, MA, and New York, 2013)
Damisch, Hubert, *A Theory of /Cloud/: Toward a History of Painting*, trans. Janet Lloyd (Stanford, CA, 2002)
Danto, Arthur, 'Ad Reinhardt', in *Embodied Meanings: Critical Essays and Aesthetic Meditations* (New York, 1994), pp. 204–11
—, 'Historical Museum of Monochrome Art', in *After the End of Art: Contemporary Art and the Pale of History* (Princeton, NJ, 1997), pp. 153–74
Davis, Whitney, *A General Theory of Visual Culture* (Princeton, NJ, and Oxford, 2011)
Deleuze, Gilles, *Francis Bacon: The Logic of Sensation*, trans. Daniel W. Smith (London, 2003)
—, and Félix Guattari, *A Thousand Plateaus: Capitalism and Schizophrenia*, trans. Brian Massumi (Minneapolis, MN, 1987)
Dezeuze, Anna, 'Nothing Works', *Tate Etc*, 21 (Spring 2011), www.tate.org.uk, accessed 11 September 2018
Dickerman, Lara, ed., *Inventing Abstraction, 1910–1925: How a Radical Idea Changed Modern Art*, exh. cat., Museum of Modern Art, New York (New York, 2012)
Didi-Huberman, Georges, *Confronting Images: Questioning the Ends of a Certain History of Art*, trans. John Goodman (University Park, PA, 2005)
—, 'The Supposition of the Aura: The Now, the Then, and Modernity', in *Negotiating Rapture: The Power of Art to Transform Lives*, ed. Richard Francis, exh. cat., Museum of Contemporary Art, Chicago (Chicago, IL, 1996), pp. 48–63
Dissanayake, Ellen, 'The Arts After Darwin: Does Art Have an Origin and Adaptive Function?', in *World Art Studies: Exploring Concepts and Approaches*, ed. Wilfried van Damme and Kitty Zijlmans (Amsterdam, 2008), pp. 241–63
Dümpelman, Britta Tanja, 'The World of Objectless: A Snapshot of an Artistic Universe', in *Kazimir Malevich: The World as Objectlessness*, ed. Simon Baier et al., (Basel, 2014), pp. 11–59
De Duve, Thierry, 'The Monochrome and the Blank Canvas', in *Reconstructing Modernism: Art in New York, Paris, and Montreal, 1945–1964*, ed. Serge Guilbaut (Cambridge, MA, and New York, 1992), pp. 244–310
Elkins, James, *The Object Stares Back: On the Nature of Seeing* (New York, 1996)
—, *On Pictures and the Words that Fail Them* (Cambridge, 1998)
—, ed., *Is Art History Global?* (New York, 2007)
—, Zhivka Valiavicharksa and Alice Kim, eds, *Art and Globalization* (University Park, PA, 2010)

Fer, Briony, *The Infinite Line: Re-making Art after Modernism* (New Haven, CT, and London, 2004)
——, *On Abstract Art* (New Haven, CT, and London, 1997)
Floyer, Ceal, Jonathan Watkins and Jeremy Millar, *Ceal Floyer*, exh. cat., Ikon Gallery, Birmingham (Birmingham, 2001)
Fontana, Lucio, *Lucio Fontana*, ed. Sarah Whitfield, exh. cat., Hayward Gallery, London (London, 2000)
Foster, Hal, 'Re: Post', in *Art After Modernism: Rethinking Representation*, ed. Brian Wallis (New York, 1984), pp. 189–201
Francis, Richard, ed., *Negotiating Rapture: The Power of Art to Transform Lives*, exh. cat., Museum of Contemporary Art, Chicago (Chicago, IL, 1996)
Fraser, Pamela, *How Color Works: Color Theory in the 21st Century* (Oxford, 2018)
Freedberg, David, 'Memory in Art: History and the Neuroscience of Art', in *The Memory Process: Neuroscience and Humanistic Perspectives*, ed. Suzanne Nalbantian et al. (Cambridge, MA, and London, 2011), pp. 337–58
Freeland, Cynthia A., 'A New Question about Color', *Journal of Aesthetics and Art Criticism*, LXXV/3 (Summer 2017), pp. 231–48
Fried, Michael, 'Three Modernist Painters: Noland, Olitski, Stella', in *Art and Objecthood* (Chicago, IL, and London, 1996), pp. 213–65
Gage, John, *Colour and Culture: Practice and Meaning from Antiquity to Abstraction* (London and New York, 1995)
——, *Colour and Meaning: Art, Science, and Symbolism* (London and New York, 2000)
Gamboni, Dario, *The Destruction of Art: Iconoclasm and Vandalism since the French Revolution* (London, 1997)
——, *Potential Images: Ambiguity and Indeterminacy in Modern Art* (London, 2002)
Gazzaley, Adam, and Larry D. Rosen, *The Distracted Mind* (Cambridge, MA, and New York, 2016)
Gibson, Ann Eden, 'Colour and Difference in Abstract Painting: The Ultimate Case of Monochrome', in *The Feminism and Visual Culture Reader*, ed. Amelia Jones (London, 2003), pp. 192–204
Gilbert-Rolfe, Jeremy, *Beauty and the Contemporary Sublime* (New York, 1999)
——, *Beyond Piety: Critical Essays on the Visual Arts, 1986–1993* (Cambridge, 1995)
Goethe, Johann Wolfgang von, *Theory of Colours*, trans. Charles Lock Eastlake (London, 1840), www.gutenberg.org, accessed 1 May 2017
Grave, Johannes, *Caspar David Friedrich*, trans. Fiona Elliott (New York, 2012)
Graw, Isabelle, *The Love of Painting: Genealogy of a Success Medium* (Berlin, 2018)
Gray, John, *Enlightenment's Wake* [1995] (London and New York, 2010)
Greenberg, Clement, 'Modernist Painting', in *Twentieth Century Theories of Art*, ed. James M. Thompson (Carleton, ON, 1990), pp. 94–103

——, 'The Recentness of Sculpture', in *Minimal Art: A Critical Anthology*, ed. Gregory Battock (Berkeley and Los Angeles, CA, 1968), pp. 180–86
Govan, Michael, and Christine K. Kim, *James Turrell: A Retrospective*, exh. cat., Los Angeles County Museum of Art, Los Angeles (Los Angeles, CA, 2013)
Groys, Boris, 'Becoming Revolutionary: On Kazimir Malevich', in *In the Flow* (London, 2016)
Guyton, Wade, *Wade Guyton: Black Paintings* (Zurich, 2010)
Hafif, Marcia, 'Beginning Again', *Artforum* (September 1978), pp. 35–40, www.marciahafif.com, accessed 17 February 2019
——, 'Monochrome in New York, Round Table Discussion with Seven Painters', *Flash Art*, 92–3 (October–November 1979)
——, et al., *Marcia Hafif, The Inventory: Painting*, exh. cat., Laguna Art Museum, Laguna Beach, (Laguna Beach, CA, 2015)
Hankins, Evelyn C., ed., *Robert Irwin: All the Rules Will Change*, exh. cat., Hirshhorn Museum, Washington, DC (Washington, DC, 2016)
Hardimann, Katherine, 'Monochromes and Mandalas', http://shuffle.rauschenbergfoundation.org, accessed 20 September 2017
Harrison, Charles, and Paul Wood, eds, *Art in Theory, 1900–2000: An Anthology of Changing Ideas* (Oxford, 2000)
Hillings, Valerie, ed., *Zero: Countdown to Tomorrow, 1950s–60s*, exh. cat., Solomon R. Guggenheim Museum, New York (New York, 2014)
Hirai, Shoichi, 'Gutai and Its Internationalism', in *Destroy the Picture: Painting the Void, 1949–1962*, ed. Paul Schimmel, exh. cat., Museum of Contemporary Art, Los Angeles (Los Angeles, CA, 2012), pp. 204–11
Hopps, Walter, *Robert Rauschenberg: The Early 1950s* (Houston, TX, 1991)
Huxley, Aldous, *The Perennial Philosophy* (London, 1950)
Inboden, Gudrun, ed., *Frank Stella: Black Paintings, 1958–1960*, exh. cat., Staatsgalerie, Stuttgart (Stuttgart, 1998)
——, and Thomas Kellein, eds, *Ad Reinhardt*, exh. cat., Staatsgalerie, Stuttgart (Stuttgart, 1985)
Ingold, Tim, *Making: Anthropology, Archaeology, Art and Architecture* (London and New York, 2013)
——, *The Perception of the Environment* (London and New York, 2010)
Irwin, Robert, *Notes Toward a Conditional Art*, ed. Matthew Simms (Los Angeles, CA, 2011)
Jarman, Derek, *Chroma: A Book of Colour* (London, 1994)
Jay, Martin, *Downcast Eyes: The Denigration of Vision in Twentieth-century French Thought* (Berkeley and Los Angeles, CA, 1994)
Johnson, Mark, *The Meaning of the Body: Aesthetics of Human Understanding* (Chicago, IL, and London, 2007)
Jones, Caroline A., *Eyesight Alone: Clement Greenberg's Modernism and the Bureaucratization of the Senses* (Chicago, IL, 2005)

Jones, Zebedee, *Zebedee Jones*, exh. cat., Agnew's Gallery, London (London, 2011)

Joselit, David, 'Painting Beside Itself', *October*, 130 (Autumn 2009), pp. 125–34

Joseph, Brandon, *Random Order: Robert Rauschenberg and the Neo-Avant-garde* (Cambridge, MA, and London, 2003)

Judd, Donald, *Donald Judd: Complete Writings, 1959–1975* (New York, 1975)

——, *Donald Judd: Early Works, 1955–1968*, ed. Thomas Kellein (New York, 2002)

Jullien, François, *Detour and Access: Strategies of Meaning in China and Greece*, trans. Sophie Hawkes (New York, 2000)

——, *The Great Image Has No Form; or, On the Nonobject through Painting*, trans. Jane Marie Todd (Chicago, IL, 2009)

——, *In Praise of Blandness: Proceeding from Chinese Thought and Aesthetics*, trans. Paula M. Varsano (New York, 2008)

Kandel, Eric R., *Reductionism in Art and Brain Science* (New York, 2016)

Kandinsky, Wassily, *Concerning the Spiritual in Art* [1911], trans. M.T.H. Sadler (New York, 1977)

Kasulis, Thomas P., *Intimacy or Integrity: Philosophy and Cultural Difference* (Honolulu, HI, 2002)

Kaufmann, Thomas DaCosta, 'The Geography of Art: Historiography, Issues, and Perspectives', in *World Art Studies: Exploring Concepts and Approaches*, ed. Wilfried van Damme and Kitty Zijlmans (Amsterdam, 2008), pp. 167–82

Kee, Joan, *Contemporary Korean Art: Tansaekhwa and the Urgency of Method* (Minneapolis, MN, 2013)

——, 'Tansaekhwa: Inside and Out', in *Resonance of Dansaekhwa*, ed. Kim Sunyoung (Seoul, 2016), pp. 34–57

Kelly, Ellsworth, *Ellsworth Kelly: A Retrospective*, ed. Diane Waldman, exh. cat., Museum of Modern Art, New York (New York, 1997)

Klein, Yves, *Overcoming the Problematics of Art: The Writings of Yves Klein*, ed. and trans. Klaus Ottmann (Putnam, CT, 2007)

——, *Yves Klein*, exh. cat., Centre Georges Pompidou, Paris (Paris, 1983)

Kosuth, Joseph, 'Comments on the Second Frame', in *Joseph Kosuth: Art After Philosophy and After: Collected Writings, 1966–90*, ed. Gabriele Guercio (Boston, MA, and New York, 1991), pp. 169–73

Kotz, M. L., *Rauschenberg: Art and Life* (New York, 1990)

Krauss, Rosalind, 'Grids', in *The Originality of the Avant-garde and Other Modernist Myths* (Cambridge, MA, and New York, 1986), pp. 8–22

——, *The Optical Unconscious* (Boston, MA, and New York, 1994)

——, 'Overcoming the Limits of Matter: On Revising Minimalism', in *American Art of the Sixties*, ed. John Elderfield, James Leggio and Susan Weiley (New York, 1991), pp. 123–41

Kristeva, Julia, *Desire in Language: A Semiotic Approach to Language and Art*, ed. Leon S. Roudiez, trans. Thomas Gora and Alice A. Jardine (New York, 1980)

Kusama, Yayoi, *Yayoi Kusama: White Infinity Nets*, exh. cat., Victoria Miro Gallery, London (London, 2013)
——, Laura Hoptman, Akira Tatehata et al., *Yayoi Kusama* (London, 2017)
Lakoff, George, and Mark Johnson, *Philosophy in the Flesh: The Embodied Mind and its Challenge to Western Thought* (New York, 1999)
Lawlor, Robert, *Sacred Geometry: Philosophy and Practice* (London, 1982)
l'Écotais, Emmanuelle de, 'In Search of a New Reality', in *Shape of Light: 100 Years of Photography and Abstract Art*, ed. Simon Baker, Emmanuelle de l'Ecotais and Shoair Movlain, exh. cat., Tate Modern, London (London, 2018), pp. 13–86
Le Bon, Laurent, ed., *Vides (Voids)*, Centre Georges Pompidou, Paris (2009)
Lee, Yongwoo, ed., *Dansaekhwa*, exh. cat., Venice Bienale and Kukje Gallery, Seoul (Seoul, 2015)
Lee Joon, ed., *Void in Korean Art*, exh. cat., Leeum Samsung Museum, Seoul (Seoul, 2008)
Lee Ufan, *Lee Ufan: The Art of Encounter*, trans. Stanley Anderson (London, 2008)
——, *Lee Ufan: Marking Infinity*, ed. Alexandra Munroe, exh. cat., Solomon R. Guggenheim Museum, New York (New York, 2011)
——, *Selected Writings by Lee Ufan, 1970–96*, ed. Jean Fisher (London, 1996)
Levine, Sherrie, *Sherrie Levine, 'After All': Works 1981–2016*, exh. cat., Neues Museum, Nürnberg (Nürnberg, 2016)
Lewison, Jeremy, *Ben Nicholson* (London, 1991)
Li Shiyan, *Le Vide dans l'art du xxe siècle: Occident/Extrême-Orient* (Marseille, 2014)
Livingstone, Margaret S., *Vision and Art: The Biology of Seeing* (New York, 2008)
Lodermeyer, Peter, ed., *Personal Structures: Works and Dialogues* (New York, 2003)
Lyotard, Jean-François, 'Presenting the Unpresentable: The Sublime', trans. Lisa Libermann, in *The Sublime: Documents of Contemporary Art*, ed. Simon Morley (London and Cambridge, MA, 2010), pp. 130–36
——, 'The Sublime and the Avant-garde', trans. Lisa Libermann, in *The Sublime: Documents of Contemporary Art*, ed. Simon Morley (London and Cambridge, MA, 2010), pp. 27–41
McEvilley, Thomas, 'Grey Geese Descending: The Art of Agnes Martin', in *The Exile's Return: Toward a Redefinition of Painting for the Post-modern Era* (Cambridge, 1993)
——, 'Heads It's Form, Tails It's Not Content', in Thomas McEvilley and G. Roger Denson, *Capacity: History, the World, and the Self in Contemporary Art Criticism* (Amsterdam, 1996), pp. 22–44
——, 'Seeking the Primal in Paint: The Monochrome Icon', in Thomas McEvilley and G. Roger Denson, *Capacity: History, the World, and the Self in*

Contemporary Art and Criticism (Amsterdam, 1996), pp. 45–87. Also printed in McEvilley, *The Exile's Return: Toward a Redefinition of Painting for the Post-modern Era* (Cambridge, 1993), pp. 9–56

—, 'Yves Klein: Conquistador of the Void', in *Yves Klein, 1928–1962: A Retrospective*, ed. Dominique Bozo et al., exh. cat., Institute of Fine Art, Rice University, Houston (Houston, TX, 1982)

Malevich, Kazimir, *Kazimir Malevich, 1878–1935*, ed. Jeanne D'Andrea, exh. cat., Stedelijk Museum, Amsterdam (Amsterdam, 1988)

—, 'The World as Objectlessness', in *Kazimir Malevich: The World as Objectlessness*, exh. cat., Kunstmuseum Basel (Berlin, 2014), pp. 145–200

Mangold, Robert, *Robert Mangold*, ed. Richard Schiff et al. (London and New York, 2000)

Manzoni, Piero, *Piero Manzoni*, ed. Germano Celant et al., exh. cat., Serpentine Gallery, London (London, 1998)

Marden, Brice, *Plane Image: A Brice Marden Retrospective*, ed. Gary Garrels, exh. cat., Museum of Modern Art, New York (New York, 2007)

Margolin, Victor, *The Struggle for Utopia: Rodchenko, Lissitzky, Moholy-Nagy, 1917–1946* (Chicago, IL, and London, 1997)

Marioni, Joseph, *Joseph Marioni: Paintings, 1970–1998. A Survey*, exh. cat., Rose Art Museum, Brandeis University, Waltham, MA (Waltham, MA, 1998)

Martin, Agnes, *Agnes Martin*, ed. Barbara Haskell, exh. cat., Whitney Museum of American Art, New York (New York, 1993)

—, *Agnes Martin*, ed. Frances Morris and Tiffany Bell, exh. cat., Tate Modern, London (London, 2015)

—, *Writings*, ed. Dieter Schwarz (Ostfildern, 1998)

Martin, Jason, and Francis Gooding, *Jason Martin*, exh. cat., Lisson Gallery, London (London, 2016)

Mavor, Carol, *Blue Mythologies: Reflections on a Colour* (London, 2013)

Merleau-Ponty, Maurice, 'Eye and Mind', in *The Merleau-Ponty Aesthetics Reader: Philosophy and Painting*, ed. Galen A. Jonson (Evanston, IL, 1993)

—, *The Phenomenology of Perception*, trans. Colin Smith (London, 1962)

Metzinger, Thomas, *The Ego Tunnel: The Science of Mind and the Myth of the Self* (New York, 2009)

Meyer, Franz, *Barnett Newman: The Stations of the Cross – Lema Sabachthani* (Düsseldorf, 2004)

Milner, John, *Kazimir Malevich and the Art of Geometry* (New Haven, CT, and London, 1996)

Mitchell, W.J.T., *Picture Theory* (Chicago, IL, and London, 1994)

Morley, Simon, '"A Shimmering Thing at the Edge of Analysis": Figure/Ground and the Paintings of Agnes Martin', *Journal of Contemporary Painting*, II/2 (2016), pp. 39–56

——, 'The Brain is Wider than the Sky', *Chaos and Awe: Painting for the 21st Century*, ed. Mark W. Scala, exh. cat., Frist Center for the Visual Arts, Nashville, TN (Cambridge, MA, and London, 2018), pp. 27–38

——, 'Dansaekhwa: Korean Monochrome Painting', in *Painting: Critical and Primary Sources*, vol. II: *Modern Painting*, ed. Beth Harland and Sunil Manghani (London, 2016)

——, '"Free and Easy Wandering": Agnes Martin and the Limits of Intercultural Dialogue', *World Art*, VI/2 (2016), pp. 247–68

——, 'In Between Lee Ufan', *Lee Ufan*, exh. cat., Lisson Gallery (London, 2015), pp. 3–12

——, 'The Paintings of Yun Hyong-Keun as "Emergent Blended Structures"', *Third Text*, XXIX/6 (2015), pp. 473–86

——, 'Retaining Plenitude: Lee Ufan and the "Indistinct", *Journal of Visual Art Practice*, XVII/2–3 (2018), pp. 173–87

——, 'Robert Ryman', *Art Monthly*, 164 (March 1993), pp. 10–12

——, 'Shaping Up to Ellsworth Kelly: An Interview', *Tate* (Summer 1997), pp. 22–9

——, 'The Translucence of the Transhistorical: The Case of Korean Dansaekhwa', *World Art*, VIII/1 (2018), pp. 59–84

——, ed., *The Sublime: Documents of Contemporary* Art (Cambridge, MA, and London, 2010)

Mosset, Olivier, *Olivier Mosset (1966–2003)*, exh. cat, Musée Cantonal des Beaux-Arts, Lausanne, and Kunstverein St Gallen (Milan, 2003)

Mudrak, Myroslava M., 'Kazimir Malevich, Symbolism, and Ecclesiastic Orthodoxy', in *Modernism and the Spiritual in Russian Art: New Perspectives*, ed. Louise Hardiman and Nicola Kozicharow (Cambridge, 2017), pp. 91–114

Newman, Barnett, *Barnett Newman*, ed. Ann Temkin, exh. cat., Philadelphia Museum of Art (New Haven, CT, and London, 2001)

——, *Barnet Newman: Selected Writings and Interviews*, ed. Paul O'Neill (Berkeley and Los Angeles, CA, 1990)

Nisbett, Richard E., *The Geography of Thought: How Asians and Westerners Think Differently – and Why* (New York, 2003)

Noë, Alva, *Strange Tools: Art and Human Nature* (New York, 2016)

Oiticica, Hélio, *Hélio Oiticica: The Body of Colour*, ed. Mari Carmen Ramírez, exh. cat., Tate Modern, London (London, 2007)

Onians, John, *European Art: A Neuroarthistory* (New Haven, CT, and London, 2016)

——, ed., *Compression vs. Expression: Containing and Explaining the World's Art* (Williamstown, MA, 2006)

Owens, Craig, 'The Allegorical Impulse: Towards a Theory of Postmodernism', in *Beyond Recognition: Representation, Power, and Culture*, ed. Barbara Kruger and Jane Weinstock (Berkeley and Los Angeles, CA, 1994), pp. 117–21

——, 'From Work to Frame; or, Is There Life After "The Death of the Author"?', in *Beyond Recognition: Representation, Power, and Culture*, ed. Barbara Kruger and Jane Weinstock (Berkeley and Los Angeles, CA, 1994), pp. 122–39

——, 'Repetition and Difference', in *Allan McCollum: Surrogates*, exh. cat., Lisson Gallery, London (London, 1985), p. 5. Also in *Beyond Recognition: Representation, Power, and Culture*, ed. Barbara Kruger and Jane Weinstock (Berkeley and Los Angeles, CA, 1994), pp. 117–21

Packer, Lelia, and Jennifer Sliwka, eds, *Monochrome: Painting in Black and White*, exh. cat. National Gallery, London (London, 2017)

Pallasmaa, Juhani, *The Eyes of the Skin: Architecture and the Senses* (Chichester, 2005)

Park Seo-bo, Soon Chun Cho and Barbara J. Bloemink, *Empty the Mind: The Art of Park Seo-bo* (Berkeley and Los Angeles, CA, 2009)

Pastoureau, Michel, *Black: The History of a Color*, trans. Jody Gladding (Princeton, NJ, 2008)

——, *Blue: The History of a Color*, trans. Mark Cruse (Princeton, NJ, 2001)

——, *Green: The History of a Color*, trans. Jody Gladding (Princeton, NJ, 2014)

——, *Red: The History of a Color*, trans. Jody Gladding (Princeton, NJ, 2016)

——, and Dominque Simonet, *Le Petit Livre des couleurs* (Paris, 2005)

Peirce, C. S., 'Logic as Semiotic: The Theory of Signs', in *Philosophical Writings of Peirce*, ed. Justin Buchler (New York, 1955), pp. 98–121

Phillips, Glenn, and Thomas Crow, eds, *Seeing Rothko* (Los Angeles, CA, 2005)

Pincus-Witten, Robert, 'Ryman, Marden, Manzoni: Theory, Sensibility, Meditation', *Artforum* (June 1972), pp. 50–53

Prina, Stephen, *Monochrome Painting*, exh. cat., Renaissance Society, Chicago (Chicago, IL, 1989)

Ragaglia, Letizia, ed., *Ceal Floyer*, exh. cat., Museion, Bolzano (Bolzano, 2014)

Ramachandran, V. S., and William Hirstein, 'The Science of Art: A Neurological Theory of Aesthetic Experience', *Journal of Consciousness Studies*, VI/6–7 (1999), pp. 15–51

Raskin, David, *Donald Judd* (New Haven, CT, and London, 2017)

Rauschenberg, Robert, *Robert Rauschenberg: The White and Black Paintings, 1949–1952*, exh. cat., Gagosian Gallery, London (London, 1990)

Reinhardt, Ad, *Art as Art: The Selected Writings of Ad Reinhardt*, ed. Barbara Rose (Berkeley and Los Angeles, CA, 1991)

Richter, Gerhard, *Gerhard Richter: Forty Years of Painting*, ed. Robert Storr, exh. cat., Museum of Modern Art, New York (New York, 2002)

——, *Texts, Writings, Interviews and Letters, 1961–2007* (London and New York, 2009)

Riley, Charles A., *Color Codes: Modern Theories of Color in Philosophy, Painting and Architecture, Literature, Music, and Psychology* (Hanover, NH, 1995)

Riout, Denys, *La Peinture monochrome: histoire et archéologie d'un genre*, revd edn (Paris, 2006)

Rose, Barbara, ed., *Monochromes: From Malevich to the Present* (Berkeley and Los Angeles, CA, 2006)

—, and Alex Bacon, ed., *Brooklyn Rail: Special Edition on Ad Reinhardt*, https://brooklynrail.org (January 2014)

Rosenblum, Robert, 'The Abstract Sublime', in *Reading Abstract Expressionism: Contexts and Critique*, ed. Ellen G. Landau (New Haven, CT, and London, 2003), pp. 273–8

——, *Frank Stella* (New York, 1971)

——, *Modern Painting and the Northern Romantic Tradition: Friedrich to Rothko* (New York, 1975)

Rosenthal, Stephanie, ed., *Black Paintings: Robert Rauschenberg, Ad Reinhardt, Mark Rothko, Frank Stella*, exh. cat., Haus der Kunst, Munich (Munich, 2006)

Rothko, Mark, *Writings on Art*, ed. Miguel López-Ramiro (New Haven, CT, and London, 2006)

Rowell, Margit, ed., *Ad Reinhardt and Color*, exh. cat., Solomon R. Guggenheim Museum, New York (New York, 1980)

Rubin, Edgar, 'Figure and Ground', in *Visual Perception: Essential Readings*, ed. Stephen Yantis (Philadelphia, PA, 2001), pp. 225–30

Rugoff, Ralph, ed., *Invisible: Art About the Unseen*, exh. cat., Hayward Gallery, London (London, 2012)

Ryman, Robert, *Robert Ryman*, ed. Robert Storr, exh. cat., Tate Gallery, London (London, 1993)

Saltz, Jerry, 'Zombie on the Walls: Why Does So Much New Abstraction Look the Same?,' *New York Magazine*, 16 June 2014, reprinted at www.vulture.com, 17 June 2014

Scharfstein, Ben-Ami, *Art without Borders: A Philosophical Exploration of Art and Humanity* (Chicago, IL, and London, 2009)

Schimmel, Paul, ed., *Destroy the Picture: Painting the Void, 1949–1962*, exh. cat., Museum of Contemporary Art, Chicago (Chicago, IL, 2012)

Shatskikh, Aleksandra, *Black Square: Malevich and the Origin of Suprematism*, trans. Marian Schwartz (New Haven, CT, and London, 2012)

Silverman, Kaja, *Flesh of My Flesh* (Stanford, CA, 2009)

Small, Irene V., *Hélio Oiticica: Folding the Frame* (Chicago, IL, and London, 2016)

Smith, Walter, 'Ad Reinhardt's Oriental Aesthetic', *Smithsonian Studies in American Art*, IV/3–4 (Summer/Autumn 1990), pp. 22–45

Solso, Robert L., *Cognition and the Visual Arts* (Cambridge, MA, and London, 1996)

Sontag, Susan, 'The Aesthetics of Silence', in *A Susan Sontag Reader* (London, 1982), pp. 181–204

Staff, Craig, *Monochrome: Darkness and Light in Contemporary Art* (London and New York, 2015)

Stafford, Barbara Maria, *Visual Analogy: Consciousness as the Art of Connecting* (Cambridge, MA, and London, 2001)
——, ed., *A Field Guide to a New Meta-field: Bridging the Humanities–Neuroscience Divide* (Chicago, IL, 2011)
Steinberg, Leo, 'The Flatbed Picture Plane', in Steinberg, *Other Criteria: Confrontations with Twentieth-century Art* (Chicago, IL, and New York, 1972), pp. 82–91
Stella, Frank, *Frank Stella*, ed. Robert Rosenblum (Harmondsworth, 1971)
——, *Frank Stella: A Retrospective*, ed. Michael Auping, exh. cat., Whitney Museum of American Art, New York (New York, 2014)
Stiles, Kristine, and Peter Selz, eds., *Theories and Documents of Contemporary Art: A Sourcebook of Artists' Writings* (Berkeley and Los Angeles, CA, 1996)
Strzemiński, Władysław, and Katarzyna Kobro, *L'Espace uniste: écrits du Constructivisme polonais*, trans. and ed. Antoine Baudin and Pierre-Maxime Jedryka (Lausanne, 1977)
Suárez, Osbel, ed., *Cold American: Geometric Abstraction in Latin America, 1934–1973*, exh. cat., Fundación Juan March, Madrid (Madrid, 2011)
Sugimoto, Hiroshi, *Hiroshi Sugimoto*, exh. cat., Leeum Samsung Museum, Seoul (Seoul, 2013)
——, *Hiroshi Sugimoto: Theaters*, trans. Giles Murray (Bologna, 2016)
Summers, David, *Real Spaces: World Art History and the Rise of Western Modernism* (London, 2003)
Suzuki, D. T., *An Introduction to Zen Buddhism* (New York, 1964)
Tempkin, Ann, ed., *Color Chart: Reinventing Color, 1950 to Today*, exh. cat., Museum of Modern Art, New York (New York, 2008)
Temple, Richard, *Icons and the Mystical Origins of Christianity* (Shaftsbury, Dorset, 1990)
Tiampo, Ming, *Gutai: Decentering Modernism* (Chicago, IL, and New York, 2011)
——, and Alexandra Munroe, eds, *Gutai: Splendid Playground*, exh. cat., Guggenheim Museum, New York (New York, 2013)
Tobey, Mark, *Mark Tobey: Threading Light*, ed. Debra Bricker Balken, exh. cat., Addison Gallery, Andover, MA (New York, 2017)
Tuchman, Maurice, ed., *The Spiritual in Art: Abstract Painting, 1890–1985*, exh. cat., Los Angeles County Museum of Art (Los Angeles, CA, 1986)
Varnedoe, Kirk, *Pictures of Nothing: Abstract Art Since Pollock* (Princeton, NJ, and Oxford, 2006)
Versluis, Arthur, *American Gurus: From Transcendentalism to New Age Religion* (Oxford, 2014)
Wall, Jeff, 'Monochrome and Photojournalism in On Kawara's *Today* Paintings', in *Jeff Wall: Works and Collected Writings*, ed. Michael Newman and Jeff Wall (Barcelona, 2007), pp. 329–40
Watson, Gay, *A Philosophy of Emptiness* (London, 2014)

Welchman, John C., *Invisible Colors: A Visual History of Titles* (New Haven, CT, and London, 1997)
Westgeest, Helen, *Zen in the Fifties: Interactions in Art between East and West* (Waanders, 1996)
Wittgenstein, Ludwig, *Remarks on Colour*, ed. G.E.M. Anscombe (Oxford, 1977)
Wollheim, Richard, *Painting as an Art* (London and New York, 1987)
Wong, Wucius, *The Tao of Chinese Landscape Painting: Principles and Methods* (New York, 1991)
Wu, Tim, *The Attention Merchants: The Epic Scramble to Get Inside Our Heads* (New York, 2016)
Yoon Jin-sup, ed., *Dansaekhwa: Korean Monochrome Painting*, exh. cat., National Museum of Contemporary Art, Seoul (Seoul, 2012)
Zeki, Semir, *Inner Vision: An Exploration of Art and the Brain* (Oxford, 1999)

ACKNOWLEDGEMENTS

Most of *The Simple Truth* was written in the Republic of Korea, where I live and work. This comparative isolation has certainly had both positive and negative effects on the book's contents. I am grateful to the Korean artists (especially Lee Ufan and Kim Taek-Sang), curators, writers and all those over here who have helped broaden my horizons. I especially thank my partner, Chang Eungbok, for her insights and patience.

Several of the ideas explored in *The Simple Truth* were first aired in essays published in *Third Text*, *World Art*, the *Journal of Visual Art Practice* and the *Journal of Contemporary Painting*, and in various catalogue essays. Many thanks to the editors and anonymous peer reviewers whose helpful feedback served to improve my work.

Thanks to the artists or their estates for permission to reproduce works. A major thanks to the team at Reaktion Books, especially my chief editor Vivian Constantinopoulos for having faith in the project, my editors Phoebe Colley and Aimee Selby for suggesting much-needed improvements, and the designer Simon McFadden. Also thanks to James Atlee for his initial support for the project.

The American painter Robert Ryman, one of the most single-minded producers of monochromes, died on 8 February 2019, as this book's manuscript was nearing completion. I had the privilege of interviewing him in 1993 during his exhibition at the Tate Gallery in London, and in many ways that interview sowed the seeds for this book. *The Simple Truth* is dedicated to Robert Ryman's memory. I hope it does him, and the monochrome in general, some kind of justice.

PHOTO ACKNOWLEDGEMENTS

The author and publishers wish to express their thanks to the below sources of illustrative material and/or permission to reproduce it. Some locations of artworks are given below, in the interest of brevity:

© ARS, NY and DACS, London, 2020, photo The Museum of Modern Art, New York/Scala, Florence: 2; The Art Institute of Chicago (Mr and Mrs Frank G. Logan Purchase Prize Fund, 1979) © Agnes Martin/DACS, London, 2020, photo The Art Institute of Chicago/Art Resource, New York/Scala, Florence: 6; courtesy the artist (David Batchelor) and Ingleby Gallery, Edinburgh: 8; courtesy the artist (David Batchelor) and Galeria Leme, São Paulo: 9; courtesy the artist (Olafur Eliasson), neugerriemschneider, Berlin, and Tanya Bonakdar Gallery, New York – © Olafur Eliasson, photo Anders Sune Berg: 10; © Succession Yves Klein c/o ADAGP, Paris, and DACS, London, 2020, photo The Museum of Modern Art, New York/Scala, Florence: 1; courtesy Kukje Gallery, Seoul: 7; Coleçao César e Claudio Oiticica, © 2015 Projeto Hélio Oiticica: 5; © Ewa Sapka-Pawliczak & Muzeum Sztuki, Łódź: 4; State Tretyakov Gallery, Moscow: 3.

INDEX

Illustration numbers are indicated by *italics*